The Wordsworth Book of
*Restoration and
Eighteenth-Century Verse*

The Wordsworth Book of
Restoration and Eighteenth-Century Verse

*Edited, with an Introduction,
by Tim Cook*

Wordsworth Poetry Library

This edition published 1997 by Wordsworth Editions Limited
Cumberland House, Crib Street, Ware, Hertfordshire SG12 9ET

ISBN 1 85326 450 4

Typeset by Antony Gray
Printed and bound in Great Britain by
Mackays of Chatham plc, Chatham, Kent

INTRODUCTION

This anthology is intended, like its companion volume, the *Wordsworth Book of Nineteenth-Century Verse,* to give anyone interested in poetry as wide and varied picture as possible of the period it covers, as seen through the eyes of its poets. It takes as its starting point the year in which Charles II was restored to the throne, and ends in 1800 when Britain was embroiled in the war with France which followed the French Revolution.

Charles's Restoration after over a decade of what many people saw as joyless repression under Cromwell led to a revival of interest in arts such as poetry and drama coupled with a relaxation of standards of morality, especially in upper-class circles. This is reflected in the sometimes sexually explicit or bawdy subject matter of the drama written in his reign and the verse of such poets as Rochester and Aphra Behn. Although writers became more restrained, under critical and social pressure, after the end of the century, Pope, Swift and others still felt justified by the practices of the Classical satirists (Horace and Juvenal) they admired in using lavatorial and other indecorous imagery to attack their targets.

In the early years of Charles's reign two of the major poets who had supported the Puritan cause, Milton and Marvell, were still writing, and poems they produced after his accession are represented here. Indeed, *Paradise Lost*'s powerful influence is felt all the way through the period, whatever the poets felt about his politics. His Satan is recognisable in Dryden's Achitophel and in Pope's Hervey, and the music of his verse is echoed in many poets from Young and Thomson to Wordsworth, the perhaps equally great poet with whose early work his volume ends.

However although there were many short lyrics, ballads and poems in blank verse written during the period, its most characteristic verse form was the five-stress, ten-syllable 'heroic' couplet, developed as a satirical weapon by Dryden through what might be called verbipuncture: the placing at a key point in a couplet of one word that completely demolishes the effect of the rest, as in his

> S[hadwell] alone my perfect image bears
> Mature in *dullness* from his earliest years

or Pope's

> Not louder screams to pitying Heaven are cast
> When husbands or when *lapdogs* breathe their last.

Pope used the internal structure of the couplet, with its opportunities for contrast and balance within and between its two lines, in various ways for different witty effects. He brought it to a very high degree of polish and perfection in such masterpieces as *The Rape of the Lock* and his various *Epistles,* while Samuel Johnson used it as a building block for his powerfully structured argument in *The Vanity of Human Wishes*. It was still very popular at the end of the century, with Coleridge in many of his unexciting early poems (not represented here) still using it frequently, though by his time it had lost its earlier elegance and power to surprise, and had been the vehicle for much dreary verse.

The Augustans

The writers of the Restoration and the earlier eighteenth century took the major poets of Augustan Rome, especially Virgil, the writer of pastoral and epic, and Horace, the genial satirist, critic and producer of well-crafted lyrics on love and other subjects, as their models. The later Roman writers Martial, the witty epigrammatist, and the savagely satirical Juvenal were also strong influences. The English 'Augustans', as they came to be called, aimed to follow neo-Classical principles of order and decorum (which meant suiting one's language and style to one's subject matter) in their work. Many of their poems were written in imitation of Classical genres such as epic, satire and didactic (i.e. educational and informative) poetry, each of which was governed by its own conventions. It was these conventions that led Dr Johnson, for instance, to object to Shakespeare's use in his tragedy *Macbeth* of 'low' words such as 'knife' and 'blanket', since the language of tragedy was supposed to be lofty if not archaic. As a result, eighteenth-century poets, in particular, often express themselves in a way that modern readers may find somewhat artificial, wordy and over-patterned at first.

Another characteristic of much of the verse of the time is that it tends to be focused on the behaviour and moral concerns of human beings. For Pope and Johnson the idea of the poet as some sort of superior being blest with visionary and prophetic powers and claiming divine inspiration was as suspect as the Puritan 'enthusiasts' (which in the eighteenth century meant 'fanatics') who claimed to speak with the voice of God. The new Augustan age saw itself as an age of reason and enlightenment which had emerged from the aftermath of a Civil War and tyrannical Commonwealth government. For Pope, 'The proper study of Mankind is Man', while for Samuel Johnson, 'The only end of writing is to enable the readers better to enjoy life or better to endure it.' Both of them in their different ways are concerned with examining the human condition, pointing out the many and varied follies of mankind and persuading us to put our trust in rational acceptance of our lot and belief that, whatever may happen to us in our lifetimes, there is an ultimately benevolent Creator.

This faith is echoed throughout the century by many other poets, including the writers of the great familiar hymns, from Isaac Watts and Joseph Addison at the start of the century to William Cowper at its end, Edward Young seeking consolation for bereavement through reaffirming over and over again in *Night Thoughts* his belief in the message of the Resurrection and Christopher Smart's ecstatic outpourings. It is only at the end of the eighteenth century that we begin to come across a new kind of religious poetry in which, in their different ways, poets such as Blake and Wordsworth offer us fresh and genuinely visionary explorations of religious experience. It is at this time, too, that poets begin to be more revolutionary in their social ideas. Though writers like Johnson, Goldsmith, Thomson and even Pope had drawn attention to the condition of the poor, their solution to the problem of alleviating their misery was to encourage the rich to be more responsible or more generous, rather than to question established hierarchies.

The Poets of Feeling

The Augustan strand in poetry, running from Dryden right through as far as some couplet poems of Burns and even, as we have seen, some early Coleridge, was of course not the only one. Literary history is always complex, and even a poet like Pope can let his feelings occasionally run away with him in an un-Augustan manner, as he does in his early *Eloisa to Abelard* and *Elegy to An Unfortunate Lady* and the closing doom-predicting pages of *The Dunciad*. However there were always poets for whom the expression of emotion was more important than rational analysis, and since the sense of shared emotion is something that attracts most of us to a poet, many readers may find these just as interesting as their orthodox Augustan contemporaries.

Many of these 'poets of feeling' preferred to express themselves in varied lyrical forms, from short songs or ballads to grand, elaborate odes, rather than through the rigid structures of the couplet or the more flexible but still metrically restrictive blank verse. Some of them, such as Thomas Gray and William Collins, experimented with form and subject matter, turning for inspiration to other cultures, such as that of the Celtic world, its beliefs and superstitions. Such poets have sometimes been called 'pre-romantic' or 'poets of sensibility'. However, for all their innovatory efforts, they lacked the imaginative unifying visions of their Romantic successors. Nor did they succeed in breaking free from the conventions in language and phrasing that the Augustans had developed. A good example of a poem seriously affected by these limitations is Gray's *Ode on a Distant Prospect of Eton College*.

So it is refreshing to come across, in the last decade of the eighteenth century, the outspokenness of Burns and the novelty of his colloquial Scots diction, the deceptive apparent simplicity and prophetic fervour of Blake, the interplay between vivid awareness of nature and visionary imagination of Wordsworth and Coleridge. A selection of the poems that they wrote before our cut-off date of 1800 will be found in appropriate places throughout this volume, and will enable you to see their achievement in its historical context. You can then continue to explore some of them in our companion anthology for the nineteenth century.

This collection also tries to do justice, within its limits of space, to the very real achievements, nearly all of them, interestingly, in the form of lyrics, of the previously often unjustly neglected women poets of the period. Aphra Behn, as has already been mentioned, rivals Rochester in her uninhibited love lyrics, and poets from the aristocratic Mary Wortley Montagu and Henrietta O'Neill, via the middle-class Mary Barber, Joanna Baillie, Charlotte Smith and

Anna Laetitia Barbauld, to the far less privileged Mary Collier all either match male achievements in traditional areas or deal effectively and often movingly with experience seen from a different and hitherto unheard point of view.

George Orwell criticised Sir Arthur Quiller Couch, editor of an older edition of the prestigious *Oxford Book of English Verse,* for including a good deal of what he saw as inferior poetry. Some readers may feel that an 'anthology', since the word means (translating the original Greek word) a 'collection of flowers', should only include a selection of the 'best' poems written during a period, whatever 'best' means, since taste in verse varies so tremendously. My aim on the other hand has been to make this collection as widely representative of the times it covers as possible. Like its companion volume, it is designed to cater for readers with historical, political or sociological interests, as well as those with either a casual or an informed interest in poetry. We hope that it manages to avoid including any really bad pieces, but clearly its scope means that most of the great long poems of the age are represented only by characteristic extracts. Some may not be included at all, and many worthwhile shorter poems have had to be sacrificed to our general purpose.

GENERAL PLAN

From Prophecy to Social Reform

As with the companion *Nineteenth-Century* volume, this anthology is divided into sections covering the various aspects of human life and other topics that tend to inspire poets. The sections are in many cases very similar to those in the other volume, so making it possible for a reader who has both to trace a favourite subject of poets right through from 1660 to 1800 and explore the various ways in which it has been treated by different people in different ages. The main omission is of a section dealing with the Classical world. The influence of Rome, especially, is so pervasive during this period that you will find it in almost all the sections, and a special one seemed unnecessary.

We begin with the prophetic voice of Milton's angel, giving Adam after the Fall faith in Divine Providence by showing how God's plan will bring about the ultimate redemption of man through Christ, though there will be much suffering in the meantime. Isaac Watts concentrates on the Day of Judgment itself, while Blake at the end of the period sees a kind of apocalyptic vengeance being inflicted on the Britain of his day. Pope in an early poem and Thomson foretell the rise of British power and influence, though the later Pope sees his country about to be plunged into a dark age of ignorance, cultural desecration and perverted values. Gray and Cowper speak up for the oppressed of the past, and Burns affirms the dignity of man, welcomes the American Revolution and temporarily submerges his nationalism (if not his radicalism!) in the face of a threat to the whole of Britain. Barbauld asserts the need for her half of the human race to be properly recognised by its male partners.

The second section begins with two of Rochester's powerful and thoughtful general satires on humanity, before moving, in the work of Dryden and Defoe, to the exploration of current political issues, while Pope comments with some compassion on the empty lives of the upper-class women with whom, because of poor health that excluded him from many masculine activities, he spent much of his time. Thomson and Goldsmith show a vivid and concerned awareness of the sufferings of the poor, while Mary Collier writes about them from personal experience. Cowper attacks the slave-trade, Hannah More the purveyors of cheap alcohol and Blake, more obliquely, the exploitation of child labour.

From Religion to Laughter

Although the period we are covering was still very much an age of faith, even if it manifested itself in many different ways, there were many occasions on which poets came close to despair, but few rejected Christian teaching as decisively as Rochester may have done before his apparent death-bed conversion. The third section on Faith, Doubt, Melancholy, Despair and Hope contains as its centrepiece the whole of Samuel Johnson's great reworking of Juvenal's examination of the futility of human desire, seeing Christian faith in a better after-life as the only consolation. It is surrounded by poems written in many different moods, ranging from Watts' wondering and doubt-free contemplation of the Cross and Smart's passionate call to worship to Gay's depression and Cowper's late, agonised cry for help.

The fourth section offers the reader some possibly needed light relief – though some of the poems here, notably those by Prior and Swift, may not appeal to people who are fastidious about what they look for in poetry. The major poem in this section, which many editors might have included in the section on Social Comment, is Pope's *Rape of the Lock*. It is here because of its marvellously witty use of language and the couplet, and the light and imaginative touch with which Pope treats his subject. The section finishes with Gray's delightful mock elegy in which a drowned cat's fate is presented in the guise of a mini-epic decorated with appropriately pompous language and Classical allusions, and finished off with a moral for young girls.

Nature, the Countryside and the City

More animals, as well as birds and flowers, usually treated in a more serious manner, greet us in the second half of the next and longest section, which covers poets' responses to nature and the non-human world. In the next century the same scenes and creatures would often be charged with a special kind of inspired meaningfulness, as in Wordsworth's *Tintern Abbey*, which just falls within the period covered. One only has to compare this with the fine but ultimately little more than effectively descriptive passages by Pope, Winchilsea, Thomson, Dyer and even Cowper (whom Wordsworth much admired) to see the difference. The flower, animal and bird poems, too, though often charming, tend to lack that extra dimension, at least until we reach the few jewel-like and infinitely suggestive poems by Blake and the remorseful reactions of Burns to his clumsy interactions with nature. However there is much to admire and enjoy here, ranging from Thomson's careful observations of bird behaviour to Cowper's lament over his stricken poplars, anticipating a similar one by Hopkins a century later.

From poems about landscape and the countryside we move into the London of the times and a short series of often witty descriptions of the dangers and problems of city life. Swift, who was to live most of his life in distant exile from the city, seems to have revelled in its sights, sounds and squalor, Gay's *Trivia* gives us a vivid picture of its inhabitants, and we know that Johnson, whose poem *London* was based on one in which Juvenal deplores the state of Rome in the first century AD, actually claimed that, 'If a man is tired of London, he is tired of life.' However he certainly identified with the misfortunes and indignities facing a poor man struggling to make his way in a rich busy and materialistic environment, while Joanna Baillie is more purely descriptive and Mary Robinson expresses her views succinctly and effectively.

From the Cradle to the Grave

Another subject favoured by nineteenth-century writers and represented by many poems included in our companion anthology is childhood, whether seen from a child's or an adult's point of view. It was also a topic to which earlier writers often turned. Henry Vaughan, who probably helped to inspire Wordsworth's great *Ode on Intimations of Immortality from Recollections of Early Childhood*, wrote his poetry too early to be included here, but the last of the seventeenth-century metaphysical poets, Thomas Traherne, whose work only became known this century, was influenced by him, and one of his striking poems, using a child's view of the world to explore his faith, begins the next section. It also includes three poems written from the point of view of motherhood, hitherto too rarely represented, as well as Cowper's criticism of the corrupting influence on society of public-school education, Gray's gloomy reflections on the likely destinies of the carefree children he sees playing near his old school, and early sketches of childhood innocence by Blake and Wordsworth.

From a section that includes two pieces about the beginnings of life, we move to reflections on death and the deaths of individuals. The major poem in this section, Gray's great *Elegy*, chooses itself, but the reader will find many different reactions to death here, They range from Dryden's effective tribute to a colleague who died young to Pope's passionate denunciation of the aristocratic family that drove a mysterious young woman to suicide, and include Swift's entertaining prediction of society's responses to his own death and Johnson's gravely indignant defence of the memory of a recently dead friend.

Love and War

Most poets at some time in their lives write poems about their amorous feelings for someone of the opposite, or possibly of the same, gender. Milton wrote love sonnets in English and Italian early in his life, and a beautiful sonnet about his dead second wife in his middle years, but these are too early for this collection. However *Paradise Lost* contains at least two great affirmations of his belief in the centrality to human experience of love, including sex, within marriage, and these are included here, before we turn to the often more cynical and amused accounts of relations between the sexes fashionable amongst his Restoration contemporaries. Pope's *Eloisa to Abelard* on the other hand, reveals his ability to identify passionately and imaginatively with a girl in an agonising conflict between her spiritual and sexual natures.

Swift's *Cadenus and Vanessa,* almost novel-like in its detail and very readable in style, describes in a charming and wryly amused way his own relationship with a much younger girl who fell for his intellectual charms. Burns reinvigorates the traditional love lyric, and he, Cowper and Anna Sawyer deal touchingly with the love and affection that can continue between people who have spent their whole lives together.

Section Ten strikes a much harsher note in its descriptions of that other favourite human activity: warfare. Charles II's reign began with some naval humiliations at the hands of the Dutch which Marvell describes in his sardonically satirical manner, very different from the sober but admiringly patriotic account of the greatest English victory of the century at Blenheim, written by Addison. A very different point of view on the same battle is provided by Southey at the century's end. Collins and Smollett react to the deaths in another military campaign, that of the '45 Jacobite Rebellion, from different national perspectives; Jane Elliot laments a much earlier military catastrophe suffered by Scotland; Cowper mourns an admiral and his crew lost in a naval disaster; Coleridge in a very striking and not well-known dramatic eclogue, of which he later repented, attacks Pitt the Younger as a warmonger.

More Humour – and an Artistic Interlude

After the violence of battle, a change of tone seems appropriate, and so we have included some more light-hearted material, some of it jocularly satirical such as the two short poems by Johnson and those by Goldsmith and Canning, some of it pure entertainment such as Cowper's *John Gilpin* and Burns's celebration of the barley that provided the basis for his favourite tipples, and some uninhibitedly uproarious in their exposure of human failings: the last poet's *Holy Willie's Prayer* and *To a Louse,* written in his favourite colloquial style.

We then turn to a section that, unlike the others, does not have a parallel in the companion volume: a series of poems related to the arts and criticism of them. Dryden's short *Ode for St Cecilia's Day* characterises the instruments of the seventeenth-century orchestra, Addison describes a contemporary theatre, Swift mocks the poets of

Grub Street (the traditional home of bad writers), Pope writes to Jervas about their shared enthusiasm for painting, lays down the law for poets and critics and gives an example of ostentatious vulgarity in the tastes of a real or imagined great landowner of his time, and Johnson deplores the quality of the work of a contemporary poet.

The Art of Portraiture

From the early seventeenth century onwards people had been attempting short character sketches, inspired originally by the Greek writer Theophrastus, who wrote in prose and confined himself to describing general types, with titles such as 'The Disagreeable Man'. It was probably from these that the art of describing specific individuals, often in a critical or satirical way, eventually developed, though the popularity in England of *Don Quixote,* with its humorous portraits of the Don himself and his 'squire' Sancho Panza, will have been another factor, and the first character in our series, Sir Hudibras, was clearly partly inspired by Cervantes. As an example of rumbustious invective this has rarely been matched in English literature, and it is a pity we have no room for more of the poem.

However it is in Dryden's and Pope's work that we find the art of character demolition in verse at its skilful best, and several famous examples are included here. To show that Pope was not always on the attack we include his courageous praise for Robert Harley, Earl of Oxford, the Tory minister who was disgraced and imprisoned by his political enemies one of whom was Walpole, described succinctly in another sketch by Pope's friend Swift. In a more positive mood we have Swift's charming picture of his friend Stella, and his own self-portrait written no doubt with posterity in mind. Besides these we have a verse portrait of a lazy man in the Theophrastan mode written for children's moral education by Isaac Watts (this was later parodied by Lewis Carroll) and some relevant pieces by Goldsmith. Finally Cowper gives us an imagined self-portrait of Alexander Selkirk (the castaway whose story inspired Defoe's *Robinson Crusoe*) in a form that resembles that favourite device of Browning and other nineteenth-century poets, the dramatic monologue.

The Antique and the Abnormal

The last section of the anthology brings in subject matter outside the preferred range of the most characteristic poets of the eighteenth century, but destined to become much more popular in the nineteenth century. The influence of Milton's portrayal of Satan would become even more pervasive, extending into the novel, and interest in the supernatural world, medieval and archaic literature and cultures intensified. Collins, together with Gray (see the reference to *The Bard* above), was one of the pioneers in this area. The researches of Bishop Percy into medieval ballads, ending in his *Reliques of Ancient English Poetry,* provided another stimulus, and he and several of his contemporaries tried their hands at imitating them.

The young Bristol poet Thomas Chatterton went further and managed to deceive some of his contemporaries into accepting his pastiches of medieval poems as genuine writings from the period – one of these is reproduced in its original spelling to demonstrate its effect. However it was only at the end of the century that poetry of real genius and impact dealing with the abnormal came to be written. Three of the greatest such poems produced then, Burns's comic masterpiece, *Tam O'Shanter,* and two of Coleridge's finest works, the mysteriously visionary *Kubla Khan* and the greatest of all poems inspired by the ballad tradition, *The Ancient Mariner,* bring this tour of a hundred and forty years of poetry in English to a striking conclusion. We hope you will enjoy it.

TIM COOK
Kingston University

N.B. Although early texts have been consulted wherever possible, spelling and presentation have often been modernised since many readers find it tiring to read poems printed in their original spelling and with the frequent use of capitals. Purists may object to this, but our aim is to enable as many people to enjoy the anthology as possible. However, in some cases, such as those of Pope's *The Rape of the Lock,* Chatterton's pastiche *Minstrel's Song* and Prior's and Rochester's poems, we have left the poems as they first appeared, so that the original effect can be seen, and, maybe, appreciated

Finally, I would like to dedicate this anthology to the memory of Professors Harold Brooks and Geoffrey Tillotson of Birkbeck College, two great teachers and scholars who believed, unusually, that their students should enjoy eighteenth-century literature rather than endure it.

CONTENTS

1 PROPHETS, PATRIOTS & REVOLUTIONARIES

2 GENERAL, SOCIAL & POLITICAL SATIRE & COMMENT

5 RESPONSES TO NATURE
PART ONE: LANDSCAPE AND NATURAL PHENOMENA

5 RESPONSES TO NATURE
PART TWO: TREES, FLOWERS, ANIMALS AND BIRDS

6 CITY LIFE

7 VIEWS OF CHILDHOOD & PARENTHOOD

8 THOUGHTS & MEMORIES OF DEATH

LIST OF KEY DATES

1
PROPHETS, PATRIOTS &
REVOLUTIONARIES

from *Paradise Lost*

The archangel Michael has told Adam about the coming of Christ which will redeem the sin originated in man by the eating of the Forbidden Fruit in the Garden of Eden.

> So spake the archangel Michael; then paused
> As at the earth's great period; and our sire
> Replete with joy and wonder, thus replied:
> 'O goodness infinite, goodness immense!
> That all this good of evil shall produce
> And evil turn to good; more wonderful
> Than that which by creation first brought forth
> Light out of darkness! Full of doubt I stand,
> Whether I should repent me now of sin
> By me done and occasion'd, or rejoice
> Much more, that much more good thereof shall spring;
> To God more glory, more goodwill to men
> From God, and over wrath grace shall abound.
> But say, if our Deliverer up to Heaven
> Must reascend, what will betide the few,
> His faithful, left among the unfaithful herd,
> The enemies of truth? Who then shall guide
> His people – who defend? Will they not deal
> Worse with His followers than with Him they dwelt?'

> 'Be sure they will,' said the angel; 'but from heaven
> He to his own a Comforter will send,
> The promise of the Father, who shall dwell
> His spirit within them; and the law of faith,
> Working through love, upon their hearts shall write.
> To guide them in all truth, and also arm
> With spiritual armour able to resist
> Satan's assaults, and quench his fiery darts;
> What man can do against them, not afraid,
> Though to the death; against such cruelties
> With inward consolations recompensed,
> And oft supported so as shall amaze
> Their proudest persecutors; for the Spirit,

Pour'd first on his apostles, whom he sends
To evangelise the nations, then on all baptised, shall
    then
With wondrous gifts endue and do all miracles,
As did their Lord before them. Thus they win
Great numbers of each nation to receive
With joy the tidings brought from heaven: at length,
Their ministry perform'd and race well run
Their doctrine and their story written left,
They die; but in their room, as they forewarn
Wolves shall succeed for teachers, grievous wolves,
Who all the sacred mysteries of heaven
To their own vile advantages shall turn
of lucre and ambition; and the truth
With superstitions and traditions taint.
Left only in those written records pure,
Though not but by the Spirit understood.
Then shall they seek to avail themselves of names,
Places and titles, and with these to join
Secular power, though feigning still to act
By spiritual, to themselves appropriating
The Spirit of God, promised alike and given
To all believers; and from that pretence,
Spiritual laws by carnal power shall force;
On every conscience, laws which none shall find
Left them enroll'd or what the Spirit within
Shall on the heart engrave. What will they, then,
But force the Spirit of Grace itself, and bind
His consort Liberty? What but unbuild
His living temples, built by faith to stand,
Their own faith, not another's? for, on earth,
Who against faith and conscience can be heard
Infallible? Yet many shall presume;
Whence heavy persecution shall arise
On all who in the worship persevere,
of spirit and truth; the rest, far greater part,
Will deem in outward rites and specious forms
Religion satisfied; truth shall retire
Bestuck with slanderous darts, and works of faith
Rarely be found. So shall the world go on

To good malignant, to bad men benign.
Under her own weight groaning, till the day
Appear of respiration to the just,
And vengeance to the wicked, at return
Of Him so lately promised to thy aid,
The woman's seed, obscurely then foretold,
Now ampler known, thy Saviour and thy Lord;
Lost in the clouds, from heaven to be reveal'd,
In glory of the Father to dissolve
Satan with his perverted world; then raise
From the conflagrant mass, purged and refined,
New heavens, new earth, ages of endless date,
Founded in righteousness, in peace and love;
To bring forth fruits, joy and eternal bliss.'

                                  JOHN MILTON (1674)

The Day of Judgment

AN ODE ATTEMPTED IN ENGLISH SAPPHIC

When the fierce north wind with his airy forces
Rears up the Baltic to a foaming fury;
And the red lightning with a storm of hail comes
                        Rushing amain down,

How the poor sailors stand amazed and tremble!
While the hoarse thunder like a bloody trumpet
Roars a loud onset to the gaping waters
                        Quick to devour them.

Such shall the noise be, and the wild disorder,
(If things eternal may be like these earthly)
Such the dire terror when the great archangel
                        Shakes the creation;

Tears the strong pillars of the vault of heaven,
Breaks up old marble, the repose of princes;
See the graves open, and the bones arising,
                    Flames all around 'em.

Hark the shrill outcries of the guilty wretches!
Lively bright horror and amazing anguish
Stare through their eye-lids, while the living worm lies
                    Gnawing within them.

Thoughts like old vultures prey upon their heartstrings,
And the smart twinges, and their eye beholds the
Lofty judge frowning, and the flood of vengeance
                    Rolling afore him.

Hopeless immortals! how they scream and shiver
While devils push them to the pit wide yawning
Hideous and gloomy, to receive them headlong
                    Down to the centre.

Stop here my fancy: (all away ye horrid
Doleful ideas) come arise to Jesus,
How he sits god-like! and the saints around him
                    Throned, yet adoring!

O may I sit there when he comes triumphant
Dooming the nations: then ascend to glory,
While our Hosannahs all along the passage
                    Shout the Redeemer.

                              ISAAC WATTS (1706)

from *Windsor Forest*

POPE PREDICTS A GLORIOUS FUTURE
FOR BRITAIN UNDER QUEEN ANNE

Hail Sacred *Peace*! hail long-expected Days,
That *Thames*'s Glory to the Stars shall raise!
Tho' *Tyber*'s Streams immortal *Rome* behold,
Tho' foaming *Hermus* swells with Tydes of Gold,
From Heav'n it self tho' sev'nfold *Nilus* flows,
And Harvests on a hundred Realms bestows;
These now no more shall be the Muse's Themes,
Lost in my Fame, as in the Sea their Streams.
Let *Volga*'s Banks with Iron Squadrons shine,
And Groves of Lances glitter on the *Rhine*,
Let barb'rous *Ganges* arm a servile Train;
Be mine the Blessings of a peaceful Reign.
No more my Sons shall dye with *British* Blood
Red *Iber*'s Sands, or *Ister*'s foaming Flood;
Safe on my Shore each unmolested Swain
Shall tend the Flocks, or reap the bearded Grain;
The shady Empire shall retain no Trace
Of War or Blood, but in the Sylvan Chace,
The Trumpets sleep, while chearful Horns are blown,
And Arms employ'd on Birds and Beasts alone.
Behold! th'ascending *Villa*'s on my Side
Project long Shadows o'er the Chrystal Tyde.
Behold! *Augusta*'s glitt'ring Spires increase,
And Temples rise, the beauteous Works of Peace.
I see, I see where two fair Cities bend
Their ample Bow, a new *White-Hall* ascend!
There mighty Nations shall inquire their Doom,
The World's great Oracle in Times to come;
There Kings shall sue, and suppliant States be seen
Once more to bend before a *British* QUEEN.
    Thy Trees, fair *Windsor*! now shall leave their Woods,
And half thy Forests rush into my Floods,
Bear *Britain*'s Thunder, and her Cross display,
To the bright Regions of the rising Day;

Tempt Icy Seas, where scarce the Waters roll,
Where clearer Flames glow round the frozen Pole;
Or under Southern Skies exalt their Sails,
Led by new Stars, and born by spicy Gales!
For me the Balm shall bleed, and Amber flow,
The Coral redden, and the Ruby glow,
The Pearly Shell its lucid Globe infold,
And *Phœbus* warm the ripening Ore to Gold.
The Time shall come, when free as Seas or Wind
Unbounded *Thames* shall flow for all Mankind,
Whole Nations enter with each swelling Tyde,
And Seas but join the Regions they divide;
Earth's distant Ends our Glory shall behold,
And the new World launch forth to seek the Old.
Then Ships of uncouth Form shall stem the Tyde,
And Feather'd People crowd my wealthy Side,
And naked Youths and painted Chiefs admire
Our Speech, our Colour, and our strange Attire!
Oh stretch thy Reign, fair *Peace*! from Shore to Shore,
Till Conquest cease, and Slav'ry be no more:
Till the freed *Indians* in their native Groves
Reap their own Fruits, and woo their Sable Loves,
Peru once more a Race of Kings behold,
And other *Mexico*'s be roof'd with Gold.
Exil'd by Thee from Earth to deepest Hell,
In Brazen Bonds shall barb'rous *Discord* dwell:
Gigantick *Pride*, pale *Terror*, gloomy *Care*,
And mad *Ambition*, shall attend her there.
There purple *Vengeance* bath'd in Gore retires,
Her Weapons blunted, and extinct her Fires:
There hateful *Envy* her own Snakes shall feel,
And *Persecution* mourn her broken Wheel:
There *Faction* roar, *Rebellion* bite her Chain,
And gasping Furies thirst for Blood in vain.

ALEXANDER POPE (1704 onwards)

From *The Dunciad*

The scene is the court of the Queen of Dullness, and the Wizard
seems to be Sir Robert Walpole, noted for his corrupt use of
political patronage and honours. Pope goes on to give various
examples of what he sees as decadence: a chef offering exotic
cuisine is followed by what he saw as some of the useless follies of
scientific enquiry and other activities he felt unworthy of cultured
human beings. The poem ends with a vision of the triumph of the
Philistines and an imminent new Dark Age.

> With that, a WIZARD OLD his *Cup* extends;
> Which who so tastes, forgets his former friends,
> Sire, Ancestors, Himself. One casts his eyes
> Up to a *Star*, and like Endymion dies:
> A *Feather* shooting from another's head,
> Extracts his brain, and Principle is fled,
> Lost is his God, his Country, ev'ry thing;
> And nothing left but Homage to a King!
> The vulgar herd turn off to roll with Hogs,
> To run with Horses, or to hunt with Dogs;
> But, sad example! never to escape
> Their Infamy, still keep the human shape.
>
> But she, good Goddess, sent to ev'ry child
> Firm Impudence, or Stupefaction mild;
> And strait succeeded, leaving shame no room,
> Cibberian forehead, or Cimmerian gloom.
>
> Kind Self-conceit to some her glass applies,
> Which no one looks in with another's eyes:
> But as the Flatt'rer or Dependant paint,
> Beholds himself a Patriot, Chief, or Saint.
>
> On others Int'rest her gay liv'ry flings,
> Int'rest, that waves on Party-colour'd wings:
> Turn'd to the Sun, she casts a thousand dyes,
> And, as she turns, the colours fall or rise.

                    *   *   *

> On some, a Priest succinct in amice white
> Attends; all flesh is nothing in his sight!

Beeves, at his touch, at once to jelly turn,
And the huge Boar is shrunk into an Urn:
The board with specious miracles he loads,
Turns Hares to Larks, and Pigeons into Toads.
Another (for in all what one can shine?)
Explains the *Seve* and *Verdeur* of the Vine.
What cannot copious Sacrifice attone?
Thy Treufles, Perigord! thy Hams, Bayonne!
With French Libation, and Italian Strain,
Wash Bladen white, and expiate Hays's stain.
Knight lifts the head, for what are crowds undone
To three essential Partriges in one?
Gone ev'ry blush, and silent all reproach,
Contending Princes mount them in their Coach.

   Next bidding all draw near on bended knees,
The Queen confers her *Titles* and *Degrees*.
Her children first of more distinguish'd sort,
Who study Shakespeare at the Inns of Court,
Impale a Glow-worm, or Vertù profess,
Shine in the dignity of F. R. S.
Some, deep Free-Masons, join the silent race
Worthy to fill Pythagoras's place:
Some Botanists, or Florists at the least,
Or issue Members of an Annual feast.
Nor past the meanest unregarded, one
Rose a Gregorian, one a Gormogon.
The last, not least in honour or applause,
Isis and Cam made Doctors of her Laws.

   Then blessing all, 'Go Children of my care!
To Practice now from Theory repair.
All my commands are easy, short and full:
My Sons! be proud, be selfish, and be dull.
Guard my Prerogative, assert my Throne:
This Nod confirms each Privilege your own.
The Cap and Switch be sacred to his Grace;
With Staff and Pumps the Marquis lead the Race;
From Stage to Stage the licens'd Earl may run,
Pair'd with his Fellow-Charioteer the Sun;
The learned Baron Butterflies design,
Or draw to silk Arachne's subtile line;

The Judge to dance his brother Sergeant call;
The Senator at Cricket urge the Ball;
The Bishop stow (Pontific Luxury!)
An hundred Souls of Turkeys in a pye;
The sturdy Squire to Gallic masters stoop,
And drown his Lands and Manors in a Soupe.
Others import yet nobler arts from France,
Teach Kings to fiddle, and make Senates dance.
Perhaps more high some daring son may soar,
Proud to my list to add one Monarch more;
And nobly conscious, Princes are but things
Born for First Ministers, as Slaves for Kings,
Tyrant supreme! shall three Estates command,
And MAKE ONE MIGHTY DUNCIAD OF THE LAND!'
    More she had spoke, but yawn'd – All Nature nods:
What Mortal can resist the Yawn of Gods?
Churches and Chapels instantly it reach'd;

(St James's first, for leaden Gilbert preach'd)
Then catch'd the Schools; the Hall scarce kept awake;
The Convocation gap'd, but could not speak:
Lost was the Nation's Sense, nor could be found,
While the long solemn Unison went round:
Wide, and more wide, it spread o'er all the realm;
Ev'n Palinurus nodded at the Helm:
The Vapour mild o'er each Committee crept;
Unfinish'd Treaties in each Office slept;
And Chiefless Armies doz'd out the Campaign;
And Navies yawn'd for Orders on the Main.
    O Muse! relate (for you can tell alone,
Wits have short Memories, and Dunces none)
Relate, who first, who last resign'd to rest;
Whose Heads she partly, whose completely blest;
What Charms could Faction, what Ambition lull,
The Venal quiet, and intrance the Dull;
'Till drown'd was Sense, and Shame, and Right, and
    Wrong –
O sing, and hush the Nations with thy Song!

*   *   *

In vain, in vain – the all-composing Hour

Resistless falls: The Muse obeys the Pow'r.
She comes! she comes! the sable Throne behold
Of *Night* Primæval, and of *Chaos* old!
Before her, *Fancy*'s gilded clouds decay,
And all its varying Rain-bows die away.
Wit shoots in vain its momentary fires,
The meteor drops, and in a flash expires.
As one by one, at dread Medea's strain,
The sick'ning stars fade off th' ethereal plain;
As Argus' eyes by Hermes' wand opprest,
Clos'd one by one to everlasting rest;
Thus at her felt approach, and secret might,
Art after *Art* goes out, and all is Night.
See skulking *Truth* to her old Cavern fled,
Mountains of Casuistry heap'd o'er her head!
Philosophy, that lean'd on Heav'n before,
Shrinks to her second cause, and is no more.
Physic of *Metaphysic* begs defence,
And *Metaphysic* calls for aid on *Sense*!
See *Mystery* to *Mathematics* fly!
In vain! they gaze, turn giddy, rave, and die.
Religion blushing veils her sacred fires,
And unawares *Morality* expires.
Nor *public* Flame, nor *private*, dares to shine;
Nor *human* Spark is left, nor Glimpse *divine*!
Lo! thy dread Empire, CHAOS! is restor'd;
Light dies before thy uncreating word:
Thy hand, great Anarch! lets the curtain fall;
And Universal Darkness buries All.

ALEXANDER POPE (1743)

Rule Britannia

When Britain first, at Heaven's command,
   Arose from out the azure main,
This was the charter of the land,
   And guardian angels sung this strain —
      'Rule, Britannia, rule the waves;
      Britons never will be slaves.'

The nations, not so blest as thee,
   Must in their turns to tyrants fall;
Whilst thou shalt flourish great and free,
   The dread and envy of them all.

Still more majestic shalt thou rise,
   More dreadful from each foreign stroke;
As the loud blast that tears the skies
   Serves but to root thy native oak.

Thee haughty tyrants ne'er shall tame;
   All their attempts to bend thee down
Will but arouse thy generous flame,
   But work their woe and thy renown.

To thee belongs the rural reign;
   Thy cities shall with commerce shine;
All thine shall be the subject main,
   And every shore it circles thine.

The Muses, still with freedom found,
   Shall to thy happy coast repair:
Blest isle! with matchless beauty crowned,
   And manly hearts to guard the fair.
      'Rule, Britannia, rule the waves;
      Britons never will be slaves.'

JAMES THOMSON (1740)

The Bard

A PINDARIC ODE

Gray is here imagining the last of the Welsh Druidic bards
confronting Edward I during his conquest of Wales, and predicting
the untimely deaths of his Plantagenet son, Edward II, murdered in
Berkeley Castle, his great grandson, the Black Prince, the latter's
son Richard II, also murdered, and the saintly Henry VI, a remoter
descendant, murdered by Richard III whose heraldic animal was a
boar. He in turn was overthrown by the Welsh Tudors, whose
future glory the bard prophesies. The Greek poet Pindar wrote long
and complex celebratory lyrics in which the train of thought was
often hard to follow, and these inspired many English imitations.

1

'Ruin seize thee, ruthless King!
    Confusion on thy banners wait!
Though fanned by Conquest's crimson wing
    They mock the air with idle state.
Helm, nor hauberk's twisted mail,
Nor e'en thy virtues, tyrant, shall avail
To save thy secret soul from nightly fears,
From Cambria's curse, from Cambria's tears!'
– Such were the sounds that o'er the crested pride
    Of the first Edward scattered wild dismay,
As down the steep of Snowdon's shaggy side
    He wound with toilsome march his long array: –
Stout Glo'ster stood aghast in speechless trance;
'To arms!' cried Mortimer, and couched his quivering
    lance.

2

On a rock, whose haughty brow
Frowns o'er old Conway's foaming flood,
    Robed in the sable garb of woe,
With haggard eyes the poet stood;
(Loose his beard and hoary hair
Streamed like a meteor to the troubled air;)

And with a master's hand and prophet's fire
Struck the deep sorrows of his lyre:
'Hark, how each giant oak and desert cave
    Sighs to the torrent's awful voice beneath!
O'er thee, O King! their hundred arms they wave
    Revenge on thee in hoarser murmurs breathe;
Vocal no more, since Cambria's fatal day,
To high-born Hoel's harp, or soft Llewellyn's lay.

3

'Cold is Cadwallo's tongue,
    That hushed the stormy main:
Brave Urien sleeps upon his craggy bed:
    Mountains, ye mourn in vain
    Modred, whose magic song
Made huge Plinlimmon bow his cloud-topt head.
    On dreary Arvon's shore they lie
Smeared with gore and ghastly pale:
Far, far aloof the affrighted ravens sail;
    The famished eagle screams, and passes by.
Dear lost companions of my tuneful art,
    Dear as the light that visits these sad eyes,
Dear as the ruddy drops that warm my heart,
    Ye died amidst your dying country's cries –
No more I weep. They do not sleep;
    On yonder cliffs, a griesly band,
I see them sit; they linger yet,
    Avengers of their native land:
With me in dreadful harmony they join;
And weave with bloody hands the tissue of thy line.

4

' "Weave the warp and weave the woof,
    The winding-sheet of Edward's race:
Give ample room and verge enough
    The characters of hell to trace.
Mark the year and mark the night
When Severn shall re-echo with affright
The shrieks of death through Berkley's roof that ring,
Shrieks of an agonizing king!

She-wolf of France, with unrelenting fangs
That tear'st the bowels of thy mangled mate,
    From thee be born, who o'er thy country hangs
The scourge of heaven! What terrors round him wait!
Amazement in his van, with flight combined,
And sorrow's faded form, and solitude behind.

5

' "Mighty victor, mighty lord,
    Low on his funeral couch he lies!
No pitying heart, no eye, afford
    A tear to grace his obsequies.
Is the sable warrior fled?
Thy son is gone. He rests among the dead.
The swarm that in thy noon-tide beam were born?
— Gone to salute the rising morn.
Fair laughs the morn, and soft the zephyr blows,
    While proudly riding o'er the azure realm
In gallant trim the gilded vessel goes:
    Youth on the prow, and Pleasure at the helm:
Regardless of the sweeping whirlwind's sway,
That, hushed in grim repose, expects his evening prey.

6

' "Fill high the sparkling bowl,
The rich repast prepare;
    Reft of a crown, he yet may share the feast:
Close by the regal chair
    Fell Thirst and Famine scowl
    A baleful smile upon their baffled guest.
Heard ye the din of battle bray,
    Lance to lance, and horse to horse?
    Long years of havoc urge their destined course,
And through the kindred squadrons mow their way.
    Ye towers of Julius, London's lasting shame,
With many a foul and midnight murder fed,
    Revere his consort's faith, his fathers fame,
And spare the meek usurper's holy head!
Above, below, the rose of snow,
    Twined with her blushing foe, we spread:

The bristled boar in infant-gore
  Wallows beneath the thorny shade.
Now, brothers, bending o'er the accursèd loom,
Stamp we our vengeance deep, and ratify his doom.

7

' "Edward, lo! to sudden fate
  (Weave we the woof; The thread is spun;)
Half of thy heart we consecrate.
  (The web is wove; The work is done.)"
Stay, 0 stay! nor thus forlorn
Leave me unblessed, unpitied, here to mourn:
In yon bright track that fires the western skies
They melt, they vanish from my eyes.
But O! what solemn scenes on Snowdon's height
  Descending slow their glittering skirts unroll?
Visions of glory, spare my aching sight,
  Ye unborn ages, crowd not on my soul!
No more our long-lost Arthur we bewail: –
All hail, ye genuine kings! Britannia's issue, hail!

8

  'Girt with many a baron bold
Sublime their starry fronts they rear;
  And gorgeous dames, and statesmen old
In bearded majesty, appear.
In the midst a form divine!
Her eye proclaims her of the Briton-line:
Her lion-port, her awe-commanding face
Attempered sweet to virgin-grace.
What strings symphonious tremble in the air,
  What strains of vocal transport round her play?
Hear from the grave, great Taliessin, hear;
  They breathe a soul to animate thy clay.
Bright Rapture calls, and soaring as she sings,
Waves in the eye of heaven her many-coloured wings.

9

'The verse adorn again
    Fierce war, and faithful love,
And Truth severe, by fairy Fiction drest.
    In buskined measures move
Pale grief, and pleasing pain,
With horror, tyrant of the throbbing breast.
A voice as of the cherub-choir
    Gales from blooming Eden bear,
And distant warblings lessen on my ear,
That lost in long futurity expire.
Fond impious man, think'st thou yon sanguine cloud
    Raised by thy breath, has quenched the orb of day?
To-morrow he repairs the golden flood
    And warms the nations with redoubled ray.
Enough for me: with joy I see
    The different doom our fates assign:
Be thine despair and sceptred care;
    To triumph and to die are mine.'
– He spoke, and headlong from the mountain's height
Deep in the roaring tide he plunged to endless night.

THOMAS GRAY (by 1757)

Boadicea: An Ode

When the British warrior Queen,
   Bleeding from the Roman rods,
Sought, with an indignant mein,
   Counsel of her country's gods,

Sage beneath a spreading oak
   Sat the Druid, hoary chief;
Every burning word he spoke
   Full of rage and full of grief.

'Princess, if our aged eyes
   Weep upon thy matchless wrongs,
'Tis because resentment ties
   All the terrors of our tongues.

Rome shall perish – write that word
   In the blood that she has spilt:
Perish hopeless and abhorr'd
   Deep in ruin, as in guilt.

Rome, for empire far renown'd
   Tramples on a thousand states;
Soon her pride shall kiss the ground –
   Hark! the Gaul is at her gates!

Other Romans shall arise,
   Heedless of a soldier's name;
Sounds, not arms, shall win the prize –
   Harmony the path to fame.

Then the progeny that springs
   From the forests of our land,
Arm'd with thunder, clad with wings,
   Shall a wider world command.

Regions Caesar never knew
  Thy posterity shall sway,
Where his eagles never flew,
  None invincible as they.'

Such the bard's prophetic words,
  Pregnant with celestial fire,
Bending, as he swept the chords
  Of his sweet but awful lyre.

She, with all a monarch's pride,
  Felt them in her bosom glow;
Rush'd to battle, fought, and died;
  Dying, hurl'd them at the foe.

'Ruffians, pitiless as proud,
  Heav'n awards the vengeance due;
Empire is on us bestow'd,
  Shame and ruin wait for you.'

WILLIAM COWPER (1780)

Boadicea (Boudicca), a Celtic queen who resisted the Romans, was
seen as an important national heroine by the predominantly Anglo-
Saxon English who had of course conquered the Celts themselves!
The sixth stanza refers to opera, seen as a product of contemporary
Roman decadence.

For A' That

Is there, for honest poverty,
   That hangs his head, and a' that?
The coward-slave, we pass him by,
   We dare be poor for a' that!
     For a' that, and a' that,
       Our toils obscure, and a' that;
     The rank is but the guinea stamp;
       The man's the gowd[1] for a' that.

What tho' on hamely fare we dine,
   Wear hodden-grey[2], and a' that;
Gie fools their silks, and knaves their wine,
   A man's a man for a' that.
     For a' that, and a' that,
       Their tinsel show, and a' that;
     The honest man, tho' e'er sae poor,
       Is king o' men for a' that.

Ye see yon birkie,[3] ca'd a lord,
   Wha struts, and stares, and a' that;
Tho' hundreds worship at his word,
   He's but a coof[4] for a' that:
     For a' that, and a' that,
       His riband, star, an' a' that,
     The man of independent mind,
       He looks and laughs at a' that.

A prince can mak a belted knight,
   A marquis, duke, an' a' that;
But an honest man's aboon his might,
   Guid faith he mauna fa' that!
     For a' that, an' a' that,
       Their dignities, and a' that,
     The pith o' sense, and pride o' worth,
       Are higher rank than a' that.

---

[1] gold   [2] cheap rough cloth   [3] brash young man   [4] a fool

Then let us pray that come it may,
　　As come it will for a' that;
That sense and worth, o'er a' the earth,
　　May bear the gree,[5] an' a' that.
　　　For a' that, and a' that,
　　　　It's comin' yet, for a' that,
　　　That man to man the warld o'er
　　　Shall brothers be for a' that.

ROBERT BURNS (1794)

[5] win the prize

This poem, written for the birthday of one champion of liberty of
English descent, reflects Burns's horror at Britain's aid to counter-
revolutionary forces in France.

Ode for General Washington's Birthday

No Spartan tube, no Attic shell
　　No lyre Aeolian I awake;
'Tis Liberty's bold note I swell
　　Thy harp, Columbia, let me take!
See gathering thousands, while I sing,
A broken chain exulting bring,
　　And dash it in a tyrant's face,
And dare him to his very beard,
And tell him he no more is feared –
　　No more the despot of Columbia's race!
A tyrant's proudest insults brav'd,
They shout – a people freed! They hail an Empire saved.

Where is man's godlike form?
　　Where is that brow erect and bold –
　　That eye that unmov'd can behold
The wildest rage, the loudest storm
That e'er created Fury dared to raise?

Avaunt! thou caitiff, servile, base,
That tremblest at a despot's rod,
Can'st laud the arm that struck th'insulting blow?
Art thou of man's Imperial line?
Dost boast that countenance divine?
  Each skulking feature answers, No!
But come, ye sons of Liberty,
Columbia's offspring, brave as free,
In danger's hour still flaming in the van,
Ye know, and dare maintain, the Royalty of Man!

Alfred! on thy starry throne,
  Surrounded by the tuneful choir
  The bards that erst have struck the patriot lyre
    And rous'd the freeborn Briton's soul of fire
No more thy England own!
Dare injur'd nations form the great design,
  To make detested tyrants bleed?
  Thy England execrates the glorious deed!
  Beneath her hostile banners waving,
  Every pang of honour braving,
England in thunder calls, 'The tyrant's cause is mine!'
  That hour accurst how did the fiends rejoice
And hell thro' all her confines, raise the exulting voice,
  That hour which saw the generous English name
Linkt with such damned deeds of everlasting shame.

Thee, Caledonia! thy wild heaths among
Fam'd for the martial deed, the heaven-taught song,
  To thee I turn with swimming eyes;
Where is that soul of Freedom fled?
Immingled with the mighty dead,
  Beneath that hallow'd turf where WALLACE lies.
Hear it not, WALLACE! in thy bed of death.
  Ye babbling winds! in silence sweep,
  Disturb not ye the hero's sleep
Nor give the coward secret breath!
Is this the ancient Caledonian form,
Firm as her rock, resistless as her storm?
Show me that eye which shot immortal hate,

>Blasting the despot's proudest bearing;
>Show me that arm which, nerv'd with thundering fate,
>Crush'd Usurpation's boldest daring! –
>Dark-quench'd as yonder sinking star,
>No more that glance lightens afar;
>That palsied arm no more whirls on the waste of war.

ROBERT BURNS (by 1795)

This is a sequel to Blake's poem *America* in which he celebrates the American Revolution. He now predicts the downfall of Albion's (i.e. England's) presiding Angel, the oppressive governing classes and those in the nation seduced by the corrupt female spirit Enitharmon before the revolutionary demon Orc. Urizen represents masculine tyranny. Palamabron and Rintrah are Enitharmon's sons, one of whom seems to be making an unsuccessful resistance, the other biding his time.

from *Europe*

>Albion's Angel rose upon the Stone of Night.
>He saw Urizen on the Atlantic;
>And his brazen book
>That kings and priests had copies on earth
>Expanded from north to south.

And the clouds and fires pale rolled round in the night of
    Enitharmon
Round Albion's cliffs and London's walls (still Enitharmon slept);
Rolling volumes of grey mist involve churches, palaces, towers,
For Urizen unclasped his book, feeding his soul with pity.
The youth of England hid in gloom curse the pained heavens,
    compelled
Into the deadly night to see the form of Albion's Angel.
Their parents brought them forth and aged ignorance preaches
    canting

On a vast rock, perceived by those senses that are closed from
    thought –
Bleak, dark, abrupt it stands and overshadows London city.
They saw his bony feet on the rock, the flesh consumed in flames;
They saw the serpent temple lifted above, shadowing the island
    white;
They heard the voice of Albion's Angel howling in flames of Orc,
Seeking the trump of the last doom.

Above the rest the howl was heard from Westminster louder and
    louder.
The Guardian of the secret codes forsook his ancient mansion,
Driven out by the flames of Orc; his furred robes and false locks
Adhered and grew one with his flesh, and nerves and veins shot
    through with them.
With dismal torment sick, hanging upon the wind, he fled
Grovelling along Great George Street through the Park gate. All the
    soldiers
Fled from his sight; he dragged his torments to the wilderness.
Thus was the howl through Europe.
For Orc rejoiced to hear the howling shadows;
But Palamabron shot his lightnings trenching down his wide back,
And Rintrah hung with all his legions in the nether deep.

Enitharmon laughed in her sleep to see (Oh? woman's triumph!)
Every house a den, every man bound; the shadows are filled
With spectres? and the windows wove over with curses of iron.
Over the doors *Thou shalt not*, and over the chimneys *Fear* is
    written.
With bands of iron round their necks fastened into the walls
The citizens, in leaden gyves the inhabitants of suburbs
Walk heavy; soft and bent are the bones of the villagers.

Between the clouds of Urizen the flames of Orc roll heavy
Around the limbs of Albion's Guardian, his flesh consuming.
Howlings and hissings, shrieks and groans, and voices of despair
Arise around him in the cloudy
Heavens of Albion. Furious
The red-limbed Angel seized, in horror and torment,
The trump of the last doom; but he could not blow the iron tube!
Thrice he assayed presumptuous to awake the dead to Judgement.

A mighty spirit leaped from the land of Albion
Named Newton; he seized the trump and blowed the enormous
    blast.

Yellow as leaves of autumn, the myriads of angelic hosts
Fell through the wintry skies seeking their graves,
Rattling their hollow bones in howling and lamentation.

WILLIAM BLAKE (1794)

London

I wander through each charter'd street,
Near where the charter'd Thames does flow,
And mark in every face I meet
Marks of weakness, marks of woe.

In every cry of every man,
In every infant's cry of fear,
In every voice, in every ban,
The mind-forged manacles I hear.

How the chimney sweeper's cry
Every blackening church appalls;
And the hapless soldier's sigh
Runs in blood down palace walls.

But most through midnight streets I hear
How the youthful harlot's curse
Blasts the new-born infant's tear,
And blights with plagues the marriage hearse.

WILLLAM BLAKE (1794)

Does haughty Gaul

Does haughty Gaul invasion threat?
   Then let the loons beware, Sir,
There's wooden walls upon our seas,
   And volunteers on shore, Sir.
The Nith shall run to Corsincon,
   And Criffel sink in Solway,
Ere we permit a foreign foe
   On British ground to rally!

O let us not like snarling tykes
   In wrangling be divided,
Till, slap! come in an unco loon
   And wi' a rung decide it.
Be Britain still to Britain true,
   Amang oursels united;
For never but by British hands
   Maun British wrangs be righted!

The kettle o the kirk and state,
   Perhaps a clout may fail in't;
But deil a foreign tinkler loon
   Shall ever ca' a nail in't.
Our father's blude the kettle bought,
   An' wha wad dare to spoil it?
By heavens! the sacrilegious dog
   Shall fuel be to boil it!

The wretch that would a tyrant own,
   And the wretch, his true-born brother,
Who'd set the mob aboon the throne –
   May they be damned together!
Who will not sing *God, save the King*!
   Shall hang as high's the steeple;
But while we sing *God save the King*!
   We'll not forget the people!

ROBERT BURNS (1795)

The Rights of Women

Yes, injured Woman! rise, assert thy right!
Woman! too long degraded, scorned, oppressed;
O born to rule in partial Law's despite,
Resume thy native empire o'er the breast!

Go forth arrayed in panoply divine,
That angel pureness which admits no stain;
Go, bid proud Man his boasted rule resign
And kiss the golden sceptre of thy reign.

Go, gird thyself with grace, collect thy store
Of bright artillery glancing from afar;
Soft melting tones thy thundering cannon's roar,
Blushes and fears thy magazine of war.

Thy rights are empire; urge no meaner claim, –
Felt, not defined, and if debated, lost;
Like sacred mysteries, which withheld from fame,
Shunning discussion, are revered the most.

Try all that wit and art suggest to bend
Of thy imperial foe the stubborn knee;
Make treacherous Man thy subject, not thy friend;
Thou mayst command, but never canst be free.

Awe the licentious and restrain the rude;
Soften the sullen, clear the cloudy brow:
Be, more than princes' gifts, thy favours sued; –
She hazards all, who will the least allow.

But hope not, courted idol of mankind,
On this proud eminence secure to stay;
Subduing and subdued, thou soon shalt find
Thy coldness soften, and thy pride give way.

Then, then, abandon each ambitious thought;
Conquest or rule thy heart shall feebly move,
In Nature's school, by her soft maxims taught
That separate rights are lost in mutual love.

ANNA LAETITIA BARBAULD (c.1795)

2
GENERAL, SOCIAL & POLITICAL
SATIRE & COMMENT

A Satyr against Mankind

   Were I (who to my cost already am
One of those strange prodigious Creatures *Man*.)
A Spirit free, to choose for my own share,
What Case of Flesh, and Blood, I pleas'd to weare,
I'd be a *Dog*, a *Monkey*, or a *Bear*.
Or any thing but that vain *Animal*,
Who is so proud of being rational.
The senses are too gross, and he'll contrive
A Sixth, to contradict the other Five;
And before certain instinct, will preferr
Reason, which Fifty times for one does err.
Reason, an *Ignis fatuus*, in the *Mind*,
Which leaving light of Nature, sense behind;
Pathless and dang'rous wandring ways it takes,
Through errors, Fenny-*Boggs*, and Thorny *Brakes*;
Whilst the misguided follower, climbs with pain,
Mountains of Whimseys, heap'd in his own *Brain*:
Stumbling from thought to thought, falls head-long
    down,
Into doubt's boundless Sea, where like to drown,
Books bear him up awhile, and makes him try,
To swim with Bladders of *Philosophy*;
In hopes still t'oretake the'escaping light,
The *Vapour* dances in his dazl[ed] sight,
Till spent, it leaves him to eternal Night.
Then Old Age, and experience, hand in hand,
Lead him to death, and make him understand,
After a search so painful, and so long,
That all his Life he has been in the wrong;
Hudled in dirt, the reas'ning *Engine* lyes,
Who was so proud, so witty, and so wise.
Pride drew him in, as *Cheats*, their *Bubbles*, catch,
And makes him venture, to be made a *Wre[t]ch*.
His wisdom did his happiness destroy,
Aiming to know [t]hat *World* he shou'd enjoy;

And *Wit*, was his vain frivolous pretence,
Of pleasing others, at his own expence.
For *Witts* are treated just like common *Whores*,
First they're enjoy'd, and then kickt out of *Doores*:
The pleasure past, a threatening doubt remains,
That frights th'enjoyer, with succeeding pains:
Women and *Men* of *Wit*, are dang'rous Tools,
And ever fatal to admiring *Fools*.
Pleasure allures, and when the *Fopps* escape,
'Tis not that they're belov'd, but fortunate,
And therefore what they fear, at least they hate.

    But now methinks some formal Band, and Beard,
Takes me to task, come on Sir I'm prepar'd.

    Then by your favour, any thing that's writ
Against this gibeing jingling knack call'd Wit,
Likes me abundantly, but you take care,
Upon this point, not to be too severe.
Perhaps my Muse, were fitter for this part,
For I profess, I can be very smart
On Wit, which I abhor with all my heart:
I long to lash it in some sharp Essay,
But your grand indiscretion bids me stay,
And turns my Tide of Ink another way.
What rage ferments in your degen'rate mind
To make you rail at Reason and Mankind?
Blest glorious Man! to whom alone kind Heav'n,
An everlasting Soul has freely giv'n;
Whom his great Maker took such care to make,
That from himself he did the Image take,
And this fair frame, in shining Reason drest,
To dignifie his Nature, above Beast.
Reason, by whose aspiring influence,
We take a flight beyond material sense,
Dive into Mysteries, then soaring pierce,
The flaming limits of the Universe.
Search Heav'n and Hell, find out what's acted there,
And give the World true grounds of hope and fear.

    Hold mighty Man, I cry, all this we know,
From the Pathetique Pen of *Ingello*;
From *P[atrick's] Pilgrim, S[ibbs'] [soliloquies],*

And 'tis this very reason I despise.
This supernatural gift, that makes a *Myte*,
Think he is the Image of the Infinite:
Comparing his short life, void of all rest,
To the *Eternal*, and the ever blest.
This busie, puzling, stirrer up of doubt,
That frames deep *Mysteries*, then finds 'em out;
Filling with Frantick Crowds of thinking *Fools*,
Those Reverend *Bedlams*, *Colledges*, and *Schools*
Borne on whose Wings, each heavy *Sot* can pierce,
The limits of the boundless Universe.
So charming Oyntments, make an Old *Witch* flie,
And bear a Crippled Carcass through the Skie.
'Tis this exalted Pow'r, whose bus'ness lies,
In *Nonsense*, and impossibilities.
This made a Whimsical *Philosopher*,
Before the spacious *World*, his *Tub* prefer,
And we have modern *Cloysterd Coxcombs*, who
Retire to think, cause they have naught to do.
But thoughts, are giv'n for Actions government,
Where Action ceases, thoughts impertinent:
Our *Sphere* of Action, is lifes happiness,
And he who thinks Beyond, thinks like an *Ass*.
Thus, whilst 'gainst false reas'ning I inveigh,
I own right *Reason*, which I wou'd obey:
That *Reason* that distinguishes by sense,
And gives us *Rules*, of good, and ill from thence:
That bounds desires, with a reforming Will,
To keep 'em more in vigour, not to kill.
Your *Reason* hinders, mine helps t'enjoy,
Renewing Appetites, yours wou'd destroy.
My Reason is my *Friend*, yours is a *Cheat*,
Hunger calls out, my Reason bids me eat;
Perversely yours, your Appetite does mock,
This asks for Food, that answers what's a Clock?
This plain distinction Sir your doubt secures,
'Tis not true Reason I despise but yours.
Thus I think Reason righted, but for *Man*,
I'le nere recant defend him if you can.
For all his Pride, and his Philosophy,

'Tis evident, *Beasts* are in their degree,
As wise at least, and better far than he.
Those *Creatures*, are the wisest who attain,
By surest means, the ends at which they aim.
If therefore *Jowler*, finds, and Kills his Hares,
Better than M[eres], supplyes Committee Chairs;
Though one's a *States-man*, th'other but a *Hound*,
Jowler, in Justice, wou'd be wiser found.
You see how far *Mans* wisedom here extends,
Look next, if humane Nature makes amends;
Whose Principles, most gen'rous are, and just,
And to whose *Moralls*, you wou'd sooner trust.
Be Judge your self, I'le bring it to the test,
Which is the basest *Creature Man*, or *Beast*?
Birds, feed on *Birds*, *Beasts*, on each other prey,
But Savage *Man* alone, does *Man*, betray:
Prest by necessity, they Kill for Food,
Man, undoes *Man*, to do himself no good.
With Teeth, and Claws by Nature arm'd they hunt,
Natures allowances, to supply their want.
But *Man*, with smiles, embraces, Friendships, praise,
Unhumanely his Fellows life betrays;
With voluntary pains, works his distress,
Not through necessity, but wantonness.
For hunger, or for Love, they fight, or tear,
Whilst wretched *Man*, is still in Arms for fear;
For fear he armes, and is of Armes afraid,
By fear, to fear, successively betray'd
Base fear, the source whence his best passion[s] came,
His boasted Honor, and his dear bought Fame.
That lust of Pow'r, to which he's such a *Slave*,
And for the which alone he dares be brave:
To which his various Projects are design'd,
Which makes him gen'rous, affable, and kind.
For which he takes such pains to be thought wise,
And screws his actions, in a forc'd disguise:
Leading a tedious life in Misery,
Under laborious, mean *Hypocrisie*.
Look to the bottom, of his vast design,
Wherein *Mans* Wisdom, Pow'r, and Glory joyn;

The good he acts, the ill he does endure,
'Tis all for fear, to make himself secure.
Meerly for safety, after Fame we thirst,
For all Men, wou'd be *Cowards* if they durst.
And honesty's against all common sense,
Men must be *Knaves*, 'tis in their own defence.
Mankind's dishonest, if you think it fair,
Amongst known *Cheats*, to play upon the square,
You'le be undone . . .
Nor can weak truth, your reputation save,
The *Knaves*, will all agree to call you *Knave*.
Wrong'd shall he live, insulted o're, opprest,
Who dares be less a *Villain*, than the rest.
Thus Sir you see what humane Nature craves,
Most Men are *Cowards*, all Men shou'd be *Knaves*:
The diff'rence lyes (as far as I can see)
Not in the thing it self, but the degree;
And all the subject matter of debate,
Is only who's a *Knave*, of the first *Rate*?
    All this with indignation have I hurl'd,
At the pretending part of the proud World,
Who swolne with selfish vanity, devise,
False freedomes, holy Cheats, and formal Lyes
Over their fellow *slaves* to tyrannize.
    But if in *Court*, so just a Man there be,
(In *Court*, a just Man, yet unknown to me.)
Who does his needful flattery direct,
Not to oppress, and ruine, but protect;
Since flattery, which way so ever laid,
Is still a Tax on that unhappy Trade.
If so upright a *States-Man*, you can find,
Whose passions bend to his unbyass'd Mind;
Who does his Arts, and *Policies* apply,
To raise his *Country*, not his *Family*;
Nor while his Pride, own'd Avarice withstands,
Receives Aureal Bribes, from *Friends* corrupted hands.
    Is there a *Church-Man* who on *God* relyes?
Whose Life, his Faith, and Doctrine Justifies?
Not one blown up, with vain Prelatigue Pride,
Who for reproof of Sins, does *Man* deride:

Whose envious heart with his obstrep'rous sawcy
   Eloquence,
Dares chide at *Kings*, and raile at Men of sense.
Who from his Pulpit, vents more peevish Lyes,
More bitter railings, scandals, Calumnies,
Than at a Gossipping, are thrown about,
When the good *Wives*, get drunk, and then fall out.
None of that sensual *Tribe*, whose Tallents lye,
In Avarice, *Pride*, *Sloth*, and *Gluttony*.
Who hunt good Livings, but abhor good Lives,
Whose Lust exalted, to that height arrives,
They act *Adultery* with their own *Wives*.
And e're a score of Years compleated be,
Can from the lofty *Pulpit* proudly see,
Half a large *Parish*, their own *Progeny*.
Nor doating B— who wou'd be ador'd,
For domineering at the *Councel Board*;
A greater *Fop*, in business at Fourscore,
Fonder of serious *Toyes*, affected more,
Than the gay glitt'ring *Fool*, at Twenty proves,
With all his noise, his tawdrey Cloths, and Loves.
   But a meek humble Man, of modest sense,
Who Preaching peace, does practice continence;
Whose pious life's a proof he does believe,
Misterious truths, which no *Man* can conceive.
If upon *Earth* there dwell such *God-like Men*,
I'le here recant my *Paradox* to them.
Adore those *Shrines* of *Virtue*, *Homage* pay,
And with the *Rabble World*, their *Laws* obey.
If such there are, yet grant me this at least,
Man differs more from *Man*, than *Man* from *Beast*.

JOHN WILMOT, EARL OF ROCHESTER (1675)

An *ignis fatuus* is a Will o' the Wisp; *Bubbles* are the victims of con-
men. The speaker arguing with the poet on the second page is
clearly a member of the clergy. Rochester was possibly an atheist at
this time, though his translation of Seneca (see Section 3) was
written not long before his death-bed conversion.

Upon Nothing

1

Nothing! thou Elder Brother ev'n to Shade,
That hadst a Being e're the World was made,
And (well fixt) art alone, of ending not afraid.

2

E're time and place were, time and place were not,
When Primitive *Nothing* something strait begot,
Then all proceeded from the great united – What?

3

Something, the Gen'ral Attribute of all,
Sever'd from thee, it's sole Original,
Into thy boundless self must undistinguish'd fall.

4

Yet something did thy mighty Pow'r command,
And from thy fruitful emptiness's hand,
Snatch'd Men, Beasts, Birds, Fire, [Water,] Air and Land.

5

Matter, the wicked'st off-spring of thy Race,
By Form assisted, flew from thy Embrace,
And Rebel Light obscur'd thy reverend dusky Face.

6

With Form, and Matter, Time and Place did joyn,
Body, thy Foe, with [these] did Leagues combine,
To spoil thy peaceful Realm, and ruine all thy Line.

7

But turn-Coat Time assists the Foe in vain,
And, brib'd by thee, [destroys their] short-liv'd Reign,
And to thy hungry Womb drives back thy Slaves again.

8

Tho' Mysteries are barr'd from Laick Eyes,
And the Divine alone, with Warrant, pryes
Into thy Bosom, where the truth in private lies,

9

Yet this of thee the wise may freely say,
Thou from the virtuous nothing tak'st away,
And to be part with thee the Wicked wisely pray.

10

Great Negative, how vainly would the Wise,
Enquire, define, distinguish, teach, devise?
Didst thou not stand to point their dull Philosophies.

11

Is, or *is not*, the two great Ends of Fate,
And, true or false, the subject of debate,
That perfect, or destroy, the vast designs of Fate,

12

When they have rack'd the *Politician*'s Breast,
Within thy Bosom most securely rest,
And, when reduc'd to thee, are least unsafe and best.

13

But, *Nothing*, why does *Something* still permit,
That Sacred Monarchs should at Council sit,
With Persons highly thought at best for nothing fit?

14

Whilst weighty *Something* modestly abstains,
From Princes Coffers, and from States-Men's Brains,
And Nothing there like stately *Nothing* reigns,

15

Nothing who dwell'st with Fools in grave Disguise,
For whom they rev'rend Shapes, and Forms devise,
Lawn Sleeves, and Furs, and Gowns, when they like thee
      look wise.

16

French Truth, *Dutch* Prowess, *Brittish* Policy,
Hibernian Learning, *Scotch* Civility,
Spaniards Dispatch, *Danes* Wit, are mainly seen in thee.

17

The great Man's Gratitude to his best Friend,
Kings Promises, Whores Vows, tow'rds thee they bend,
Flow swiftly into thee, and in thee ever end.

JOHN WILMOT, EARL OF ROCHESTER (c.1679)

from *Absalom and Achitophel*

This great political satire, using biblical parallels, was written on the eve
of the trial of the Earl of Shaftesbury (Achitophel) for high treason in
1681. David is Charles II, well known for his many mistresses (which
explains the opening of the poem) and Absalom his illegitimate son, the
Duke of Monmouth. The handsome and popular Monmouth was in fact
later to lead an unsuccessful rebellion against Charles's brother James
II, for which he was executed. The poem was written in the aftermath of
the alleged Popish plot, when the informer Titus Oates caused the ruin
or death of many people said to be plotting against the State. The
atmosphere was very similar to that prevailing in McCarthyite America.
The extracts below describe Monmouth and Shaftesbury and the latter's
initial approach to the Duke. Saul is Cromwell and the Jews are the
English. Further extracts will be found in Section 13.

   In pious times, ere priestcraft did begin,
Before polygamy was made a sin;
When man on many multiplied his kind,
Ere one to one was cursedly confined;
When nature prompted and no law denied
Promiscuous use of concubine and bride;
Then Israel's monarch after Heaven's own heart,
His vigorous warmth did variously impart
To wives and slaves; and, wide as his command,
Scattered his Maker's image through the land.
Michal, of royal blood, the crown did wear,
A soil ungrateful to the tiller's care:
Not so the rest; for several mothers bore

To godlike David several sons before.
But since like slaves his bed they did ascend,
No true succession could their seed attend.
Of all this numerous progeny was none
So beautiful, so brave, as Absalom:
Whether, inspired by some diviner lust,
His father got him with a greater gust,
Or that his conscious destiny made way,
By manly beauty, to imperial sway.
Early in foreign fields he won renown,
With kings and states allied to Israel's crown:
In peace the thoughts of war he could remove,
And seemed as he were only born for love.
Whate'er he did, was done with so much ease,
In him alone 'twas natural to please;
His motions all accompanied with grace;
And paradise was opened in his face.
With secret joy indulgent David viewed
His youthful image in his son renewed:
To all his wishes nothing he denied;
And made the charming Annabel his bride.
What faults he had (for who from faults is free?)
His father could not, or he would not see.
Some warm excesses which the law forbore,
Were construed youth that purged by boiling o'er:
And Amnon's murther, by a specious name,
Was called a just revenge for injured fame.
Thus praised and loved the noble youth remained,
While David, undisturbed, in Sion reigned.
But life can never be sincerely blest;
Heaven punishes the bad, and proves the best.
The Jews, a headstrong, moody, murmuring race,
As ever tried the extent and stretch of grace;
God's pampered people, whom, debauched with ease,
No king could govern, nor no God could please
(Gods they had tried of every shape and size
That god-smiths could produce, or priests devise);
These Adam-wits, too fortunately free,
Began to dream they wanted liberty;
And when no rule, no precedent was found,

Of men by laws less circumscribed and bound,
They led their wild desires to woods and caves,
And thought that all but savages were slaves.
They who, when Saul was dead, without a blow,
Made foolish Ishbosheth the crown forgo;
Who banished David did from Hebron bring,
And with a general shout proclaimed him king:
Those very Jews, who, at their very best,
Their humor more than loyalty expressed,
Now wondered why so long they had obeyed
An idol monarch, which their hands had made;
Thought they might ruin him they could create,
Or melt him to that golden calf, a state.

*   *   *

   Of these the false Achitophel was first;
A name to all succeeding ages cursed:
For close designs, and crooked counsels fit;
Sagacious, bold, and turbulent of wit;
Restless, unfixed in principles and place;
In power unpleased, impatient of disgrace:
A fiery soul, which, working out its way,
Fretted the pygmy body to decay,
And o'er-informed the tenement of clay.
A daring pilot in extremity;
Pleased with the danger, when the waves went high,
He sought the storms; but, for a calm unfit,
Would steer too nigh the sands, to boast his wit.
Great wits are sure to madness near allied,
And thin partitions do their bounds divide;
Else why should he, with wealth and honor blest,
Refuse his age the needful hours of rest?
Punish a body which he could not please;
Bankrupt of life, yet prodigal of ease?
And all to leave what with his toil he won,
To that unfeathered two-legged thing, a son;
Got, while his soul did huddled notions try;
And born a shapeless lump, like anarchy.
In friendship false, implacable in hate,
Resolved to ruin or to rule the state.

To compass this the triple bond he broke,
The pillars of the public safety shook,   }
And fitted Israel for a foreign yoke;
Then seized with fear, yet still affecting fame,
Usurped a patriot's all-atoning name.
So easy still it proves in factious times,
With public zeal to cancel private crimes.
How safe is treason, and how sacred ill,
Where none can sin against the people's will!
Where crowds can wink, and no offense be known,
Since in another's guilt they find their own!
Yet fame deserved, no enemy can grudge;
The statesman we abhor, but praise the judge.
In Israel's courts ne'er sat an Abbethdin
With more discerning eyes, or hands more clean;
Unbribed, unsought, the wretched to redress;
Swift of dispatch, and easy of access.
Oh, had he been content to serve the crown,
With virtues only proper to the gown;
Or had the rankness of the soil been freed
From cockle, that oppressed the noble seed;
David for him his tuneful harp had strung,
And Heaven had wanted one immortal song.
But wild Ambition loves to slide, not stand,
And Fortune's ice prefers to Virtue's land.
Achitophel, grown weary to possess
A lawful fame, and lazy happiness,
Disdained the golden fruit to gather free,
And lent the crowd his arm to shake the tree.
Now, manifest of crimes contrived long since,
He stood at bold defiance with his prince;
Held up the buckler of the people's cause
Against the crown, and skulked behind the laws.
The wished occasion of the Plot he takes;
Some circumstances finds, but more he makes.
By buzzing emissaries fills the ears
Of listening crowds with jealousies and fears
Of arbitrary counsels brought to light,
And proves the king himself a Jebusite.

Weak arguments! which yet he knew full well
Were strong with people easy to rebel.
For, governed by the moon, the giddy Jews
Tread the same track when she the prime renews;
And once in twenty years, their scribes record,
By natural instinct they change their lord.
Achitophel still wants a chief, and none
Was found so fit as warlike Absalom:
Not that he wished his greatness to create
(For politicians neither love nor hate),
But, for he knew his title not allowed,
Would keep him still depending on the crowd,
That kingly power, thus ebbing out, might be
Drawn to the dregs of a democracy.
Him he attempts with studied arts to please,
And sheds his venom in such words as these:
    'Auspicious prince, at whose nativity
Some royal planet ruled the southern sky;
Thy longing country's darling and desire;
Their cloudy pillar and their guardian fire:
Their second Moses, whose extended wand
Divides the seas, and shows the promised land;
Whose dawning day in every distant age
Has exercised the sacred prophet's rage:
The people's prayer, the glad diviners' theme,
The young men's vision, and the old men's dream!
Thee, savior, thee, the nation's vows confess,
And, never satisfied with seeing, bless:
Swift unbespoken pomps thy steps proclaim,
And stammering babes are taught to lisp thy name.
How long wilt thou the general joy detain,
Starve and defraud the people of thy reign?
Content ingloriously to pass thy days
Like one of Virtue's fools that feeds on praise;
Till thy fresh glories, which now shine so bright,
Grow stale and tarnish with our daily sight.
Believe me, royal youth, thy fruit must be
Or gathered ripe, or rot upon the tree.
Heaven has to all allotted, soon or late,
Some lucky revolution of their fate;

Whose motions if we watch and guide with skill
(For human good depends on human will),
Our Fortune rolls as from a smooth descent,
And from the first impression takes the bent;
But, if unseized, she glides away like wind,
And leaves repenting Folly far behind . . . '

JOHN DRYDEN (published 1681)

Absalom is then persuaded by Achitophel (called, in Miltonic terms, 'Hell's dire angel') with psychologically powerful arguments to lead a movement to force his father's abdication. The prince wins over the crowds with his attractive personality. After the general observations on the foolishness of the people and the need for enlightened monarchy as a guarantee of political stability, Dryden portrays, under Hebrew names, some of the King's loyal supporters, before David makes a speech and restores order. A second part of the poem, mostly not by Dryden was published later.

from *The True-Born Englishman*

Defoe points out that ever since the Norman conquest people have been arriving and intermingling with those already here and defends new immigrants under William III against prejudice.

These are the Heroes that despise the *Dutch*,
And rail at new-come Foreigners so much;
Forgetting that themselves are all deriv'd
From the most Scoundrel Race that ever liv'd.
A horrid Medly of Thieves and Drones,
Who ransack'd Kingdoms, and dispeopl'd Towns.
The *Pict* and Painted *Britain*, Treach'rous *Scot*,
By Hunger, Theft, and Rapine, hither brought.
Norwegian Pirates, Buccaneering *Danes*,
Whose Red-hair'd Offspring ev'ry where remains.
Who join'd with *Norman-French*, compound the Breed
From whence your *True-Born Englishmen* proceed.

And lest by Length of Time it be pretended,
The Climate may this Modern Breed ha' mended,
Wise Providence, to keep us where we are,
Mixes us daily with exceeding Care:
We have been *Europe's* Sink, *the Jakes* where she
Voids all her Offal Out-cast Progeny.
From our Fifth *Henry's* time, the Strolling Bands
Of banish'd Fugitives from Neighb'ring Lands,
Have here a certain Sanctuary found:
The Eternal Refuge of the Vagabond.
Where in but half a common Age of Time,
Borr'wing new Blood and Manners from the Clime,
Proudly they learn all Mankind to contemn,
And all their Race are *True-Born Englishmen*.

   Dutch, *Walloons*, *Flemings*, *Irishmen*, and *Scots*,
Vaudois and *Valtolins*, and *Hugonots*,
In good Queen *Bess's* Charitable Reign,
Suppli'd us with Three hundred thousand Men.
Religion, *God we thank thee*, sent them hither,
Priests, Protestants, the Devil and all together:
Of all Professions, and of ev'ry Trade,
All that were persecuted or afraid;
Whether for Debt or other Crimes they fled,
David at *Hackelah* was still their Head.

   The Offspring of this Miscellaneous Crowd,
Had not their new Plantations long enjoy'd,
But they grew *Englishmen*, and rais'd their Votes
At Foreign Shoals of *Interloping Scots*.
The Royal Branch from *Pict-land* did succeed,
With Troops of *Scots* and Scabs from *North-by-Tweed*.
The Seven first Years of his Pacifick Reign,
Made him and half his Nation *Englishmen*.
Scots from the *Northern* Frozen Banks of Tay,
With Packs and Plods came *Whigging* all away:
Thick as the Locusts which in *Egypt* swarm'd,
With Pride and hungry Hopes compleatly arm'd:
With Native Truth, Diseases, and No Money,
Plunder'd our *Canaan* of the Milk and Honey.

Here they grew quickly Lords and Gentlemen,
And all their Race are *True-Born Englishmen*.

    The Civil Wars, the common Purgative,
Which always use to make the Nation thrive,
Made way for all that strolling Congregation,
Which throng'd in Pious *Ch[arle]s's* Restoration.
The *Royal Refugee* our Breed restores,
With *Foreign Courtiers*, and with *Foreign Whores*:
And carefully repeopled us again,
Throughout his Lazy, Long, Lascivious Reign,
With such a blest and True-born *English* Fry,
As much Illustrates our Nobility.
A Gratitude which will so black appear,
As future Ages must abhor to hear:
When they look back on all that Crimson Flood,
Which stream'd in *Lindsey's*, and *Caernarvon's* Blood:
Bold *Strafford*, *Cambridge*, *Capel*, *Lucas*, *Lisle*,
Who crown'd in Death his Father's Fun'ral Pile.
The Loss of whom, in order to supply
With True-Born *English* Nobility,
Six Bastard Dukes survive his Luscious Reign,
The Labours of *Italian C[astlemai]n*,
French P[ortsmout]h, *Tabby S[co]t*, and *Cambrian*.
Besides the Num'rous Bright and Virgin Throng,
Whose Female Glories shade them from my Song.

    This Offspring, if one Age they multiply,
May half the House with *English* Peers supply:
There with true *English* Pride they may contemn
S[chomber]g and *P[ortlan]d*, new-made Noblemen.

    French Cooks, *Scotch* Pedlars, and *Italian* Whores,
Were all made Lords, or Lords Progenitors.
Beggars and Bastards by his new Creation,
Much multipli'd the Peerage of the Nation;
Who will be all, e're one short Age runs o're,
As True-Born Lords as those we had before.

    Then to recruit the Commons he prepares,
And heal the latent Breaches of the Wars:
The Pious Purpose better to advance,

H' invites the banish'd Protestants of *France*:
Hither for God's sake and their own they fled,
Some for Religion came, and some for Bread:
Two hundred thousand Pair of Wooden Shooes,
Who, God be thank'd, had nothing left to lose;
To Heav'n's great Praise did for Religion fly,
To make us starve our Poor in Charity.
In ev'ry Port they plant their fruitful Train,
To get a Race of *True-Born Englishmen*:
Whose Children will, when riper Years they see,
Be as Ill-natur'd and as Proud as we:
Call themselves *English*, Foreigners despise,
Be surly like us all, and just as wise.

    Thus from a Mixture of all Kinds began,
That Het'rogeneous Thing, *An Englishman*:
In eager Rapes, and furious Lust begot,
Betwixt a Painted *Britton* and a *Scot*:
Whose gend'ring Offspring quickly learnt to bow,
And yoke their Heifers to the *Roman* Plough:
From whence a Mongrel half-bred Race there came,
With neither Name nor Nation, Speech or Fame.
In whose hot Veins new Mixtures quickly ran,
Infus'd betwixt a *Saxon* and a *Dane*.
While their Rank Daughters, to their Parents just,
Receiv'd all Nations with Promiscuous Lust.
This Nauseous Brood directly did contain
The well-extracted Blood of *Englishmen*.

    Which Medly canton'd in a Heptarchy,
A Rhapsody of Nations to supply,
Among themselves maintain'd eternal Wars,
And still the Ladies lov'd the Conquerors.

    The *Western* Angles all the rest subdu'd;
A bloody Nation, barbarous and rude:
Who by the Tenure of the Sword possest
One part of *Britain*, and subdu'd the rest.
And as great things denominate the small,
The Conqu'ring Part gave Title to the Whole.
The *Scot*, *Pict*, *Britain*, *Roman*, *Dane* submit,

And with the *English-Saxon* all unite:
And these the Mixture have so close pursu'd,
The very Name and Memory's subdu'd;
No *Roman* now, no *Britain* does remain;
Wales strove to separate, but strove in vain:
The silent Nations undistinguish'd fall,
And *Englishman*'s the common Name for all.
Fate jumbl'd them together, *God knows how*;
Whate're they were, they're *True-Born English* now.

DANIEL DEFOE (1701)

from the *Epistle to A Lady*

Pope comments to a valued female friend on the empty lives
of society women.

Men, some to business, some to pleasure take;
But every woman is at heart a rake;
Men, some to quiet, some to public strife;
But every lady would be queen for life.
Yet mark the fate of a whole sex of queens:
Power all their end, but beauty all the means.
In youth they conquer, with so wild a rage,
As leaves them scarce a subject in their age:
For foreign glory, foreign joy, they roam;
No thought of peace or happiness at home.
But wisdom's triumph is well-timed retreat,
As hard a science to the fair as great!
Beauties, like tyrants, old and friendless grow,
Yet hate repose, and dread to be alone,
Worn out in public, weary every eye,
Nor leave one sigh behind them when they die.
Pleasures the sex, as children birds, pursue
Still out of reach, yet never out of view,
Sure, if they catch, to spoil the toy at most,

To covet flying, and regret when lost:
At last, to follies youth could scarce defend,
It grows their age's prudence to pretend;
Ashamed to own they gave delight before,
Reduced to feign it, when they give no more;
As hags hold sabbaths, less for joy than spite,
So these their merry, miserable night;
Still round and round the ghosts of beauty glide
And haunt the places where their honor died.
      See how the world its veterans rewards
A youth of frolics, an old age of cards;
Fair to no purpose, artful to no end,
Young without lovers, old without a friend;
A fop their passion, but their prize a sot;
Alive, ridiculous, and dead, forgot!
      Ah friend! to dazzle let the vain design;
To raise the thought, and touch the heart be thine!
That charm shall grow, while what fatigues the Ring
Flaunts and goes down, an unregarded thing:
So when the sun's broad beam has tired the sight,
All mild ascends the moon's more sober light,
Serene in virgin modesty she shines,
And unobserved the glaring orb declines.
      Oh! blest with temper, whose unclouded ray
Can make tomorrow cheerful as today;
She, who can love a sister's charms, or hear
Sighs for a daughter with unwounded ear;
She, who ne'er answers till a husband cools
Or, if she rules him, never shows she rules;
Charms by accepting, by submitting sways,
Yet has her humor most, when she obeys;
Lets fops or fortune fly which way they will;
Disdains all loss of tickets or Codille;
Spleen, vapors, or smallpox, above them all,
And mistress of herself, though China fall.
      And yet, believe me, good as well as ill,
Woman's at best a contradiction still.
Heaven, when it strives to polish all it can
Its last best work, but forms a softer man;
Picks from each sex, to make the favorite blest.

Your love of pleasure, our desire of rest:
Blends, in exception to all general rules,
Your taste of follies, with our scorn of fools:
Reserve with frankness, art with truth allied,
Courage with softness, modesty with pride;
Fixed principles, with fancy ever new;
Shakes all together, and produces – you.
   Be this a woman's fame: with this unblest,
Toasts live a scorn, and queens may die a jest.
This Phoebus promised (I forget the year)
When those blue eyes first opened on the sphere:
Ascendant Phoebus watched that hour with care.
Averted half your parents' simple prayer;
And gave you beauty, but denied the pelf
That buys your sex a tyrant o'er itself.
The generous god, who wit and gold refines,
And ripens spirits as he ripens mines,
Kept dross for duchesses, the world shall know it.
To you gave sense, good humor, and a poet.

ALEXANDER POPE (1735)

The Ring was the circuit in Hyde Park where the fashionable world
rode or drove to show itself off. The tickets mentioned are lottery
tickets. Codille was the end of the game of ombre, as played in *The
Rape of the Lock* (see Section 4). 'China' had been a word with a
double meaning since a famous scene in Wycherley's *The Country
Wife*, where it was used as a code word for sex.

from *The Seasons – Winter*

THOUGHTS ON POVERTY

Ah! little think the gay licentious proud,
Whom pleasure, power, and affluence surround –
They, who their thoughtless hours in giddy mirth,
And wanton, often cruel, riot waste –
Ah! little think they, while they dance along,
How many feel, this very moment, death
And all the sad variety of pain;
How many sink in the devouring flood,
Or more devouring flame; how many bleed,
By shameful variance betwixt man and man;
How many pine in want, and dungeon-glooms,
Shut from the common air and common use
Of their own limbs; how many drink the cup
Of baleful grief, or eat the bitter bread
Of misery; sore pierced by wintry winds,
How many shrink into the sordid hut
Of cheerless poverty; how many shake
With all the fiercer tortures of the mind,
Unbounded passion, madness, guilt, remorse –
Whence, tumbled headlong from the height of life,
They furnish matter for the tragic muse;
Even in the vale, where wisdom loves to dwell,
With friendship, peace, and contemplation joined,
How many, racked with honest passions, droop
In deep retired distress; how many stand
Around the death-bed of their dearest friends,
And point the parting anguish! Thought fond man
Of these, and all the thousand nameless ills
That one incessant struggle render life,
One scene of toil, of suffering, and of fate,
Vice in his high career would stand appalled.
And heedless rambling Impulse learn to think;
The conscious heart of Charity would warm,
And her wide wish Benevolence dilate;
The social tear would rise, the social sigh;

And, into clear perfection, gradual bliss,
Refining still, the social passions work.
    And here can I forget the generous band
Who, touched with human woe, redressive searched
Into the horrors of the gloomy jail?
Unpitied and unheard where misery moans,
Where sickness pines, where thirst and hunger burn,
And poor misfortune feels the lash of vice;
While in the land of liberty – the land
Whose every street and public meeting glow
With open freedom – little tyrants raged,
Snatched the lean morsel from the starving mouth.
Tore from cold wintry limbs the tattered weed,
Even robbed them of the last of comforts, sleep,
The free-born Briton to the dungeon chained
Or, as the lust of cruelty prevailed,
At pleasure marked him with inglorious stripes,
And crushed out lives, by secret barbarous ways,
That for their country would have toiled or bled.
O great design! if executed well.
With patient care and wisdom-tempered zeal.
Ye sons of mercy! yet resume the search;
Drag forth the legal monsters into light,
Wrench from their hands Oppression's iron rod,
And bid the cruel feel the pains they give.
Much still untouched remains; in this rank age,
Much is the patriot's weeding hand required.
The toils of law – what dark insidious men
Have cumbrous added to perplex the truth
And lengthen simple justice into trade –
How glorious were the day that saw these broke,
And every man within the reach of right!

JAMES THOMSON (1726)

from *The Washerwoman's Labour*

THE CONDITION OF WORKING WOMEN
(AN ANSWER TO STEPHEN DUCK)

'Tis true, that when our Morning's work is done,
And all our Grass expos'd unto the Sun.
While that his scorching Beams do on it shine.
As well as you we have a Time to dine:
I hope, that since we freely toil and sweat
To earn our Bread, you'll give us Time to eat.
That over, soon we must get up again,
And nimbly turn our Hay upon the Plain;
Nay, rake and prow it in, the Case is clear;
Or how should Cocks in equal Rows appear?
But if you'd have what you wrote believ'd
I find that you to hear us talk are griev'd:
In this, I hope you do not speak your Mind,
For none but Turks, that ever I could find
Have Mutes to serve them, or did e'er deny
Their Slaves at Work, to chat it merrily
Since you have Liberty to speak your Mind,
And are to talk, as well as we, inclin'd,
Why should you thus repine, because that we,
Like you enjoy that pleasing Liberty?
What! would you lord it quite, and take away
The only Privilege our Sex employ?

When Ev'ning does approach, we homeward hie,
And our domestick Toils incessant ply:
Against your coming Home prepare to get
Our Work all done, our House in order set;
Bacon and Dumpling in the Pot we boil;
Our Beds we make, our Swine we feed the while;
Then wait at Door to see you coming Home,
And set the Table out against you come:
Early next Morning we on you attend;
Our Children dress and feed, their Cloaths we mend;
And in the Field our daily Task renew

Soon as the rising Sun has dried the Dew.
When Harvest comes, into the Field we'll go,
And help to reap the Wheat as well as you;
Or else we go the Ears of Corn to glean;
No Labour scorning, be it e'er so mean;
But in the Work we freely bear a Part,
And what we can perform with all our Heart.

To get a Living we so willing are
Our tender Babes into the Field we bear,
And wrap them in our Cloaths to keep them Warm,
When round about we gather up the Corn;
And often unto them our Course do bend,
To came them safe, that nothing them offend:
Our Children that are able, bear a Share,
In gleaning Corn, such is our frugal Fare.
When night comes on, unto our Home to we go,
Our Corn we carry, and our Infant too;
Weary, indeed, but 'tis not worth our while
Once to complain, or *rest at ev'ry Stile*;
We must make haste, for when we Home are come,
We find again our Work has just begun;
So many Things for our Attendance call,
Had we ten Hands, we could employ them all.
Our Children put to Bed, with greatest Care
We all Things for your coming Home prepare:
You sup, and go to Bed without Delay,
And rest yourself until the ensuing Day;
While we, alas!, but little Sleep can have,
Because our froward Children cry and rave;
Yet, without Fail, as soon as Daylight doth spring,
We in the Field again our Work begin,
And there, with all our Strength, our Toil renew,
Till Titan's golden Rays have dry'd the Dew;
Then Home we go unto our Children dear,
Dress, feed, and bring them to the Field with Care . . .

The Harvest ended, Respite none we find;
The Hardest of our Toil is still behind:
Hard Labour we most cheerfully pursue,

And out, abroad, a chairing often go:
Of which I now will briefly tell in part,
What fully to declare is past my Art;
So many Hardships daily we go through,
I boldly say, the like you never knew.

MARY COLLIER (published 1762)

Mary Collier, a self-taught Hampshire woman, is responding
vigorously to criticisms of woman's idleness made by the 'thresher
poet' Stephen Duck. Her poem goes on to describe in vivid detail
the slave-like and poorly paid conditions in which washerwomen
worked. A Gloucestershire Exciseman who doubted her authorship
was answered in similarly forthright verse.

from *The Deserted Village*

Ye friends to truth, ye statesmen who survey
The rich man's joys increase, the poor's decay,
'Tis yours to judge how wide the limits stand
Between a splendid and a happy land.
Proud swells the tide with loads of freighted ore,
And shouting Folly hails them from her shore;
Hoards, even beyond the miser's wish, abound,
And rich men flock from all the world around.
Yet count our gains. This wealth is but a name
That leaves our useful products still the same.
Not so the loss. The man of wealth and pride
Takes up a space that many poor supplied;
Space for his lake, his park's extended bounds,
Space for his horse, his equipage and hounds;
The robe that wraps his limbs in silken sloth,
Has robbed the neighbouring field of half their growth;
His seat? where solitary sports are seen,
Indignant spurns the cottage from the green;
Around the world each needful product flies,

For all the luxuries the world supplies:
While thus the land, adorned for pleasure all,
In barren splendour feebly waits the fall.

*   *   *

Where, then, ah where, shall poverty reside
To scape the pressure of contiguous pride?
If to some common's fenceless limits strayed,
He drives his flock to pick the scanty blade,
Those fenceless fields the sons of wealth divide,
And even the bare-worn common is denied.

    If to the city sped – What waits him there?
To see profusion that he must not share;
To see ten thousand baleful arts combined
To pamper luxury, and thin mankind;
To see those joys the sons of pleasure know
Extorted from his fellow creature's woe.
Here, while the courtier glitters in brocade,
There the pale artist plies his sickly trade;
Here, while the proud their long-drawn pomps display.
There the black gibbet glooms beside the way,
The dome where Pleasure holds her midnight reign
Here, richly decked, admits the gorgeous train;
Tumultuous grandeur crowds the blazing square,
The rattling chariots clash, the torches glare.
Sure, scenes like these no troubles e'er annoy!
Sure, these denote one universal joy!
Are these thy serious thoughts? – Ah, turn thine eyes
Where the poor, houseless, shivering female lies.
She once, perhaps, in village plenty blest,
Has wept at tales of innocence distressed;
Her modest looks the cottage might adorn,
Sweet as the primrose peeps beneath the thorn;
Now, lost to all; her friends, her virtue fled,
Near her betrayer's door she lays her head,
And, pinched with cold and shrinking from the shower,
With heavy heart deplores that luckless hour,
When idly first, ambitious of the town,
She left her wheel and robes of country brown.

Do thine, sweet Auburn, thine, the loveliest train
Do thy fair tribes participate her pain?
Even now, perhaps, by cold and hunger led,
At proud men's doors they ask a little bread!

Ah, no. To distant climes, a dreary scene,
Where half the convex world intrudes between,
Through torrid tracts with fainting steps they go,
Where wild Altama murmurs to their woe.
Far different there from all that charmed before
The various terrors of that horrid shore:
Those blazing suns that dart a downward ray,
And fiercely shed intolerable day;
Those matted woods where birds forget to sing,
And silent bats in drowsy clusters cling;
Those poisonous fields with rank luxuriance crowned,
Where the dark scorpion gathers death around;
Where, at each step, the stranger fears to wake
The rattling terrors of the vengeful snake;
Where crouching tigers wait their hapless prey,
And savage men, more murderous still than they;
While oft in whirls the mad tornado flies
Mingling the ravaged landscape with the skies.
Far different these from every former scene,
The cooling brook, the grassy-vested green,
The breezy covert of the warbling grove,
That only sheltered thefts of harmless love.

Good Heaven! what sorrows gloomed that parting day,
And called them from their native walks away;
When the poor exiles, every pleasure past,
Hung round their bowers and fondly looked their last,
And took a last farewell and wished in vain
For seat like these beyond the western main;
And, shuddering still to face the distant deep,
Returned and wept, and still returns to weep.
The good old sire the first prepared to go
To new-found worlds, and wept for others' woe;
But for himself, in conscious virtue brave,
He only wished for worlds beyond the grave.
His lovely daughter, lovelier in her tears,

The fond companion of his helpless years,
Silent went next, neglectful of her charms,
And left a lover's for a father's arms.
With louder plaints the mother spoke her woes,
And blessed the cot where every pleasure rose;
And kissed her thoughtless babes with many a tear,
And clasped them close, in sorrow doubly dear;
While her fond husband strove to lend relief
In all the silent manliness of grief

O luxury! thou cursed by Heaven's decree,
How ill exchanged are things like these for thee!
How do thy potions with insidious joy
Diffuse their pleaures only to destroy!
Kingdoms by thee to sickly greatness grown,
Boast of a florid vigour not their own.
At every draught more large and large they grow,
A bloated mass of rank unwieldy woe;
Till sapped their strength, and every part unsound,
Down, down they sink and spread a ruin round.

Even now the devastation is begun,
And half the business of destruction done;
Even now, methinks, as pondering here I stand,
I see the rural virtues leave the land.
Down where yon anchoring vessel spreads the sail,
That idly waiting flaps with every gale,
Downward they move, a melancholy band,
Pass from the shore and darken all the strand.
Contented toil and hospitable care,
And kind connubial tenderness are there;
And piety with wishes placed above,
And steady loyalty and faithful love.

OLIVER GOLDSMITH (1768–70)

Goldsmith has been claimed by scholars to be describing a particular
village, either his childhood one of Lissoy in his native Ireland, or one
of a number of English alternatives. However, it is more likely that,
although any of these may have supplied some of the details, he is
actually writing about a composite fictional one in order to protest at
the often brutal way in which the peasantry were expelled from the

villages in order to create great estates and enclose land for what landlords saw as more productive farming to raise their income. Rural communities throughout the whole of Britain and Ireland went on being dispossessed in a similar way for over a century, with many of the villagers going to America, as here. The 'tigers' that they would encounter there would have been cougars, otherwise called 'mountain lions', which were sometimes called 'tigers' (though far from being as dangerous to man) by people in the eighteenth century. The 'pale artist' in the second extract is not a painter living in a garret but an underpaid and overworked artisan or craftsman! There are further extracts from the poem in Section 13.

The Negro's Complaint

Forc'd from home, and all its pleasures,
　　Afric's coast I left forlorn;
To increase a stranger's treasures,
　　O'er the raging billows borne.
Men from England bought and sold me,
　　Paid my price in paltry gold;
But, though theirs they have enroll'd me,
　　Minds are never to be sold.

Still in thought as free as ever,
　　What are England's rights, I ask,
Me from my delights to sever,
　　Me to torture, me to task?
Fleecy locks, and black complexion
　　Cannot forfeit nature's claim;
Skills may differ, but affection
　　Dwells in white and black the same.

Why did all-creating Nature
　　Make the plant for which we toil?
Sighs must fan it, tears must water,
　　Sweat of ours must dress the soil.
Think, ye masters, iron-hearted,
　　Lolling at your jovial boards;
Think how many backs have smarted
　　For the sweets your cane affords.

Is there, as ye sometimes tell us,
   Is there one who reigns on high?
Has he bid you buy and sell us,
   Speaking from his throne the sky?
Ask him, if your knotted scourges,
   Fetters, blood-extorting screws,
Are the means which duty urges
   Agents of his will to use?

Hark! he answers – Wild tornadoes,
   Strewing yonder sea with wrecks;
Wasting towns, plantations, meadows,
   Are the voice with which he speaks.
He, forseeing what vexations
   Afric's sons should undergo,
Fix'd their tyrants' habitations
   Where his whirlwinds answer – No.

By our blood in Afric wasted,
   Ere our necks receiv'd the chain;
By the mis'ries we have tasted,
   Crossing in your barks the main;
By our suff'rings since ye brought us
   To the man-degrading mart;
All sustain'd by patience, taught us
   Only by a broken heart:

Deem our nation brutes no longer
   Till some reason ye shall find
Worthier of regard and stronger
   Than the colour of our kind.
Slaves of gold, whose sordid dealings
   Tarnish all your boasted pow'rs,
Prove that you have human feelings,
Ere you proudly question ours!

WILLIAM COWPER (1788)

The Chimney Sweeper

When my mother died I was very young,
And my father sold me while yet my tongue
Could scarcely cry ' 'weep 'weep, 'weep 'weep!'
So your chimneys I sweep, and in soot I sleep.

There's little Tom Dacre, who cried when his head,
That curled like a lamb's back, was shaved; so I said,
'Hush, Tom, never mind it, for when your head's bare,
You know that soot cannot spoil your white hair.'

And so he was quiet, and that very night,
As Tom was a-sleeping he had such a sight –
That thousands of sweepers, Dick, Joe, Ned and Jack,
Were all of them locked up in coffins of black;

And by came an angel who had a bright key,
And he opened the coffins and set them all free;
And down a green plain leaping, laughing they run,
And wash in a river and shine in the sun.

Then, naked and white, all their bags left behind,
They rise upon clouds and sport in the wind,
And the angel told Tom, if he'd be a good boy,
He'd have God for his father and never want joy.

And so Tom awoke, and we rose in the dark,
And got with our bags and our brushes to work.
Though the morning was cold, Tom was happy and warm:
So if all do their duty, they need not fear harm.

WILLIAM BLAKE (1789)

The 'harm' they need not fear is clearly in the after-life! In a second poem on the same subject, Blake lays the blame for the appalling conditions endured by Tom and his fellow-sweeps firmly on their parents, the Church and the State as represented in the King.

From *The Gin-Shop; or, A Peep into Prison*

Come, neighbour, take a walk with me
    Through many a London street,
And see the cause of penury
    In hundreds we shall meet.

We shall not need to travel far –
    Behold that great man's door;
He well discerns that idle crew
    From the deserving poor.

He will relieve with liberal hand
    The child of honest thrift;
But where long scores at Gin-Shops stand
    He will withhold his gift.

Behold that shivering female there,
    Who plies her woeful trade!
'Tis ten to one you'll find that Gin
    That hopeless wretch has made.

Look down these steps, and view below
    Yon cellar under ground;
There every want and every woe,
    And every sin is found.

Those little wretches, trembling there
    With hunger and with cold,
Were by their parents' love of Gin
    To sin and misery sold . . .

To prison dire misfortune oft
    The guiltless debtor brings;
Yet oftener far it will be found
    From Gin the misery springs.

See the pale manufacturer there,
   How lank and lean he lies!
How haggard is his sickly cheek!
   How dim his hollow eyes!

He plied the loom with good success,
   His wages still were high;
Twice what the village-labourer gains
   His master did supply.

No book-debts kept him from his cash,
   All paid as soon as due;
His wages on the Saturday
   To fail he never knew.

How amply had his gains sufficed,
   On wife and children spent!
But all must for his pleasures go;
   All to the Gin-Shop went.

See that apprentice, young in years,
   But hackneyed long in sin;
What made him rob his master's till?
   Alas! 'twas love of Gin.

That serving-man – I knew him once,
   So jaunty, spruce and smart!
Why did he steal, then pawn the plate?
   'Twas Gin ensnared his heart.

But hark! what dismal sound is that?
   'Tis Saint Sepulchre's bell!
It tolls, alas! for human guilt,
   Some malefactor's knell.

O! woeful sound, O! what could cause
   Such punishment and sin?
Hark! hear his words, he owns the cause –
   Bad Company and Gin.

And when the future lot is fixed
   Of darkness, fire and chains,
How can the drunkard hope to 'scape
   Those everlasting pains?

For if the murderer's doomed to woe,
   As holy writ declares,
The drunkard with Self-murderers
   That dreadful portion shares.

HANNAH MORE (*c.* 1796)

Gin had been a social menace since early in the century, as Hogarth's famous painting *Gin Lane* shows.

3
FAITH, DOUBT, DESPAIR, MELANCHOLY & HOPE

from *Paradise Lost*

INVOCATION TO HEAVENLY LIGHT

Hail, holy Light! offspring of heaven first born!
Or of the Eternal coeternal beam,
May I express thee unblamed? since God is light,
And never but in unapproached light
Dwelt from eternity, dwelt then in thee,
Bright effluence of bright essence increate!
Or hear'st thou rather, pure ethereal stream,
Whose fountain who shall tell? Before the sun,
Before the heavens thou wert, and at the voice
Of God as with a mantle didst invest
The rising world of waters dark and deep
Won from the void and formless infinite.
Thee I revisit now with bolder wing,
Escaped the Stygian pool, though long detained
In that obscure sojourn, while in my flight
Through utter and through middle darkness borne,
With other notes than to the Orphean lyre,
I sang of Chaos and eternal night;
Taught by the heavenly muse to venture down
The dark descent, and up to reascend,
Though hard and rare: Thee I revisit safe,
And feel thy sovereign vital lamp; but thou
Revisit'st not these eyes, that roll in vain
To find thy piercing ray, and find no dawn;
So thick a drop serene hath quench'd their orbs,
Or dim suffusion veil'd. Yet not the more
Cease I to wander where the Muses haunt,
Clear spring or shady grove or sunny hill,
Smit with the love of sacred song; but chief
Thee, Sion, and the flowery brooks beneath,
That wash thy hallow'd feet and warbling flow,
Nightly I visit; nor sometimes forget
Those other two equalled with me in fate
So were I equalled with them in renown,
Blind Thamyris and blind Maeonides,

And Tiresias and Phineus, prophets old:
Then feed on thoughts that voluntary move
Harmonious numbers; as the wakeful bird
Sings darkling, and in shadiest covert hid
Tunes her nocturnal note. Thus with the year
Seasons return, but not to me returns
Day, or the sweet approach of even or morn,
Or sight of vernal bloom, or summer's rose,
Or flocks or herds or human face divine;
But cloud instead, and ever during dark
Surrounds me, from the cheerful ways of men
Cut off, and for the book of nature fair
Presented with an universal blank
Of nature's works, to me expunged and rased
And wisdom at one entrance quite shut out.
So much the rather thou, celestial light,
Shine inward, and the mind through all her powers
Irradiate; there plant eyes, all mist from thence
Purge and disperse, that I may see and tell
Of things invisible to mortal sight.

JOHN MILTON (published 1674)

Milton's invocation (to be found in Book III) derives special force
and pathos from the fact that he had been blind for some years,
possibly with cataract ('drop serene'), yet intended in *Paradise Lost*
to justify the ways of the God who might have been seen as
inflicting blindness upon him, despite his efforts to serve the divine
cause through his writing all his life. Thamyris, a legendary poet,
Homer, the writer of the greatest Greek epics, Tiresias, the prophet
who appears in Greek tragedy, and Phineus, another mythical
figure, were all blind. The 'wakeful bird' is the nightingale.

To Be a Pilgrim

Who would true valour see
Let him come hither;
One here will constant be,
Come wind, come weather;
There's no discouragement
Shall make him once relent
His first avow'd intent
To be a pilgrim.

Whoso beset him round
With dismal stories,
Do but themselves confound;
His strength the more is.
No lion can him fright;
He'll with a giant fight,
But he will have the right
To be a pilgrim.

Hobgoblin nor foul fiend
Can daunt his spirit;
He knows he at the end
Shall life inherit.
Then fancies flee away;
He'll fear not what men say;
He'll labour night and day
To be a pilgrim.

JOHN BUNYAN (published 1676)

Translation from Seneca

After Death nothing is and nothing Death;
The utmost Limits of a gasp of Breath.
Let the ambitious Zealot lay aside
His hopes of Heav'n; (whose Faith is but his Pride)
Let slavish Souls lay by their Fear,
Nor be concern'd which way or where,
After this life they shall be hurl'd:
Dead, we become the Lumber of the World;
And to that Mass of Matter shall be swept,
Where things destroy'd with things unborn are kept;
Devouring time swallows us whole,
Impartial Death confounds Body and Soul.
For Hell and the foul Fiend that rules
The everlasting fiery Gaols
Devis'd by Rogues, dreaded by Fools,
With his grim griesly Dog that keeps the Door
Are senseless Stories, idle Tales,
Dreams, Whimseys, and no more.

JOHN WILMOT, EARL OF ROCHESTER (1680)

Crucifixion to the World by the Cross of Christ

When I survey the wondrous cross
On which the Prince of Glory died,
My richest gain I count but loss,
And pour contempt on all my pride.

Forbid it, Lord, that I should boast
Save in the death of Christ my God;
All the vain things that charm me most,
I sacrifice them to his blood.

See from his head, his hands, his feet,
Sorrow and love flow mingled down;
Did e'er such love and sorrow meet?
Or thorns compose so rich a crown?

His dying crimson like a robe
Spreads o'er his body on the tree,
Then am I dead to all the globe,
And all the globe is dead to me.

Were the whole realm of nature mine,
That were a present far too small;
Love so amazing, so divine
Demands my soul, my life, my all.

ISAAC WATTS (c.1707)

Life's Progress

How gaily is at first begun
    Our life's uncertain race!
Whilst yet that sprightly morning sun,
With which we just set out to run,
    Enlightens all the place.

How smiling the world's prospect lies,
    How tempting to go through!
Not Canaan to the prophet's eyes,
From Pisgah with a sweet surprise,
    Did more inviting show.

How promising's the book of fate,
    Till throughly understood!
Whilst partial hopes such lots create
As may the youthful fancy treat
    With all that's great and good.

How soft the first ideas prove,
    Which wander through our minds!
How full of joys, how free the love
Which does that early season move,
    As flowers the western winds!

Our sighs are then but vernal air,
    But April-drops our tears,
Which swiftly passing, all grows fair,
Whilst beauty compensates our care,
    And youth each vapour clears.

But oh! too soon, alas, we climb;
    Scarce feeling, we ascend
The gently rising hill of time,
From whence with grief we see that prime,
    And all its sweetness end.

The die now cast, our station known,
   Fond expectation past;
The thorns, which former days had sown,
To crops of late repentance grown,
   Through which we toil at last.

Whilst every care's a driving harm
   That helps to bear us down,
Which faded smiles no more can charm,
But every tear's a winter-storm,
   And every look's a frown.

Till with succeeding ills oppressed,
   For joys we hoped to find;
By age too rumpled and undressed,
We, gladly sinking down to rest,
   Leave following crowds behind.

ANNE FINCH, COUNTESS OF WINCHILSEA (1709)

The Dying Christian to His Soul

Vital spark of heavenly flame!
Quit, O quit this mortal frame:
Trembling, hoping, ling'ring, flying,
O the pain, the bliss of dying!
Cease, fond Nature, cease thy strife,
And let me languish into life.

Hark! they whisper; angels say,
Sister Spirit, come away!
What is this absorbs me quite?
Steals my senses, shuts my sight,
Drowns my spirits, draws my breath?
Tell me, my soul, can this be death?

The world recedes; it disappears!
Heaven opens on my eyes! my ears
   With sounds seraphic ring!
Lend, lend your wings! I mount! I fly!
O Grave! where is thy victory?
   O Death! where is thy sting?

ALEXANDER POPE

from An Essay on Man

DIVINE ORDER

See, thro' this air, this ocean, and this earth,
All matter quick, and bursting into birth.
Above, how high, progressive life may go!
Around, how wide! how deep extend below!
Vast chain of Being, which from God began,
Natures ethereal, human, angel, man,
Beast, bird, fish, insect! what no eye can see,
No glass can reach! from Infinite to thee,
From thee to Nothing! – On superior pow'rs
Were we to press, inferior might on ours:
Or in the full creation leave a void,
Where, one step broken, the great scale's destroy'd:
From Nature's chain whatever link you strike,
Tenth or ten thousandth, breaks the chain alike.
   And if each system in gradation roll,
Alike essential to th'amazing whole;
The least confusion but in one, not all
That system only, but the whole must fall.
Let Earth unbalanc'd from her orbit fly,
Planets and Suns run lawless thro' the sky,
Let ruling Angels from their spheres be hurl'd,
Being on being wreck'd, and world on world,
Heav'n's whole foundations to their centre nod,
And Nature tremble to the throne of God:
All this dread ORDER break – for whom ? for thee ?
Vile worm! – oh Madness, Pride, Impiety !

What if the foot, ordain'd the dust to tread,
Or hand to toil, aspir'd to be the head ?
What if the head, the eye, or ear repin'd
To serve mere engines to the ruling Mind ?
Just as absurd for any part to claim
To be another, in this gen'ral frame:
Just as absurd, to mourn the tasks or pains
The great directing MIND of ALL ordains.

All are but parts of one stupendous whole,
Whose body Nature is, and God the soul;
That, chang'd thro' all, and yet in all the same,
Great in the earth, as in th'ethereal frame,
Warms in the sun, refreshes in the breeze,
Glows in the stars, and blossoms in the trees,
Lives thro' all life, extends thro' all extent,
Spreads undivided, operates unspent,
Breathes in our soul, informs our mortal part,
As full, as perfect, in a hair as heart;
As full, as perfect, in vile Man that mourns,
As the rapt Seraph that adores and burns;
To him no high, no low, no great, no small;
He fills, he bounds, connects, and equals all.

Cease then, nor ORDER Imperfection name:
Our proper bliss depends on what we blame.
Know thy own point: This kind, this due degree
Of blindness, weakness, Heav'n bestows on thee.
Submit – in this, or any other sphere,
Secure to be as blest as thou canst bear:
Safe in the hand of one disposing Pow'r,
Or in the natal, or the mortal hour.
All Nature is but Art, unknown to thee;
All Chance, Direction, which thou canst not see;
All Discord, Harmony, not understood;
All partial Evil, universal Good:
And, spite of Pride, in erring Reason's spite,
One truth is clear, 'Whatever is, is RIGHT.'

Epistle I, 233–94

MAN SHOULD NOT PRY INTO GOD

Know then thyself, presume not God to scan;
The proper study of Man kind is Man.
Plac'd on this isthmus of a middle state,
A being darkly wise, and rudely great:
With too much knowledge for the Sceptic side,
With too much weakness for the Stoic's pride,
He hangs between; in doubt to act, or rest,
In doubt to deem himself a God, or Beast;
In doubt his Mind or Body to prefer,
Born but to die, and reas'ning but to err;
Alike in ignorance, his reason such,
Whether he thinks too little, or too much:
Chaos of Thought and Passion, all confus'd;
Still by himself abus'd, or disabus'd;
Created half to rise, and half to fall;
Great lord of all things, yet a prey to all;
Sole judge of Truth, in endless Error hurl'd:
The glory, jest, and riddle of the world !

    Go, wond'rous creature! mount where Science guides,
Go, measure earth, weigh air, and state the tides;
Instruct the planets in what orbs to run,
Correct old Time, and regulate the Sun;
Go, soar with Plato to th'empyreal sphere,
To the first good, first perfect, and first fair;
Or tread the mazy round his follow'rs trod,
And quitting sense call imitating God;
As Eastern priests in giddy circles run,
And turn their heads to imitate the Sun.
Go, teach Eternal Wisdom how to rule –
Then drop into thyself, and be a fool!

    Superior beings, when of late they saw
A mortal Man unfold all Nature's law,
Admir'd such wisdom in an earthly shape,
And shew'd a NEWTON as we shew an Ape.
Could he, whose rules the rapid Comet bind,
Describe or fix one movement of his Mind ?
Who saw its fires here rise, and there descend,

Explain his own beginning, or his end ?
Alas what wonder! Man's superior part
Uncheck'd may rise, and climb from art to art:
But when his own great work is but begun,
What Reason weaves, by Passion is undone.

Epistle II, lines 1–42

THE FOLLIES OF MANKIND

Whate'er the Passion, knowledge, fame, or pelf,
Not one will change his neighbour with himself.
The learn'd is happy nature to explore,
The fool is happy that he knows no more;
The rich is happy in the plenty giv'n,
The poor contents him with the care of Heav'n.
See the blind beggar dance, the cripple sing,
The sot a hero, lunatic a king;
The starving chemist in his golden views
Supremely blest, the poet in his Muse.
See some strange comfort ev'ry state attend,
And Pride bestow'd on all, a common friend;
See some fit Passion ev'ry age supply,
Hope travels thro', nor quits us when we die.
Behold the child, by Nature's kindly law,
Pleas'd with a rattle, tickled with a straw:
Some livelier play-thing gives his youth delight,
A little louder, but as empty quite:
Scarfs, garters, gold, amuse his riper stage;
And beads and pray'r-books are the toys of age:
Pleas'd with this bauble still, as that before;
'Till tir'd he sleeps, and Life's poor play is o'er!
Meanwhile Opinion gilds with varying rays
Those painted clouds that beautify our days;
Each want of happiness by Hope supply'd,
And each vacuity of sense by Pride:
These build as fast as knowledge can destroy;
In Folly's cup still laughs the bubble, joy;
One prospect lost, another still we gain;

And not a vanity is giv'n in vain;
Ev'n mean Self-love becomes, by force divine,
The scale to measure others wants by thine.
See! and confess, one comfort still must rise,
'Tis this, Tho' Man's a fool, yet GOD IS WISE.

Epistle II, lines 249–94

ALEXANDER POPE (1733)

Ode

The spacious firmament on high,
With all the blue ethereal sky,
And spangled heavens, a shining frame,
Their great original proclaim:
The unwearied sun, from day to day,
Does his creator's power display,
And publishes to every land
The work of an almighty hand.

Soon as the evening shades prevail,
The moon takes up the wondrous tale,
And nightly to the listening earth
Repeats the story of her birth:
Whilst all the stars that round her burn,
And all the planets, in their turn,
Confirm the tidings as they roll,
And spread the truth from pole to pole.

What though, in solemn silence, all
Move round the dark terrestrial ball?
What though nor real voice nor sound
Amid their radiant orbs be found?
In reason's ear they all rejoice,
And utter forth a glorious voice,
For ever singing, as they shine,
'The hand that made us is divine.'

JOSEPH ADDISON

On the Difficulties of Religion

O wretched world! but wretched above all,
Is man; the most unhappy animal!
Not knowing to what state he shall belong,
He tugs the heavy chain of life along.
So many ages pass, yet no experience shows
From whence man comes, nor, after, where he goes.

We are instructed of a future state,
Of just rewards, and punishments in that;
But ign'rant how, or where, or when, or what.
I'm show'd a book, in which these things are writ;
And, by all hands, assur'd all's true in it;
But in this book, such mysteries I find,
Instead of healing, oft corrode the mind.
Sometimes our faith must be our only guide,
Our senses and our reason laid aside:
Again to reason we our faith submit,
This spurs, that checks, we curvet, champ the bit,
And make our future hopes uneasy sit!
Now faith, now reason, now good-works, does all;
Betwixt these opposites our virtues fall,
Each calling each false and heretical.

And, after all; what rule have we to show,
Whether these writings sacred be, or no?
If we allege the truths that we find there,
Are to themselves a testimony clear,
By the same rule, such all good morals are.
Thus we by doubts, and hopes, and fears, are tost,
And in the lab'rinth of disputes are lost.
Unhappy who with any doubts are curst!
But of all doubts, religious doubts are worst!
Wou'd I were dead! or wou'd I had no soul!
Had ne'er been born! or else been born a fool!

Then future fears wou'd not my thoughts annoy,
I'd use what's truly mine, the present joy.
Oh! happy brutes! I envy much your state,

Whom nature, one day, shall annihilate;
Compar'd to which, wretched is human fate!

JANE BARKER (1723)

An Elegiac Epistle to a Friend

**WRITTEN BY MR GAY, WHEN HE LABOURED
UNDER A DEJECTION OF SPIRITS**

1

Friend of my youth, shedd'st thou the pitying tear
  O'er the sad relics of my happier days,
Of nature tender, as of soul sincere,
  Pour'st thou for me the melancholy lays?

2

Oh! truly said! – the distant landscape bright,
  Whose vivid colours glitter'd on the eye
Is faded now, and sunk in shades of night,
  As, on some chilly eve, the closing flow'rets die.

3

Yet had I hop'd, when first, in happier times,
  I trod the magic paths where Fancy led,
The Muse to foster in more friendly climes,
  Where never Mis'ry rear'd its hated head.

4

How vain the thought! Hope after hope expires!
Friend after friend, joy after joy is lost;
My dearest wishes feed the fun'ral fires,
And life is purchas'd at too dear a cost.

5

Yet, could my heart the selfish comfort know,
  That not alone I murmur and complain;
Well might I find companions in my woe,
  All born to Grief, the family of Pain!

6

Full well I know, in life's uncertain road,
    The thorns of mis'ry are profusely sown;
Full well I know, in this low vile abode,
    Beneath the chast'ning rod what numbers groan.

7

Born to a happier state, how many pine
    Beneath th' oppressor's pow'r, or feel the smart
Of bitter want, or foreign evils join
    To the sad symptoms of a broken heart!

8

How many, fated from their birth to view
    Misfortunes growing with their rip'ning years;
The same sad track, through various scenes, pursue,
    Still journeying onward through a vale of tears.

9

To them, alas! what boots the light of heav'n,
    While still new mis'ries mark their destin'd way,
Whether to their unhappy lot be giv'n
    Death's long, sad night, or life's short busy day!

10

Me not such themes delight; – I more rejoice,
    When chance some happier, better change I see,
Though no such change await *my* luckless choice,
    And mountains rise between my hopes and me.

11

For why should he who roves the dreary waste,
    Still joy on ev'ry side to view the gloom,
Or when upon the couch of sickness plac'd,
    Well pleas'd survey a hapless neighbour's tomb?

12

If e'er a gleam of comfort glads my soul,
    If e'er my brow to wonted smiles unbends,
'Tis when the fleeting minutes, as they roll,
    Can add one gleam of pleasure to my friends.

13

Ev'n in these shades, the last retreat of grief,
    Some transient blessings will that thought bestow;
To Melancholy's self yield some relief,
    And ease the breast surcharg' d with mortal woe.

14

Long has my bark in rudest tempests toss'd,
    Buffetted seas, and stemm'd life's hostile wave;
Suffice it now, in all my wishes cross'd,
    To seek a peaceful harbour in the grave.

15

And when that hour shall come, (as come it must,)
    Ere many moons their waning horns increase,
When this frail frame shall mix with kindred dust,
    And all its fond pursuits and troubles cease:

16

When those black gates that ever open stand,
    Receive me on th' irremeable shore,
When Life's frail glass has run its latest sand,
    And the dull jest repeated charms no more:

17

Then may my friend weep o'er the fun'ral hearse,
    Then may his presence gild the awful gloom,
And his last tribute be some mournful verse,
    To mark the spot that holds my silent tomb.

18

This – and no more: – the rest let Heav'n provide,
    To which, resign' d, I trust my weal or woe,
Assur'd howe'er its justice shall decide,
    To find nought worse than I have left below.

JOHN GAY (*d.*1732)

from *Night Thoughts on Life, Death, and Immortality*

A CHRISTIAN'S FAITH IN THE RESURRECTION

See thou? Lorenzo! where hangs all our hope!
Touch'd by the Cross, we live, or more than die;
That touch which touch'd not angels; more divine
Than that which touch'd confusion into form,
And darkness into glory; partial touch!
Ineffably pre-eminent regard!
Sacred to man and sovereign through the whole
Long golden chain of miracles, which hangs
From heaven thro' all duration, and supports
In one illustrious and amazing plan,
Thy welfare, nature! and thy God's renown;
That touch? with charm celestial, heals the soul
Diseas'd, drives pain from guilt, lights life in death,
Turns earth to heaven, to heavenly thrones transforms
The ghastly ruins of the mould'ring tomb.

Dost ask me when? When he who died returns;
Returns how chang'd! Where then the man of woe?
In glory's terrors all the godhead burns;
And all his courts, exhausted by the tide
Of deities triumphant in his train,
Leave a stupendous solitude in heaven;
Replenisht soon, replenisht with increase
Of pomp and multitude; a radiant band
Of angels new; of angels from the tomb.

Is this by fancy thrown remote? and rise
Dark doubts between the promise and event?
I send thee not to volumes for thy cure;
Read Nature; Nature is a friend to truth;
Nature is Christian; preaches to mankind;
And bids dead matter aid us in our creed.
Hast thou not seen the comet's flaming flight?
The illustrious stranger, passing, terror sheds
On gazing nations, from his fiery train
Of length enormous, takes his ample round

Thro' depths of ether; coasts unnumbered worlds
Of more than solar glory; doubles wide
Heaven's mighty cape; and then revisits earth,
From the long travel of a thousand years.
Thus, at the destined period shall return
He, once on earth, who bids the comet blaze;
And, with him, all our triumph o'er the tomb.

EDWARD YOUNG (by 1745)

from *A Song for David*

For ADORATION, in the dome
Of Christ the swallows find a home;
      And on his olives perch:
The swallow also dwells with thee,
O man of God's humility,
      Within his Saviour CHURCH.

Sweet is the dew that falls betimes,
And drops upon the leafy limes;
      Sweet Hermon's fragrant air:
Sweet is the lily's silver bell
And sweet the wakeful tapers smell
      That watch for early prayer.

Sweet the young nurse with love intense,
Which smiles o'er sleeping innocence;
      Sweet when the lost arrive:
Sweet the musician's ardour beats,
While his vague mind's in quest of sweets,
      The choicest flow'rs to hive.

Sweeter, in all the strains of love,
The language of thy turtle dove,
      Pair'd to thy swelling chord;
Sweeter with ev'ry grace endu'd,
The glory of thy gratitude,
      Respir'd unto the Lord.

Strong is the horse upon his speed;
Strong in pursuit the rapid glede
    Which makes at once his game:
Strong the tall ostrich on the ground;
Strong through the turbulent profound
    Shoots xiphias to his aim.

Strong is the lion – like a coal
His eyeball – like a bastion's mole
    His chest against the foes:
Strong the gier-eagle on his sail,
Strong against tide th'enormous whale
    Emerges as he goes.

But stronger still, in earth and air,
And in the sea, the man of pray'r
    And far beneath the tide;
And in the sea to faith assign'd,
Where ask is have, where seek is find,
    Where knock is open wide.

Beauteous the fleet before the gale;
Beauteous the multitudes in mail,
    Rank'd arms and crested heads:
Beauteous the garden's umbrage mild,
Walk, water, meditated wild,
    And all the bloomy beds.

Beauteous the moon full on the lawn;
And beauteous, when the veil's withdrawn,
    The virgin to her spouse;
Beauteous the temple, decked and filled,
When to the heaven of heavens they build
    Their heart-directed vows.

Beauteous, yea, beauteous more than these,
The shepherd king upon his knees,
    For his momentous trust;
With wish of infinite conceit,
For man, beast, mute, the small and great,
    And prostrate dust to dust.

Precious the bounteous widow's mite;
And precious for extreme delight,
       The largess from the churl:
Precious the ruby's blushing blaze,
And alba's blest imperial rays,
         And pure cerulean pearl.

Precious the penitential tear;
And precious is the sigh sincere,
       Acceptable to God:
And precious are the winning flow'rs
In gladsome Israel's feast of bow'rs,
       Bound on the hallow'd sod.

More precious that diviner part
Of David, ev'n the Lord's own heart,
       Great, beautiful and new:
In all things where it was intent.
In all extremes, in each event,
       Proof, answering true to true.

Glorious the sun in mid career;
Glorious th'assembled fires appear;
       Glorious the comet's train:
Glorious the trumpet and alarm;
Glorious th' almighty stretched out arm;
       Glorious th'enraptured main:

Glorious the northern lights astream;
Glorious the song, when God's the theme;
       Glorious the thunder's roar:
Glorious hosanna from the den;
Glorious the catholic amen;
       Glorious the martyr's gore:

Glorious – more glorious is the crown
Of him that brought salvation down
       By meekness, call'd thy Son;
Thou at stupendous truth believ'd,
And now the matchless deed's achieved,
       DETERMINED, DARED, and DONE.

CHRISTOPHER SMART (1763)

In this great poem, following a famous Roman model, Johnson looks in turn at the chief things that people ask for in life and shows the disadvantages of each.

The Vanity of Human Wishes

IN IMITATION OF THE TENTH SATIRE OF JUVENAL

Let Observation, with extensive view,
Survey mankind, from China to Peru;
Remark each anxious toil, each eager strife,
And watch the busy scenes of crowded life;
Then say how hope and fear, desire and hate
O'erspread with snares the clouded maze of fate,
Where wavering man, betrayed by venturous pride
To tread the dreary paths without a guide,
As treacherous phantoms in the mist delude,
Shuns fancied ills, or chases airy good;
How rarely Reason guides the stubborn choice,
Rules the bold hand, or prompts the suppliant voice;
How nations sink, by darling schemes oppressed,
When Vengeance listens to the fool's request.
Fate wings with every wish the afflictive dart,
Each gift of nature, and each grace of art;
With fatal heat impetuous courage glows,
With fatal sweetness elocution flows,
Impeachment stops the speaker's powerful breath,
And restless fire precipitates on death.

Wealth   But scarce observed, the knowing and the bold
Fall in the general massacre of gold;
Wide-wasting pest! that rages unconfined,
And crowds with crimes the records of mankind;
For gold his sword the hireling ruffian draws,
For gold the hireling judge distorts the laws;
Wealth heaped on wealth, nor truth nor safety buys,
The dangers gather as the treasures rise.
Let History tell where rival kings command,

And dubious title shakes the madded land,
When statutes glean the refuse of the sword,
How much more safe the vassal than the lord,
Low skulks the hind beneath the rage of power,
And leaves the wealthy traitor in the Tower,
Untouched his cottage, and his slumbers sound,
Though Confiscation's vultures hover round.

The needy traveler, serene and gay,
Walks the wild heath, and sings his toil away.
Does envy seize thee? crush the upbraiding joy,
Increase his riches and his peace destroy;
New fears in dire vicissitude invade,
The rustling brake alarms, and quivering shade,
Nor light nor darkness bring his pain relief,
One shows the plunder, and one hides the thief.

Status   Yet still one general cry the skies assails,
And gain and grandeur load the tainted gales;
Few know the toiling statesman's fear or care,
The insidious rival and the gaping heir.

Once more Democritus, arise on earth,
With cheerful wisdom and instructive mirth,
See motley life in modern trappings dressed,
And feed with varied fools the eternal jest:
Thou who couldst laugh where Want enchained Caprice,
Toil crushed Conceit, and man was of a piece;
Where Wealth unloved without a mourner died;
And scarce a sycophant was fed by Pride;
Where ne'er was known the form of mock debate,
Or seen a new-made mayor's unwieldy state;
Where change of favorites made no change of laws,
And senates heard before they judged a cause;
How wouldst thou shake at Britain's modish tribe,
Dart the quick taunt, and edge the piercing gibe?
Attentive truth and nature to descry,
And pierce each scene with philosophic eye,
To thee were solemn toys or empty show
The robes of pleasures and the veils of woe:
All aid the farce, and all thy mirth maintain,
Whose joys are causeless, or whose griefs are vain.

Such was the scorn that filled the sage's mind,

Renewed at every glance on human kind;
How just that scorn ere yet thy voice declare,
Search every state and canvass every prayer.

    Unnumbered suppliants crowd Preferment's gate,
Athirst for wealth, and burning to be great;
Delusive Fortune hears the incessant call,
They mount, they shine, evaporate, and fall.
On every stage the foes of peace attend,
Hate dogs their flight, and Insult mocks their end.
Love ends with hope, the sinking statesman's door
Pours in the morning worshiper no more;
For growing names the weekly scribbler lies,
To growing wealth the dedicator flies;
From every room descends the painted face,
That hung the bright palladium of the place;
And smoked in kitchens, or in auctions sold,
To better features yields the frame of gold;
For now no more we trace in every line
Heroic worth, benevolence divine:
The form distorted justifies the fall,
And Detestation rids the indignant wall.

    But will not Britain hear the last appeal,
Sign her foes' doom, or guard her favorites' zeal?
Through Freedom's sons no more remonstrance rings,
Degrading nobles and controlling kings;
Our supple tribes repress their patriot throats,
And ask no questions but the price of votes,
With weekly libels and septennial ale,
Their wish is full to riot and to rail.

    In full-blown dignity, see Wolsey stand,
Law in his voice, and fortune in his hand:
To him the church, the realm their powers consign,
Through him the rays of regal bounty shine;
Turned by his nod the stream of honor flows,
His smile alone security bestows:
Still to new heights his restless wishes tower,
Claim leads to claim, and power advances power;
Till conquest unresisted ceased to please
And rights submitted, left him none to seize.
At length his sovereign frowns – the train of state

Mark the keen glance and watch the sign to hate.
Where'er he turns, he meets a stranger's eye,
His suppliants scorn him, and his followers fly;
At once is lost the pride of awful state,
The golden canopy, the glittering plate,
The regal palace, the luxurious board,
The liveried army, and the menial lord.
With age, with cares, with maladies oppressed,
He seeks the refuge of monastic rest.
Grief aids disease, remembered folly stings,
And his last sighs reproach the faith of kings.

   Speak thou, whose thoughts at humble peace repine,
Shall Wolsey's wealth, with Wolsey's end be thine?
Or liv'st thou now, with safer pride content,
The wisest justice on the banks of Trent?
For why did Wolsey, near the steeps of fate,
On weak foundations raise the enormous weight?
Why but to sink beneath misfortune's blow,
With louder ruin to the gulfs below?

   What gave great Villiers to the assassin's knife,
And fixed disease on Harley's closing life?
What murdered Wentworth, and what exiled Hyde,
By kings protected and to kings allied?
What but their wish indulged in courts to shine,
And power too great to keep or to resign?

   When first the college rolls receive his name,
The young enthusiast quits his ease for fame;
Academic   Resistless burns the fever of renown
distinction   Caught from the strong contagion of the gown:
O'er Bodley's dome his future labors spread,
And Bacon's mansion trembles o'er his head.
Are these thy views? proceed, illustrious youth,
And Virtue guard thee to the throne of Truth!
Yet should thy soul indulge the generous heat,
Till captive Science yields her last retreat;
Should Reason guide thee with her brightest ray,
And pour on misty Doubt resistless day;
Should no false kindness lure to loose delight,
Nor praise relax, nor difficulty fright;
Should tempting Novelty thy cell refrain,

And Sloth effuse her opiate fumes in vain;
Should Beauty blunt on fops her fatal dart,
Nor claim the triumph of a lettered heart;
Should no disease thy torpid veins invade,
Nor Melancholy's phantoms haunt thy shade;
Yet hope not life from grief or danger free
Nor think the doom of man reversed for thee.
Deign on the passing world to cast thine eyes,
And pause a while from letters to be wise;
There mark what ills the scholar's life assail,
Toil, envy, want, the patron and the jail.
See nations slowly wise and meanly just,
To buried merit raise the tardy bust.
If dreams once flatter, once again attend,
Hear Lydiat's life and Galileo's end.

   Nor deem, when Learning her last prize bestows,
The glittering eminence exempt from foes;
See, when the vulgar 'scapes, despised or awed,
Rebellion's vengeful talons seize on Laud.
From meaner minds though smaller fines content,
The plundered palace or sequestered rent,
Marked out by dangerous parts[1] he meets the shock,
And fatal learning leads him to the block:
Around his tomb let Art and Genius weep;
But hear his death, ye blockheads, hear and sleep.

   The festal blazes, the triumphal show,
The ravished standard, and the captive foe,
The senate's thanks, the gazettes pompous tale,
With force resistless o'er the brave prevail.
Such bribes the rapid Greek[2] o'er Asia whirled,
For such the steady Romans shook the world;
For such in distant lands the Britons shine,
And stain with blood the Danube or the Rhine;
This power has praise that virtue scarce can warm,
Till fame supplies the universal charm.
Yet Reason frowns on War's unequal game,
Where wasted nations raise a single name,
And mortgaged states their grandsires' wreaths regret

---

[1] talents   [2] Alexander the Great

From age to age in everlasting debt;
Wreaths which at last the dear-bought right convey
To rust on medals, or on stones decay.

Military glory

    On what foundations stands the warrior's pride,
How just his hopes, let Swedish Charles decide;
A frame of adamant, a soull of fire
No dangers fright him, and no labours tire;
O'er love, o'er fear, extends his wide domain,
Unconquered lord of pleasure and of pain;
No joys to him pacific scepters yield,
War sounds the trump, he rushes to the field;
Behold surrounding kings their powers combine,
And one capitulate, and one resign;
Peace courts his hand, but spreads her charms in vain;
'Think nothing gained,' he cries, 'till naught remain,
On Moscow's walls till Gothic standards fly,
And all be mine beneath the polar sky.'
The march begins in military state,
And nations on his eye suspended wait;
Stern Famine guards the solitary coast,
And Winter barricades the realms of Frost;
He comes, nor want nor cold his course delay –
Hide, blushing Glory, hide Pultowa's day:
The vanquished hero leaves his broken bands,
And shows his miseries in distant lands;
Condemned a needy supplicant to wait,
While ladies interpose, and slaves debate.
But did not Chance at length her error mend?
Did no subverted empire mark his end?
Did rival monarchs give the fatal wound?
Or hostile millions press him to the ground?
His fall was destined to a barren strand,
A petty fortress, and a dubious hand;
He left the name at which the world grew pale,
To point a moral, or adorn a tale.

    All times their scenes of pompous woes afford,
From Persia's tyrant to Bavaria's lord.
In gay hostility, and barbarous pride,
With half mankind embattled at his side,
Great Xerxes comes to seize the certain prey,

And starves exhausted regions in his way;
Attendant Flattery counts his myriads o'er,
Till counted myriads soothe his pride no more:
Fresh praise is tried till madness fires his mind,
The waves he lashes, and enchains the wind;
New powers are claimed, new powers are still bestowed,
Till rude resistance lops the spreading god;
The daring Greeks deride the martial show,
And heap their valleys with the gaudy foe;
The insulted sea with humbler thought he gains,
A single skiff to speed his flight remains;
The encumbered oar scarce leaves the dreaded coast
Through purple billows and a floating host.
  The bold Bavarian, in a luckless hour,
Tries the dread summits of Caesarean power,
With unexpected legions bursts away,
And sees defenseless realms receive his sway;
Short sway! fair Austria spreads her mournful charms,
The queen, the beauty, sets the world in arms;
From hill to hill the beacon's rousing blaze
Spreads wide the hope of plunder and of praise;
The fierce Croatian, and the wild Hussar,
With all the sons of ravage crowd the war;
The baffled prince, in honor's flattering bloom
Of hasty greatness finds the fatal doom;
His foes' derision, and his subjects' blame,
And steals to death from anguish and from shame.

Long life   Enlarge my life with multitude of days!
In health, in sickness, thus the suppliant prays;
Hides from himself his state, and shuns to know
That life protracted is protracted woe.
Time hovers o'er, impatient to destroy,
And shuts up all the passages of joy;
In vain their gifts the bounteous seasons pour,
The fruit autumnal, and the vernal flower;
With listless eyes the dotard views the store,
He views, and wonders that they please no more;
Now pall the tasteless meats, and joyless wines,
And Luxury with sighs her slave resigns.
Approach, ye minstrels, try the soothing strain,

Diffuse the tuneful lenitives of pain:
No sounds, alas! would touch the impervious ear,
Though dancing mountains witnessed Orpheus near;
Nor lute nor lyre his feeble powers attend,
Nor sweeter music of a virtuous friend,
But everlasting dictates crowd his tongue,
Perversely grave, or positively wrong.
The still returning tale, and lingering jest,
Perplex the fawning niece and pampered guest,
While growing hopes scarce awe the gathering sneer,
And scarce a legacy can bribe to hear;
The watchful guests still hint the last offense;
The daughter's petulance, the son's expense,
Improve his heady rage with treacherous skill,
And mold his passions till they make his will.

Unnumbered maladies his joints invade,
Lay siege to life and press the dire blockade;
But unextinguished avarice still remains,
And dreaded losses aggravate his pains;
He turns, with anxious heart and crippled hands,
His bonds of debt, and mortgages of lands;
Or views his coffers with suspicious eyes,
Unlocks his gold, and counts it till he dies.
But grant, the virtues of a temperate prime
Bless with an age exempt from scorn or crime;
An age that melts with unperceived decay,
And glides in modest innocence away;
Whose peaceful day Benevolence endears,
Whose night congratulating Conscience cheers;
The general favorite as the general friend:
Such age there is, and who shall wish its end?

Yet even on this her load Misfortune flings,
To press the weary minutes' flagging wings;
New sorrow rises as the day returns,
A sister sickens, or a daughter mourns.
Now kindred Merit fills the sable bier,
Now lacerated Friendship claims a tear;
Year chases year, decay pursues decay,
Still drops some joy from withering life away;
New forms arise, and different views engage,

Superfluous lags the veteran on the stage,
Till pitying Nature signs the last release,
And bids afflicted Worth retire to peace.
But few there are whom hours like these await,
Who set unclouded in the gulfs of Fate.
From Lydia's monarch should the search descend,
By Solon cautioned to regard his end,
In life's last scene what prodigies surprise,
Fears of the brave, and follies of the wise!
From Marlborough's eyes the streams of dotage flow,
And Swift expires a driv'ler and a show.

Good   The teeming mother, anxious for her race,
looks Begs for each birth the fortune of a face:
Yet Vane could tell what ills from beauty spring;
And Sedley cursed the form that pleased a king.
Ye nymphs of rosy lips and radiant eyes,
Whom Pleasure keeps too busy to be wise,
Whom Joys with soft varieties invite,
By day the frolic, and the dance by night;
Who frown with vanity, who smile with art,
And ask the latest fashion of the heart;
What care, what rules your heedless charms shall save,
Each nymph your rival, and each youth your slave?
Against your fame with Fondness Hate combines,
The rival batters, and the lover mines.
With distant voice neglected Virtue calls,
Less heard and less, the faint remonstrance falls;
Tired with contempt, she quits the slippery reign,
And Pride and Prudence take her seat in vain.
In crowd at once, where none the pass defend,
The harmless freedom, and the private friend.
The guardians yield, by force superior plied:
To Interest, Prudence; and to Flattery, Pride.
Now Beauty falls betrayed, despised, distressed,
And hissing Infamy proclaims the rest.

Where then shall Hope and Fear their objects find?
Must dull Suspense corrupt the stagnant mind?
Must helpless man, in ignorance sedate,
Roll darkling down the torrent of his fate?
Must no dislike alarm, no wishes rise,

No cries invoke the mercies of the skies?
Inquirer, cease; petitions yet remain
Which Heaven may hear, nor deem religion vain.
Still raise for good the supplicating voice,
But leave to Heaven the measure and the choice.
Safe in His power, whose eyes discern afar
The secret ambush of a specious prayer.
Implore His aid, in His decisions rest,
Secure, whate'er He gives, He gives the best.
Yet when the sense of sacred presence fires,
And strong devotion to the skies aspires,
Pour forth thy fervors for a healthful mind,
Obedient passions, and a will resigned;
For love, which scarce collective man can fill;
For patience sovereign o'er transmuted ill;
For faith, that panting for a happier seat,
Counts death kind Nature's signal of retreat:
These goods for man the laws of Heaven ordain,
These goods He grants, who grants the power to gain;
With these celestial Wisdom calms the mind,
And makes the happiness she does not find.

SAMUEL JOHNSON (1749)

Each section gives examples of people whose lives have ended
disastrously. For example Cardinal Wolsey, Henry VIII's chief minister,
was dismissed by the king and possibly only escaped execution by
death; Villiers was the Duke of Buckingham, favoured by James I and
Charles I but assassinated in 1628; Harley, the disgraced political
leader of Queen Anne's reign; Wentworth the Earl of Strafford,
executed under Charles I; Hyde was the impeached Earl of Clarendon;
Galileo died in 1642 after his discoveries were condemned by the
Inquisition; Archbishop Laud was executed; Charles XII of Sweden's
brilliant military career ended in disaster at Pultowa and Xerxes'
invading fleet was annihilated by the Athenians at Salamis. Vane and
Sedley were both deserted by their powerful lovers.

The Shrubbery

WRITTEN IN A TIME OF AFFLICTION

Oh, happy shades – to me unblest!
   Friendly to peace, but not to me!
How ill the scene that offers rest,
   And heart that cannot rest, agree!

This glassy stream, that spreading pine,
   Those alders quiv'ring to the breeze,
Might sooth a soul less hurt than mine,
   And please, if any thing could please.

But fix'd unalterable care
   Foregoes not what she feels within,
Shows the same sadness ev'ry where,
   And slights the season and the scene.

For all that pleas'd in wood or lawn,
   While peace possess'd these silent bow'rs,
Her animating smile withdrawn,
   Has lost its beauties and its pow'rs.

The saint or moralist should tread
   This moss-grown alley, musing, slow;
They seek, like me, the secret shade,
   But not, like me, to nourish woe!

Me fruitful scenes and prospects waste
   Alike admonish not to roam;
These tell me of enjoyments past,
   And those of sorrows yet to come.

        WILLIAM COWPER (1773, published 1782)

The Castaway

Obscurest night involv'd the sky,
   Th' Atlantic billows roar'd,
When such a destin'd wretch as I,
   Wash'd headlong from on board,
Of friends, of hope, of all bereft,
His floating home for ever left.

No braver chief could Albion boast
   Than he with whom he went,
Nor ever ship left Albion's coast,
   With warmer wishes sent.
He lov'd them both, but both in vain,
Nor him beheld, nor her again.

He shouted: nor his friends had fail'd
   To check the vessel's course,
But so the furious blast prevail'd,
   That, pitiless perforce,
They left their outcast mate behind,
And scudded still before the wind.

Some succour yet they could afford;
   And, such as storms allow,
The cask, the coop, the floated cord,
   Delay'd not to bestow.
But he (they knew) nor ship, nor shore,
Whate'er they gave, should visit more.

Nor, cruel as it seem'd, could he
   Their haste himself condemn,
Aware that flight, in such a sea,
   Alone could rescue them;
Yet bitter felt it still to die
Deserted, and his friends so nigh.

He long survives, who lives an hour
    In ocean, self-upheld;
And so long he, with unspent pow'r,
    His destiny repell'd;
And ever, as the minutes flew,
Entreated help, or cried – Adieu!

At length, his transient respite past,
    His comrades, who before
Had heard his voice in ev'ry blast,
    Could catch the sound no more.
For then, by toil subdued, he drank
The stifling wave; and then he sank.

No poet wept him: but the page
    Of narrative sincere,
That tells his name, his worth, his age,
    Is wet with Anson's tear.
And tears by bards or heroes shed
Alike immortalize the dead.

I therefore purpose not, or dream,
    Descanting on his fate,
To give the melancholy theme
    A more enduring date:
But misery still delights to trace
Its semblance in another's case.

No voice divine the storm allay'd,
    No light propitious shone;
When, snatch'd from all effectual aid,
    We perish'd, each alone:
But I beneath a rougher sea,
And whelm'd in deeper gulphs than he.

WILLIAM COWPER (1799)

The Fall of the Leaf

The lazy mist hangs from the brow of the hill,
Concealing the course of the dark winding rill;
How languid the scenes, late so sprightly, appear,
As Autumn to Winter resigns the pale year!

The forests are leafless, the meadows are brown,
And all the gay foppery of summer has flown:
Apart let me wander, apart let me muse,
How quick Time is flying, how keen Fate pursues!

How long I have lived – but how much lived in vain;
How little of life's scanty span may remain;
What aspects old Time in his progress has worn,
What ties cruel Fate in my bosom has torn!

How foolish, or worse, till our summit is gained!
And downward how weaken'd, how darken'd, how pain'd!
Life is not worth having, with all it can give –
For something beyond it poor man sure must live.

ROBERT BURNS (published 1796)

Turn the Carpet, or The Two Weavers

A DIALOGUE BETWEEN DICK AND JOHN

As at their work two weavers sat,
Beguiling time with friendly chat;
They touch'd upon the price of meat,
So high, a weaver scarce could eat.

'What with my brats and sickly wife,'
Quoth Dick, 'I'm almost tired of life;
So hard my work, so poor my fare,
'Tis more than mortal man can bear.

How glorious is the rich man's state!
His house so fine! his wealth so great!
Heaven is unjust, you must agree,
Why all to him? why none to me?

In spite of what the scripture teaches,
In spite of all the parson preaches,
This world (indeed, I've thought so long)
Is ruled, methinks, extremely wrong.

Where'er I look, howe'er I range,
'Tis all confused, and hard, and strange;
The good are troubled and oppress'd,
And all the wicked are the bless'd.'

Quoth John, 'Our ignorance is the cause
Why thus we blame our Maker's laws;
Parts of his ways alone we know,
'Tis all that man can see below.

Seest thou that carpet, not half done,
Which thou, dear Dick, hast well begun?
Behold the wild confusion there,
So rude the mass it makes one stare!

A stranger, ignorant of the trade,
Would say, no meaning's there convey'd;
For where's the middle, where's the border?
Thy carpet now is all disorder.'

Quoth Dick, 'My work is yet in bits,
But still in every part it fits;
Besides, you reason like a lout,
Why, man, that carpet's inside out.'

Says John, 'Thou sayst the thing I mean,
And now I hope to cure thy spleen;
This world, which clouds thy soul with doubt,
Is but a carpet inside out.

As when we view these shreds and ends,
We know not what the whole intends;
So when on earth things look but odd,
They're working still some scheme of God.

No plan, no pattern, can we trace,
All wants proportion, truth, and grace;
The motley mixture we deride,
Nor see the beauteous upper side.

But when we reach that world of light,
And view those works of God aright,
Then shall we see the whole design,
And own the workman is divine.

What now seem random strokes, will there
All order and design appear;
Then shall we praise what here we spurn'd,
For then the carpet shall be turn'd.'

'Thou'rt right,' quoth Dick, 'no more I'll grumble
That this sad world's so strange a jumble;
My impious doubts are put to flight,
For my own carpet sets me right.'

HANNAH MORE (1796)

4
THE LIGHTER SIDE
Part One

The Despairing Lover

Distracted with care,
For Phillis the fair;
Since nothing could move her,
Poor Damon, her lover,
Resolves in despair
No longer to languish,
Nor bear so much anguish;
But, mad with his love,
To a precipice goes;
Where, a leap from above
Would soon finish his woes.

When in rage he came there,
Beholding how steep
The sides did appear,
And the bottom how deep;
His torments projecting,
And sadly reflecting,
That a lover forsaken
A new love may get;
But a neck, when once broken,
Can never be set:
And, that he could die
Whenever he would;
But, that he could live
But as long as he could:
How grievous so ever
The torment might grow,
He scorned to endeavour
To finish it so.
But bold, unconcerned
At thoughts of the pain,
He calmly returned
To his cottage again.

WILLIAM WALSH (d.1708)

from *Paulo Purganti and His Wife*

AN HONEST, BUT A SIMPLE PAIR

A Doctor of great Skill and Fame,
PAULO PURGANTI was his Name,
Had a good, comely, virtuous Wife:
No Woman led a better Life:
She to Intrigues was ev'n hard-hearted:
She chuckl'd when a Bawd was carted:
And thought the Nation ne'er wou'd thrive
'Till all the Whores were burnt alive.

On marry'd Men, that dare be bad,
She thought no Mercy should be had;
They should be hang'd, or starv'd, or flead,
Or serv'd like ROMISH Priests in SWEDE.
In short, all Lewdness She defy'd:
And stiff was her Parochial Pride.

Yet in an honest Way, the Dame
Was a great Lover of That same;
And could from Scripture take her Cue,
That Husbands should give Wives their Due.

Her Prudence did so justly steer
Between the Gay and the Severe,
That if in some Regards She chose
To curb poor PAULO in too close;
In others She relax'd again,
And govern'd with a looser Rein.

Thus tho' She strictly did confine
The Doctor from Excess of Wine;
With Oysters, Eggs, and Vermicelli
She let Him almost burst his Belly:
Thus drying Coffee was deny'd;
But Chocolate that Loss supply'd:
And for Tobacco (who could bear it?)

Filthy Concomitant of Claret!
(Blest Revolution!) one might see
Eringo Roots, and Bohé Tea.

She often set the Doctor's Band,
And strok'd his beard, and squeezd his Hand:
Kindly complain'd, that after Noon
He went to pore on Books too soon:
She held it wholesomer by much,
To rest a little on the Couch:
About his Waste in Bed a-nights
She clung so close for fear of Sprites.

The Doctor understood the Call;
But had not always wherewithal.

The Lion's Skin too short, you know,
(As PLUTARCH's Morals finely show)
Was lengthen'd by the Fox's Tail:
And Art supplies, where Strength may fail.

Unwilling then in Arms to meet
The Enemy, He could not beat;
He strove to lengthen the Campaign,
And save his Forces by Chicane.
FABIUS, the ROMAN Chief, who thus
By fair Retreat grew MAXIMUS,
Shows us, that all that Warrior can do
With Force inferior, is *Cunctando*.

One Day then, as the Foe drew near,
With Love, and Joy, and Life, and Dear;
Our Don, who knew this Tittle Tattle
Did, sure as Trumpet, call to Battel;
Thought it extreamly *à propos*,
To ward against the coming Blow:
To ward: but how? Ay, there's the Question:
Fierce the Assault, unarm'd the Bastion.

The Doctor feign'd a strange Surprise:
He felt her Pulse: he view'd her Eyes:
That beat too fast: These rowl'd too quick:
She was, He said, or would be Sick:

He judg'd it absolutely good,
That She should purge and cleanse her Blood.
SPAW Waters for that end were got:
If they past easily or not,
What matters it? the Lady's Feaver
Continu'd violent as ever.

For a Distemper of this, Kind,
(BLACKMORE and HANS are of my Mind)
If once it youthful Blood infects,
And chiefly of the Female Sex;
Is scarce remov'd by Pill or Potion;
What-e'er might be our Doctor's Notion.

One luckless Night then, as in Bed
The Doctor and the Dame were laid;
Again this cruel Feaver came,
High Pulse, short Breath, and Blood in Flame.
What Measures shall poor PAULO keep
With Madam, in this piteous taking?
She, like MACBETH, has murder'd Sleep,
And won't allow Him Rest, tho' waking.
Sad State of Matters! when We dare
Nor ask for Peace, nor offer War:
Nor LIVY nor COMINES have shown,
What in this Juncture may be done.
GROTIUS might own, that PAULO's Case is
Harder, than any which He places
Amongst his BELLI and his PACIS.

He strove, alas! but strove in vain,
By dint of Logic to maintain,
That all the Sex was born to grieve,
Down to her Ladyship from EVE.
He rang'd his Tropes, and preach'd up Patience;
Back'd his Opinion with Quotations,
Divines, and Moralists; and run ye on
Quite thro' from SENECA to BUNYAN.
As much in vain He bid her try
To fold her Arms, to close her Eye;
Telling Her, Rest would do Her Good;

If any thing in Nature cou'd:
So held the GREEKS quite down from GALEN,
Masters and princes of the Calling:
So all our Modern Friends maintain
(Tho' no great GREEKS) in WARWICK-LANE.

Reduce, my Muse, the wand'ring Song:
A Tale should never be too long.

The more He talk'd, the more she burn'd,
And sigh'd, and tost, and groan'd, and turn'd:
At last, I wish, said She, my Dear —
(And whisper'd something in his Ear.)
You wish! wish on, the Doctor cries:
Lord! when will Womankind be wise?
What, ill your Waters? are You mad?
Why Poyson is not half so bad.
I'll do it — But I give You Warning:
You'll die before To-morrow Morning.
'Tis kind, my Dear, what You advise;
The Lady with a sigh replies:
But Life, You know, at best is Pain:
And Death is what We should disdain.
So do it therefore, and Adieu:
For I will die for Love of You:
Let wanton Wives by Death be scar'd:
But, to my Comfort, I'm prepar'd.

MATTHEW PRIOR (published 1709)

Quintus Fabius Maximus Cunctator (the Delayer) was a Roman general who won great praise for his tactics in avoiding the destruction of his army by the great Carthaginian general Hannibal. Spaw (spa) waters were prescribed for various maladies. The Doctor pretends to be alarmed that his wife wishes to engage in certain activities while under treatment! Galen was a famous Greek doctor; Warwick Lane would seem to be the eighteenth-century City equivalent of today's Harley Street.

To Mr John Moore, Author of the Celebrated Worm-Powder

How much, egregious *Moore*, are we
    Deceiv'd by Shews and Forms!
Whate'er we think, whate'er we see,
    All Humankind are Worms.

Man is a very Worm by Birth,
    Vile Reptile, weak, and vain!
A while he crawls upon the Earth,
    Then shrinks to Earth again.

That Woman is a Worm we find,
    E'er since our Grandame's Evil;
She first convers'd with her own Kind,
    That antient Worm, the Devil.

The Learn'd themselves we Book-Worms name;
    The Blockhead is a Slow-worm;
The Nymph whose Tail is all on Flame
    Is aptly term'd a Glow-worm:

The Fops are painted Butterflies,
    That flutter for a Day;
First from a Worm they take their Rise,
    And in a Worm decay:

The Flatterer an Earwig grows;
    Thus Worms suit all Conditions;
Misers are Muckworms, Silk-worms Beaus,
    And Death-watches Physicians.

That Statesmen have the Worm, is seen
    By all their winding Play;
Their Conscience is a Worm within,
    That gnaws them Night and Day.

Ah *Moore*! thy Skill were well employ'd,
   And greater Gain would rise,
If thou could'st make the Courtier void
   The Worm that never dies!

O learned Friend of *Abchurch-Lane*,
   Who sett'st our Entrails free!
Vain is thy Art, thy Powder vain,
   Since Worms shall eat ev'n thee.

Our Fate thou only can'st adjourn
   Some few short Years, no more!
Ev'n *Button*'s Wits to Worms shall turn,
   Who Maggots were before.

ALEXANDER POPE (1716)

Buttons was one of the fashionable coffee shops where men gathered for witty conversation and political discussion.

from *The Rape of the Lock*

This comic masterpiece tells the true story of Arabella Fermor's loss of a curl at the hands of a young admirer, which caused a minor uproar at the time. It parodies the conventions of Classical epic, with Belinda (Miss Femor) at her dressing table compared to a hero setting out to do battle. Classical epics (and Milton's *Paradise Lost*) featured supernatural beings intervening in the action; Pope brilliantly substitutes for these his delightful Sylphs, the spirits of dead society women guarding the interests of their living successors in the battle of the sexes, at a time when keeping up with the fashion and preserving one's reputation were all important. At the same time he makes some serious points about the intellectual shallowness of the social world he describes.

CANTO 1

What dire Offence from am'rous Causes springs,
What mighty Contests rise from trivial Things,
I sing – This Verse to *Caryll*, Muse! is due;
This, ev'n *Belinda* may vouchsafe to view:
Slight is the Subject, but not so the Praise,
If She inspire, and He approve my Lays.
　　Say what strange Motive, Goddess! cou'd compel
A well-bred *Lord* t'assault a gentle *Belle*?
Oh say what stranger Cause, yet unexplor'd,
Cou'd make a gentle *Belle* reject a *Lord*?
In Tasks so bold, can Little Men engage,
And in soft Bosoms dwells such mighty Rage?
　　Sol thro' white Curtains shot a tim'rous Ray,
And op'd those Eyes that must eclipse the Day;
Now Lapdogs give themselves the rowzing Shake,
And sleepless Lovers, just at Twelve, awake:
Thrice rung the Bell, the Slipper knock'd the Ground,
And the press'd Watch return'd a silver Sound.
Belinda still her downy Pillow prest,
Her Guardian *Sylph* prolong'd the balmy Rest.
'Twas he had summon'd to her silent Bed
The Morning-Dream that hover'd o'er her Head.

A Youth more glitt'ring than a *Birth-night Beau*,
(That ev'n in Slumber caus'd her Cheek to glow)
Seem'd to her Ear his winning Lips to lay,
And thus in Whispers said, or seem'd to say.
　Fairest of Mortals, thou distinguish'd Care
Of thousand bright Inhabitants of Air!
If e'er one Vision touch'd thy infant Thought,
Of all the Nurse and all the Priest have taught,
Of airy Elves by Moonlight Shadows seen,
The silver Token, and the circled Green,
Or Virgins visited by Angel-Pow'rs,
With Golden Crowns and Wreaths of heavn'ly Flow'rs,
Hear and believe! thy own Importance know,
Nor bound thy narrow Views to Things below.
Some secret Truths from Learned Pride conceal'd,
To Maids alone and Children are reveal'd:
What tho' no Credit doubting Wits may give?
The Fair and Innocent shall still believe.
Know then, unnumber'd Spirits round thee fly,
The light *Militia* of the lower Sky;
These, tho' unseen, are ever on the Wing,
Hang o'er the *Box*, and hover round the *Ring*.
Think what an Equipage thou hast in Air,
And view with scorn *Two Pages* and a *Chair*.
As now your own, our Beings were of old,
And once inclos'd in Woman's beauteous Mold;
Thence, by a soft Transition, we repair
From earthly Vehicles to these of Air.
Think not, when Woman's transient Breath is fled,
That all her Vanities at once are dead:
Succeeding Vanities she still regards,
And tho' she plays no more, o'erlooks the Cards.
Her Joy in gilded Chariots, when alive,
And Love of *Ombre*, after Death survive.
For when the Fair in all their Pride expire,
To their first Elements their Souls retire:
The Sprights of fiery Termagants in Flame
Mount up, and take a *Salamander*'s Name.
Soft yielding Minds to Water glide away,
And sip with *Nymphs*, their Elemental Tea.

The graver Prude sinks downward to a *Gnome*,
In search of Mischief still on Earth to roam.
The light Coquettes in *Sylphs* aloft repair,
And sport and flutter in the Fields of Air.

    Know farther yet; Whoever fair and chaste
Rejects Mankind, is by some *Sylph* embrac'd:
For Spirits, freed from mortal Laws, with ease
Assume what Sexes and what Shapes they please.
What guards the Purity of melting Maids,
In Courtly Balls, and Midnight Masquerades,
Safe from the treach'rous Friend, the daring Spark,
The Glance by Day, the Whisper in the Dark;
When kind Occasion prompts their warm Desires,
When Musick softens, and when Dancing fires?
'Tis but their *Sylph*, the wise Celestials know,
Tho' *Honour* is the Word with Men below.

    Some Nymphs there are, too conscious of their Face,
For Life predestin'd to the *Gnomes*' Embrace.
These swell their Prospects and exalt their Pride,
When Offers are disdain'd, and Love deny'd.
Then gay Ideas crowd the vacant Brain;
While Peers and Dukes, and all their sweeping Train,
And Garters, Stars and Coronets appear,
And in soft Sounds, *Your Grace* salutes their Ear.
'Tis these that early taint the Female Soul,
Instruct the Eyes of young *Coquettes* to roll,
Teach Infant-Cheeks a bidden Blush to know,
And little Hearts to flutter at a *Beau*.

    Oft when the World imagine Women stray,
The *Sylphs* thro' mystick Mazes guide their Way,
Thro' all the giddy Circle they pursue,
And old Impertinence expel by new.
What tender Maid but must a Victim fall
To one Man's Treat, but for another's Ball?
When *Florio* speaks, what Virgin could withstand,
If gentle *Damon* did not squeeze her Hand?
With varying Vanities, from ev'ry Part,
They shift the moving Toyshop of their Heart;
Where Wigs with Wigs, with Sword-knots Sword-knots
    strive,

Beaus banish Beaus, and Coaches Coaches drive.
This erring Mortals Levity may call,
Oh blind to Truth! the *Sylphs* contrive it all.
　Of these am I, who thy Protection claim,
A watchful Sprite, and *Ariel* is my Name.
Late, as I rang'd the Crystal Wilds of Air,
In the clear Mirror of thy ruling *Star*
I saw, alas! some dread Event impend,
Ere to the Main this Morning Sun descend.
But Heav'n reveals not what, or how, or where:
Warn'd by thy *Sylph*, oh Pious Maid beware! ·
This to disclose is all thy Guardian can.
Beware of all, but most beware of Man!
　He said; when *Shock*, who thought she slept too long,
Leapt up, and wak'd his Mistress with his Tongue.
'Twas then *Belinda*! if Report say true,
Thy Eyes first open'd on a *Billet-doux*;
Wounds, *Charms*, and *Ardors*, were no sooner read,
But all the Vision vanish'd from thy Head.
　And now, unveil'd, the *Toilet* stands display'd,
Each Silver Vase in mystic Order laid.
First, rob'd in White, the Nymph intent adores
With Head uncover'd, the *Cosmetic* Pow'rs.
A heav'nly Image in the Glass appears,
To that she bends, to that her Eyes she rears;
Th'inferior Priestess, at her Altar's side,
Trembling, begins the sacred Rites of Pride.
Unnumber'd Treasures ope at once, and here
The various Off'rings of the World appear;
From each she nicely culls with curious Toil,
And decks the Goddess with the glitt'ring Spoil.
This Casket *India*'s glowing Gems unlocks,
And all *Arabia* breathes from yonder Box.
The Tortoise here and Elephant unite,
Transform'd to *Combs*, the speckled and the white.
Here Files of Pins extend their shining Rows,
Puffs, Powders, Patches, Bibles, Billet-doux.
The busy *Sylphs* surround their darling Care;
These set the Head, and those divide the Hair,
Some fold the Sleeve, whilst others plait the Gown;

And *Betty*'s prais'd for Labours not her own.
Now awful Beauty puts on all its Arms;
The Fair each moment rises in her Charms,
Repairs her Smiles, awakens ev'ry Grace,
And calls forth all the Wonders of her Face;
Sees by Degrees a purer Blush arise,
And keener Lightnings quicken in her Eyes.

CANTO 2

Not with more Glories, in th' Etherial Plain,
The Sun first rises o'er the purpled Main,
Than issuing forth, the Rival of his Beams
Lanch'd on the Bosom of the Silver *Thames*.
Fair Nymphs, and well-drest Youths around her shone,
But ev'ry Eye was fix'd on her alone.
On her white Breast a sparkling *Cross* she wore,
Which *Jews* might kiss, and Infidels adore.
Her lively Looks a sprightly Mind disclose,
Quick as her Eyes, and as unfix'd as those:
Favours to none, to all she Smiles extends,
Oft she rejects, but never once offends.
Bright as the Sun, her Eyes the Gazers strike,
And, like the Sun, they shine on all alike.
Yet graceful Ease, and Sweetness void of Pride,
Might hide her Faults, if *Belles* had Faults to hide:
If to her share some Female Errors fall,
Look on her Face, and you'll forget 'em all.
    This Nymph, to the Destruction of Mankind,
Nourish'd two Locks, which graceful hung behind
In equal Curls, and well conspir'd to deck
With shining Ringlets the smooth Iv'ry Neck.
Love in these Labyrinths his Slaves detains,
And mighty Hearts are held in slender Chains.
With hairy Sprindges we the Birds betray,
Slight Lines of Hair surprize the Finny Prey,
Fair Tresses Man's Imperial Race insnare,
And Beauty draws us with a single Hair.

Th' Adventrous *Baron* the bright Locks admir'd,
He saw, he wish'd, and to the Prize aspir'd:
Resolv'd to win, he meditates the way,
By Force to ravish, or by Fraud betray;
For when Success a Lover's Toil attends,
Few ask, if Fraud or Force attain'd his Ends.

For this, ere *Phœbus* rose, he had implor'd
Propitious Heav'n, and ev'ry Pow'r ador'd,
But chiefly *Love* – to *Love* an Altar built,
Of twelve vast *French* Romances, neatly gilt.
There lay three Garters, half a Pair of Gloves;
And all the Trophies of his former Loves.
With tender *Billet-doux* he lights the Pyre,
And breathes three am'rous Sighs to raise the Fire.
Then prostrate falls, and begs with ardent Eyes
Soon to obtain, and long possess the Prize:
The Pow'rs gave Ear, and granted half his Pray'r,
The rest, the Winds dispers'd in empty Air.

But now secure the painted Vessel glides,
The Sun-beams trembling on the floating Tydes,
While melting Musick steals upon the Sky,
And soften'd Sounds along the Waters die.
Smooth flow the Waves, the Zephyrs gently play,
Belinda smil'd, and all the World was gay.
All but the *Sylph* – With careful Thoughts opprest,
Th'impending Woe sate heavy on his Breast.
He summons strait his Denizens of Air;
The lucid Squadrons round the Sails repair:
Soft o'er the Shrouds Aerial Whispers breathe,
That seem'd but *Zephyrs* to the Train beneath.
Some to the Sun their Insect-Wings unfold,
Waft on the Breeze, or sink in Clouds of Gold.
Transparent Forms, too fine for mortal Sight,
Their fluid Bodies half dissolv'd in Light.
Loose to the Wind their airy Garments flew,
Thin glitt'ring Textures of the filmy Dew;
Dipt in the richest Tincture of the Skies,
Where Light disports in ever-mingling Dies,
While ev'ry Beam new transient Colours flings,
Colours that change whene'er they wave their Wings.

Amid the Circle, on the gilded Mast,
Superior by the Head, was *Ariel* plac'd;
His Purple Pinions opening to the Sun,
He rais'd his Azure Wand, and thus begun.

Ye *Sylphs* and *Sylphids*, to your Chief give Ear,
Fays, *Fairies*, *Genii*, *Elves*, and *Dæmons* hear!
Ye know the Spheres and various Tasks assign'd,
By Laws Eternal, to th' Aerial Kind.
Some in the Fields of purest *Æther* play,
And bask and whiten in the Blaze of Day.
Some guide the Course of wandring Orbs on high,
Or roll the Planets thro' the boundless Sky.
Some less refin'd, beneath the Moon's pale Light
Pursue the Stars that shoot athwart the Night,
Or suck the Mists in grosser Air below,
Or dip their Pinions in the painted Bow,
Or brew fierce Tempests on the wintry Main,
Or o'er the Glebe distill the kindly Rain.
Others on Earth o'er human Race preside,
Watch all their Ways, and all their Actions guide:
Of these the Chief the Care of Nations own,
And guard with Arms Divine the *British Throne*.

Our humbler Province is to tend the Fair,
Not a less pleasing, tho' less glorious Care.
To save the Powder from too rude a Gale,
Nor let th' imprison'd Essences exhale,
To draw fresh Colours from the vernal Flow'rs,
To steal from Rainbows ere they drop in Show'rs
A brighter Wash; to curl their waving Hairs,
Assist their Blushes, and inspire their Airs;
Nay oft, in Dreams, Invention we bestow,
To change a *Flounce*, or add a *Furbelo*.

This Day, black Omens threat the brightest Fair
That e'er deserv'd a watchful Spirit's Care;
Some dire Disaster, or by Force, or Slight,
But what, or where, the Fates have wrapt in Night.
Whether the Nymph shall break *Diana*'s Law,
Or some frail *China* Jar receive a Flaw,
Or stain her Honour, or her new Brocade,
Forget her Pray'rs, or miss a Masquerade,

Or lose her Heart, or Necklace, at a Ball;
Or whether Heaven has doom'd that *Shock* must fall.
Haste then ye Spirits! to your Charge repair;
The flutt'ring Fan be *Zephyretta*'s Care;
The Drops to thee, *Brillante*, we consign;
And, *Momentilla*, let the Watch be thine;
Do thou, *Crispissa*, tend her fav'rite Lock;
Ariel himself shall be the Guard of Shock.
　　To Fifty chosen *Sylphs*, of special Note,
We trust th' important Charge, the *Petticoat*:
Oft have we known that sev'nfold Fence to fail,
Tho' stiff with Hoops, and arm'd with Ribs of Whale.
Form a strong Line about the Silver Bound,
And guard the wide Circumference around.
　　Whatever Spirit, careless of his Charge,
His Post neglects, or leaves the Fair at large,
Shall feel sharp Vengeance soon o'ertake his Sins,
Be stopt in *Vials*, or transfixt with *Pins*;
Or plung'd in Lakes of bitter *Washes* lie,
Or wedg'd whole Ages in a *Bodkin*'s Eye:
Gums and *Pomatums* shall his Flight restrain,
While clog'd he beats his silken Wings in vain;
Or Alom-*Stypticks* with contracting Power
Shrink his thin Essence like a rivell'd Flower.
Or as *Ixion* fix'd, the Wretch shall feel
The giddy Motion of the whirling Mill,
In Fumes of burning Chocolate shall glow,
And tremble at the Sea that froaths below!
　　He spoke; the Spirits from the Sails descend;
Some, Orb in Orb, around the Nymph extend,
Some thrid the mazy Ringlets of her Hair,
Some hang upon the Pendants of her Ear;
With beating Hearts the dire Event they wait,
Anxious, and trembling for the Birth of Fate.

CANTO 3

Close by those Meads for ever crown'd with Flow'rs,
Where *Thames* with Pride surveys his rising Tow'rs,
There stands a Structure of Majestick Frame,
Which from the neighb'ring *Hampton* takes its Name.
Here *Britain*'s Statesmen oft the Fall foredoom
Of Foreign Tyrants, and of Nymphs at home;
Here Thou, *Great Anna*! whom three Realms obey,
Dost sometimes Counsel take – and sometimes *Tea*.

    Hither the Heroes and the Nymphs resort,
To taste awhile the Pleasures of a Court;
In various Talk th' instructive hours they past,
Who gave the *Ball*, or paid the *Visit* last:
One speaks the Glory of the *British Queen*,
And one describes a charming *Indian Screen*;
A third interprets Motions, Looks, and Eyes;
At ev'ry Word a Reputation dies.
Snuff, or the *Fan*, supply each Pause of Chat,
With singing, laughing, ogling, and all that.

    Mean while declining from the Noon of Day,
The Sun obliquely shoots his burning Ray;
The hungry Judges soon the Sentence sign,
And Wretches hang that Jury-men may Dine;
The Merchant from th' *Exchange* returns in Peace,
And the long Labours of the *Toilette* cease –

Belinda and her friends then play a game of ombre (a game similar
to whist) which is described in terms appropriate to an epic battle
and which she wins. She rejoices in her triumph before they all
adjourn for coffee. The next extract begins at that point.

    Oh thoughtless Mortals! ever blind to Fate,
Too soon dejected, and too soon elate!
Sudden these Honours shall be snatch'd away,
And curs'd for ever this Victorious Day.
    For lo! the Board with Cups and Spoons is crown'd,
The Berries crackle, and the Mill turns round.
On shining Altars of *Japan* they raise

The silver Lamp; the fiery Spirits blaze.
From silver Spouts the grateful Liquors glide,
While *China*'s Earth receives the smoking Tyde.
At once they gratify their Scent and Taste,
And frequent Cups prolong the rich Repast.
Strait hover round the Fair her Airy Band;
Some, as she sip'd, the fuming Liquor fann'd,
Some o'er her Lap their careful Plumes display'd,
Trembling, and conscious of the rich Brocade.
Coffee, (which makes the Politician wise,
And see thro' all things with his half-shut Eyes)
Sent up in Vapours to the *Baron*'s Brain
New Stratagems, the radiant Lock to gain.
Ah cease rash Youth! desist ere 'tis too late,
Fear the just Gods, and think of *Scylla*'s Fate!
Chang'd to a Bird, and sent to flit in Air,
She dearly pays for *Nisus*' injur'd Hair!

But when to Mischief Mortals bend their Will,
How soon they find fit Instruments of Ill!
Just then, *Clarissa* drew with tempting Grace
A two-edg'd Weapon from her shining Case;
So Ladies in Romance assist their Knight,
Present the Spear, and arm him for the Fight.
He takes the Gift with rev'rence, and extends
The little Engine on his Fingers' Ends,
This just behind *Belinda*'s Neck he spread,
As o'er the fragrant Steams she bends her Head:
Swift to the Lock a thousand Sprights repair,
A thousand Wings, by turns, blow back the Hair,
And thrice they twitch'd the Diamond in her Ear,
Thrice she look'd back, and thrice the Foe drew near.
Just in that instant, anxious *Ariel* sought
The close Recesses of the Virgin's Thought;
As on the Nosegay in her Breast reclin'd,
He watch'd th' Ideas rising in her Mind,
Sudden he view'd, in spite of all her Art,
An Earthly Lover lurking at her Heart.
Amaz'd, confus'd, he found his Pow'r expir'd,
Resign'd to Fate, and with a Sigh retir'd.

The Peer now spreads the glitt'ring *Forfex* wide,

T'inclose the Lock; now joins it, to divide.
Ev'n then, before the fatal Engine clos'd,
A wretched *Sylph* too fondly interpos'd;
Fate urg'd the Sheers, and cut the *Sylph* in twain,
(But Airy Substance soon unites again)
The meeting Points the sacred Hair dissever
From the fair Head, for ever and for ever!

Then flash'd the living Lightning from her Eyes,
And Screams of Horror rend th' affrighted Skies.
Not louder Shrieks to pitying Heav'n are cast,
When Husbands or when Lap-dogs breathe their last,
Or when rich *China* Vessels, fal'n from high,
In glittring Dust and painted Fragments lie!

Let Wreaths of Triumph now my Temples twine,
(The Victor cry'd) the glorious Prize is mine!
While Fish in Streams, or Birds delight in Air,
Or in a Coach and Six the *British* Fair,
As long as *Atalantis* shall be read,
Or the small Pillow grace a Lady's Bed,
While *Visits* shall be paid on solemn Days,
When numerous Wax-lights in bright Order blaze,
While Nymphs take Treats, or Assignations give,
So long my Honour, Name, and Praise shall live!

What Time wou'd spare, from Steel receives its date,
And Monuments, like Men, submit to Fate!
Steel cou'd the Labour of the Gods destroy,
And strike to Dust th' Imperial Tow'rs of *Troy*;
Steel cou'd the Works of mortal Pride confound,
And hew Triumphal Arches to the Ground.
What Wonder then, fair Nymph! thy Hairs shou'd feel
The conqu'ring Force of unresisted Steel?

CANTO 4

But anxious Cares the pensive Nymph opprest,
And secret Passions labour'd in her Breast.
Not youthful Kings in Battel seiz'd alive,
Not scornful Virgins who their Charms survive,
Not ardent Lovers robb'd of all their Bliss,

Not ancient Ladies when refus'd a Kiss,
Not Tyrants fierce that unrepenting die,
Not *Cynthia* when her *Manteau's* pinn'd awry,
E'er felt such Rage, Resentment and Despair,
As Thou, sad Virgin! for thy ravish'd Hair.

For, that sad moment, when the *Sylphs* withdrew,
And *Ariel* weeping from *Belinda* flew,
Umbriel, a dusky melancholy Spright,
As ever sully'd the fair face of Light,
Down to the Central Earth, his proper Scene,
Repair'd to search the gloomy Cave of *Spleen*.

Swift on his sooty Pinions flitts the *Gnome*,
And in a Vapour reach'd the dismal Dome.
No cheerful Breeze this sullen Region knows,
The dreaded *East* is all the Wind that blows.
Here, in a Grotto, sheltred close from Air,
And screen'd in Shades from Day's detested Glare,
She sighs for ever on her pensive Bed,
Pain at her Side, and *Megrim* at her Head.

Two Handmaids wait the Throne: Alike in Place,
But diff'ring far in Figure and in Face.
Here stood *Ill-nature* like an *ancient Maid*,
Her wrinkled Form in *Black* and *White* array'd;
With store of Pray'rs, for Mornings, Nights, and Noons,
Her Hand is fill'd; her Bosom with Lampoons.

There *Affectation* with a sickly Mien
Shows in her Cheek the Roses of Eighteen,
Practis'd to Lisp, and hang the Head aside,
Faints into Airs, and languishes with Pride;
On the rich Quilt sinks with becoming Woe,
Wrapt in a Gown, for Sickness, and for Show.
The Fair-ones feel such Maladies as these,
When each new Night-Dress gives a new Disease.

A constant *Vapour* o'er the Palace flies;
Strange Phantoms rising as the Mists arise;
Dreadful, as Hermit's Dreams in haunted Shades,
Or bright as Visions of expiring Maids.
Now glaring Fiends, and Snakes on rolling Spires,
Pale Spectres, gaping Tombs, and Purple Fires:
Now Lakes of liquid Gold, *Elysian* Scenes,

And Crystal Domes, and Angels in Machines.
   Unnumber'd Throngs on ev'ry side are seen
Of Bodies chang'd to various Forms by *Spleen*.
Here living *Teapots* stand, one Arm held out,
One bent; the Handle this, and that the Spout:
A Pipkin there like *Homer's Tripod* walks;
Here sighs a Jar, and there a Goose-pye talks;
Men prove with Child, as pow'rful Fancy works,
And Maids turn'd Bottels, call aloud for Corks.

This Canto corresponds to the visits to the underworld which have
traditionally been included in epic since Virgil's *Aeneid* (Book VI).
Here it is the gnome Umbriel (a name reminiscent of Milton's
angels) who descends into what is clearly the world of gloomy,
melancholy, angry and hysterical feelings, with some elements of
subconscious desire, which Sigmund Freud would have little difficulty
in interpreting. He obtains a bag of Sighs, Sobs and Passions,
equivalent to the bag of winds received by Ulysses in the *Odyssey*,
and then returns to arouse one of Belinda's friends the 'fierce
Thalestris' (comparable with the Amazons of Classical legend) who
urges her to action, and at this point goes off to seek masculine help.

   She said; then raging to *Sir Plume* repairs,
And bids her *Beau* demand the precious Hairs:
(*Sir Plume*, of *Amber Snuff-box* justly vain,
And the nice Conduct of a *clouded Cane*)
With earnest Eyes, and round unthinking Face,
He first the Snuff-box open'd, then the Case,
And thus broke out – 'My Lord, why, what the Devil?
Z—ds! damn the Lock! 'fore Gad, you must be civil!
Plague on't! 'tis past a Jest – nay prithee, Pox!
Give her the Hair' – he spoke, and rapp'd his Box.
   It grieves me much (reply'd the Peer again)
Who speaks so well shou'd ever speak in vain.
But by this Lock, this sacred Lock I swear,
(Which never more shall join its parted Hair,
Which never more its Honours shall renew,
Clipt from the lovely Head where late it grew)
That while my Nostrils draw the vital Air,

This Hand, which won it, shall for ever wear.
He spoke, and speaking, in proud Triumph spread
The long-contended Honours of her Head.

But *Umbriel*, hateful *Gnome!* forbears not so;
He breaks the Vial whence the Sorrows flow.
Then see! the *Nymph* in beauteous Grief appears,
Her Eyes half-languishing, half-drown'd in Tears;
On her heav'd Bosom hung her drooping Head,
Which, with a Sigh, she rais'd; and thus she said.

For ever curs'd be this detested Day,
Which snatch'd my best, my fav'rite Curl away!
Happy! ah ten times happy, had I been,
If *Hampton-Court* these Eyes had never seen!
Yet am not I the first mistaken Maid,
By Love of *Courts* to num'rous Ills betray'd.
Oh had I rather un-admir'd remain'd
In some lone Isle, or distant *Northern* Land;
Where the gilt *Chariot* never marks the Way,
Where none learn *Ombre*, none e'er taste *Bohea!*
There kept my Charms conceal'd from mortal Eye,
Like Roses that in Desarts bloom and die.
What mov'd my Mind with youthful Lords to rome?
O had I stay'd, and said my Pray'rs at home!
'Twas this, the Morning *Omens* seem'd to tell;
Thrice from my trembling hand the *Patch-box* fell;
The tott'ring *China* shook without a Wind,
Nay, *Poll* sate mute, and *Shock* was most Unkind!
A *Sylph* too warn'd me of the Threats of Fate,
In mystic Visions, now believ'd too late!
See the poor Remnants of these slighted Hairs!
My hands shall rend what ev'n thy Rapine spares:
These, in two sable Ringlets taught to break,
Once gave new Beauties to the snowie Neck.
The Sister-Lock now sits uncouth, alone,
And in its Fellow's Fate foresees its own;
Uncurl'd it hangs, the fatal Sheers demands;
And tempts once more thy sacrilegious Hands.
Oh hadst thou, Cruel! been content to seize
Hairs less in sight, or any Hairs but these!

CANTO 5

She said: the pitying Audience melt in Tears,
But *Fate* and *Jove* had stopp'd the Baron's Ears.
In vain *Thalestris* with Reproach assails,
For who can move when fair *Belinda* fails?
Not half so fixt the *Trojan* cou'd remain,
While *Anna* begg'd and *Dido* rag'd in vain.
Then grave *Clarissa* graceful wav'd her Fan;
Silence ensu'd, and thus the Nymph began.

  Say, why are Beauties prais'd and honour'd most,
The wise Man's Passion, and the vain Man's Toast?
Why deck'd with all that Land and Sea afford,
Why Angels call'd, and Angel-like ador'd?
Why round our Coaches crowd the white-glov'd Beaus,
Why bows the Side-box from its inmost Rows?
How vain are all these Glories, all our Pains,
Unless good Sense preserve what Beauty gains:
That Men may say, when we the Front-box grace,
Behold the first in Virtue, as in Face!
Oh! if to dance all Night, and dress all Day,
Charm'd the Small-pox, or chas'd old Age away;
Who would not scorn what Huswife's Cares produce,
Or who would learn one earthly Thing of Use?
To patch, nay ogle, might become a Saint,
Nor could it sure be such a Sin to paint.
But since, alas! frail Beauty must decay,
Curl'd or uncurl'd, since Locks will turn to grey,
Since painted, or not painted, all shall fade,
And she who scorns a Man, must die a Maid;
What then remains, but well our Pow'r to use,
And keep good Humour still whate'er we lose?
And trust me, Dear! good Humour can prevail,
When Airs, and Flights, and Screams, and Scolding fail.
Beauties in vain their pretty Eyes may roll;
Charms strike the Sight, but Merit wins the Soul.

Clarissa, who originally provided the miscreant lord with the scissors (the 'glittering Forfex') with which he did the 'rape' (Pope clearly had in mind the original and very different rape of Helen which began the Trojan War), utterly fails in her appeal to everyone's good sense. Her speech was inspired by a famous one by Sarpedon to Glaucus in Homer's *Iliad* where he reminds him of what is expected of a hero. Everyone then joins in the quarrel, with some physical aggression, again corresponding to epic warfare, until Jupiter decides the outcome in proper epic manner, as Belinda draws a weapon whose tongue-in-cheek history Pope delights in giving. The lock, in the confusion, disappears, with the suggestion that like many of the creatures in mythology it has become a new constellation.

> Now *Jove* suspends his golden Scales in Air,
> Weighs the Men's Wits against the Lady's Hair;
> The doubtful Beam long nods from side to side;
> At length the Wits mount up, the Hairs subside.
>   See fierce *Belinda* on the *Baron* flies,
> With more than usual Lightning in her Eyes;
> Nor fear'd the Chief th' unequal Fight to try,
> Who sought no more than on his Foe to die.
> But this bold Lord, with manly Strength indu'd,
> She with one Finger and a Thumb subdu'd:
> Just where the Breath of Life his Nostrils drew,
> A Charge of *Snuff* the wily Virgin threw;
> The *Gnomes* direct, to ev'ry Atome just,
> The pungent Grains of titillating Dust.
> Sudden, with starting Tears each Eye o'erflows,
> And the high Dome re-ecchoes to his Nose.
>   Now meet thy Fate, incens'd *Belinda* cry'd,
> And drew a deadly *Bodkin* from her Side.
> (The same, his ancient Personage to deck,
> Her great great Grandsire wore about his Neck
> In three *Seal-Rings*; which after, melted down,
> Form'd a vast *Buckle* for his Widow's Gown:
> Her infant Grandame's *Whistle* next it grew.
> The *Bells* she gingled, and the *Whistle* blew;
> Then in a *Bodkin* grac'd her Mother's Hairs,
> Which long she wore, and now *Belinda* wears.)
>   Boast not my Fall (he cry'd) insulting Foe!

Thou by some other shalt be laid as low.
Nor think, to die dejects my lofty Mind;
All that I dread, is leaving you behind!
Rather than so, ah let me still survive,
And burn in *Cupid*'s Flames, – but burn alive.

    Restore the Lock! she cries; and all around
Restore the Lock! the vaulted Roofs rebound.
Not fierce *Othello* in so loud a Strain
Roar'd for the Handkerchief that caus'd his Pain.
But see how oft Ambitious Aims are cross'd,
And Chiefs contend 'till all the Prize is lost!
The Lock, obtain'd with Guilt, and kept with Pain,
In ev'ry place is sought, but sought in vain:
With such a Prize no Mortal must be blest,
So Heav'n decrees! with Heav'n who can contest?

    Some thought it mounted to the Lunar Sphere,
Since all things lost on Earth, are treasur'd there.
There Heroes' Wits are kept in pondrous Vases,
And Beaus' in *Snuff-boxes* and *Tweezer-Cases*.
There broken Vows, and Death-bed Alms are found,
And Lovers' Hearts with Ends of Riband bound;
The Courtier's Promises, and Sick Man's Pray'rs,
The Smiles of Harlots, and the Tears of Heirs,
Cages for Gnats, and Chains to Yoak a Flea;
Dry'd Butterflies, and Tomes of Casuistry.

    But trust the Muse – she saw it upward rise,
Tho' mark'd by none but quick Poetic Eyes:
(So *Rome*'s great Founder to the Heav'ns withdrew,
To *Proculus* alone confess'd in view.)
A sudden Star, it shot thro' liquid Air,
And drew behind a radiant *Trail of Hair*.
Not *Berenice*'s Locks first rose so bright,
The Heav'ns bespangling with dishevel'd Light.
The *Sylphs* behold it kindling as it flies,
And pleas'd pursue its Progress thro' the Skies.

    This the *Beau-monde* shall from the *Mall* survey,
And hail with Musick its propitious Ray.
This, the blest Lover shall for *Venus* take,
And send up Vows from *Rosamonda*'s Lake.
This *Partridge* soon shall view in cloudless Skies,

When next he looks thro' *Galileo*'s Eyes;
And hence th' Egregious Wizard shall foredoom
The Fate of *Louis*, and the Fall of *Rome*.

  Then cease, bright Nymph! to mourn thy ravish'd Hair
Which adds new Glory to the shining Sphere!
Not all the Tresses that fair Head can boast
Shall draw such Envy as the Lock you lost.
For, after all the Murders of your Eye,
When, after Millions slain, your self shall die;
When those fair Suns shall sett, as sett they must,
And all those Tresses shall be laid in Dust;
This Lock, the Muse shall consecrate to Fame,
And mid'st the Stars inscribe *Belinda*'s Name!

ALEXANDER POPE (1712–17)

Partridge was a prominent astrologer of the period, savagely mocked by Pope's friend Swift, who pretended to be a rival astrologer, Isaac Bickerstaff, and published a comic prediction of Partridge's death. When the date arrived and Partridge apparently protested that he was still alive, Swift implied that he was, in modern terms, brain-dead anyway, to discredit him.

A New Song of New Similes

My Passion is as Mustard strong;
    I sit, all sober sad;
Drunk as a Piper all day long,
    Or like a *March*-Hare mad.

Round as a Hoop the Bumpers flow;
    I drink, yet can't forget her;
For tho' as drunk as *David*'s Sow,
    I love her still the better.

Pert as a Pear-Monger I'd be,
    If *Molly* were but kind;
Cool as a Cucumber could see
    The rest of Womankind.

Like a stuck Pig I gaping stare,
    And eye her o'er and o'er;
Lean as a Rake with Sighs and Care,
    Sleek as a Mouse before.

Plump as a Partridge was I known,
    And soft as Silk my Skin,
My Cheeks as fat as Butter grown;
    But as a Groat now thin!

I melancholy, as a Cat,
    Am kept awake to weep;
But she insensible of that,
    Sound as a Top can sleep.

Hard is her Heart as Flint or Stone,
    She laughs to see me pale,
And merry as a Grig is grown,
    And brisk as Bottled-Ale.

The God of Love at her Approach
   Is busy as a Bee,
Hearts sound as any Bell or Roach,
   Are smit and sigh like me.

Ay me, as thick as Hops or Hail,
   The fine Men crowd about her;
But soon as dead as a Door-Nail
   Shall I be if without her.

Strait as my Leg her Shape appears;
   O were we join'd together!
My Heart would be scot-free from Cares,
   And lighter than a Feather.

As fine as Five-pence is her Mien,
   No Drum was ever tighter;
Her Glance is as the Razor keen,
   And not the Sun is brighter.

As soft as Pap her kisses are,
   Methinks I taste them yet.
Brown as a Berry is her Hair,
   Her Eyes as black as Jet;

As smooth as glass, as white as Curds,
   Her pretty Hand invites;
Sharp as a needle are her Words,
   Her Wit, like Pepper, bites:

Brisk as a Body-Louse she trips,
   Clean as a Penny drest;
Sweet as a Rose her Breath and Lips,
   Round as the Globe her Breast.

Full as an Egg was I with Glee;
   And happy as a King.
Good Lord! how all Men envy'd me!
She lov'd like any thing.

But false as Hell, she, like the Wind,
    Chang'd, as her Sex must do.
Tho' seeming as the Turtle kind,
    And like the Gospel true;

If I and *Molly* could agree,
    Let who would take *Peru*!
Great as an Emp'ror should I be,
    And richer than a *Jew*;

Till you grow tender as a Chick,
    I'm dull as any Post;
Let us, like Burs, together stick,
    And warm as any Toast.

You'll know me truer than a Dye,
    And wish me better sped;
Flat as a Flounder when I lie,
    And as a Herring dead.

Sure as a Gun, she'll drop a Tear
    And sigh perhaps, and wish,
When I am rotten as a Pear,
    And mute as any fish.

            Attributed to JOHN GAY (published 1727)

The Lady and the Wasp

FABLE 8

What whispers must the Beauty bear!
What hourly nonsense haunts her ear!
Where-e'er her eyes dispense their charms
Impertinence around her swarms.
Did not the tender nonsense strike,
Contempt and scorn might look dislike,
Forbidding airs might thin the place,
The slightest flap a fly can chase.
But who can drive the num'rous breed?
Chase one, another will succeed.
Who knows a fool, must know his brother;
One fop will recommend another;
And with this plague she's rightly curst,
Because she listen'd to the first.

As *Doris*, at her toilette's duty,
Sate meditating on her beauty,
She now was pensive, now was gay,
And loll'd the sultry hours away.
    As thus in indolence she lyes,
A giddy wasp around her flies,
He now advances, now retires,
Now to her neck and cheek aspires;
Her fan in vain defends her charms,
Swift he returns, again alarms,
For by repulse he bolder grew,
Perch'd on her lip and sipt the dew.
    She frowns, she frets. Good Gods she crys,
Protect me from these teazing flys!
Of all the plagues that heav'n hath sent
A wasp is most impertinent.
    The hov'ring insect thus complain'd,
Am I then slighted, scorn'd, disdain'd?
Can such offence your anger wake?
'Twas beauty caus'd the bold mistake.

Those cherry lips that breathe perfume,
That cheek so ripe with youthful bloom
Made me with strong desire pursue
The fairest peach that ever grew.

    Strike him not, *Jenny*, *Doris* crys,
Nor murder wasps, like vulgar flys,
For though he's free (to do him right)
The creature's civil and polite.

    In ecstasies away he posts,
Where-e'er he came the favour boasts,
Brags how her sweetest tea he sips,
And shows the sugar on his lips.

    The hint alarm'd the forward crew.
Sure of success, away they flew;
They share the daintys of the day,
Round her with airy musick play,
And now they flutter, now they rest,
Now soar again and skim her breast,
Nor were they banish'd, 'till she found
That wasps have stings, and felt the wound.

JOHN GAY (1727)

from *Strephon and Chloe*

This is an extract from one of several poems in which Swift mocks human beings who pretend they have no physical needs. Strephon has hitherto worshipped Chloe as a goddess without such human failings. This is their wedding night.

> Now, ponder well, ye parents dear;
> Forbid your daughters guzzling beer;
> And make them every afternoon
> Forbear their tea, or drink it soon;
> That, e'er to bed they venture up,
> They may discharge it every sup;
> If not, they must in evil plight
> Be often forced to rise at night;
> Keep them to wholesome food confined,
> Nor let them taste what causes wind;
> ('Tis this the sage of Samos means,
> Forbidding his disciples beans)
> O, think what evils must ensue;
> Miss Moll the jade will burn it blue:[1]
> And when she once has got the art,
> She cannot help it for her heart;
> But, out it flies, even when she meets
> Her bridegroom in the wedding-sheets.
> Carminative and diuretic,
> Will damp all passions sympathetic;
> And, love such niceties requires,
> One blast will put out all his fires.
> Since husbands get behind the scene,
> The wife should study to be clean;
> Nor give the smallest room to guess
> The time when wants of nature press;
> But, after marriage, practise more
> Decorum than she did before;

[1] act outrageously (OED)

To keep her spouse deluded still,
And make him fancy what she will.

In bed we left the married pair;
'Tis time to show how things went there.
Strephon, who often had been told,
That fortune still assists the bold,
Resolved to make his first attack:
But, Chloe drove him fiercely back.
How could a nymph so chaste as Chloe,
With constitution cold and snowy,
Permit a brutish man to touch her;
Even lambs by instinct fly the butcher.
Resistance on the wedding night
Is what our maidens claim by right:
And, Chloe, 'tis by all agreed,
Was maid in thought, and word, and deed.
Yet some assign a different reason;
That Strephon chose no proper season.

Say, fair ones, must I make a pause?
Or freely tell the secret cause.

Twelve cups of tea, (with grief I speak)
Had now constrained the nymph to leak.
This point must needs be settled first:
The bride must either void or burst.
Then, see the dire effect of pease,
Think what can give the colic ease.
The nymph oppressed before, behind,
As ships are tossed by waves and wind,
Steals out her hand by nature led,
And brings a vessel into bed:
Fair utensil, as smooth and white
As Chloe's skin, almost as bright.

Strephon who heard the foaming rill
As from a mossy cliff distil;
Cried out, 'Ye gods, what sound is this?
Can Chloe, heavenly Chloe, piss?'

But when he smelt a noisome steam
Which oft attends that lukewarm stream;
(Salerno both together joins
As sovereign medicines for the loins)
And, though contrived, we may suppose
To slip his ears, yet struck his nose:
He found her, while the scent increased
As *mortal* as himself at least.

JONATHAN SWIFT (1731)

Ode on the Death of a Favorite Cat

DROWNED IN A TUB OF GOLDFISHES

'Twas on a lofty vase's side,
Where China's gayest art had dyed
   The azure flowers that blow;
Demurest of the tabby kind,
The pensive Selima reclined,
   Gazed on the lake below.

Her conscious tail her joy declared;
The fair round face, the snowy beard,
   The velvet of her paws,
Her coat, that with the tortoise vies,
Her ears of jet, and emerald eyes,
   She saw; and purred applause.

Still had she gazed; but 'midst the tide
Two angel forms were seen to glide,
   The genii of the stream:
Their scaly armor's Tyrian hue
Through richest purple to the view
   Betrayed a golden gleam.

The hapless nymph with wonder saw:
A whisker first and then a claw,
    With many an ardent wish,
She stretched in vain to reach the prize.
What female heart can gold despise?
    What cat's averse to fish?

Presumptuous maid! with looks intent
Again she stretched, again she bent,
    Nor knew the gulf between.
(Malignant Fate sat by and smiled)
The slippery verge her feet beguiled,
    She tumbled headlong in.

Eight times emerging from the flood
She mewed to every watery god,
    Some speedy aid to send.
No dolphin came, no Nereid stirred:
Nor cruel Tom, nor Susan heard.
    A favorite has no friend!

From hence, ye beauties, undeceived,
Know, one false step is ne'er retrieved.
    And be with caution bold.
Not all that tempts your wandering eyes
And heedless hearts is lawful prize;
    Nor all that glisters gold.

THOMAS GRAY (1747)

5
RESPONSES TO NATURE
Part One: Landscape and
Natural Phenomena

A Nocturnal Reverie

In such a night, when every louder wind
Is to its distant cavern safe confined;
And only gentle Zephyr fans his wings,
And lonely Philomel, still waking, sings;
Or from some tree, famed for the owl's delight,
She, hollowing clear, directs the wanderer right;
In such a night, when passing clouds give place,
Or thinly veil the heaven's mysterious face;
When in some river overhung with green,
The waving moon and trembling leaves are seen;
When freshened grass now bears itself upright,
And makes cool banks to pleasing rest invite,
Whence springs the woodbind and the bramble-rose,
And where the sleepy cowslip sheltered grows;
Whilst now a paler hue the foxglove takes,
Yet chequers still with red the dusky brakes;
When scattered glow-worms, but in twilight fine,
Show trivial beauties, watch their hour to shine;
Whilst Salisb'ry stands the test of every light,
In perfect charms and perfect virtue bright;
When odours, which declined repelling day,
Through temperate air uninterrupted stray;
When darkened groves their softest shadows wear,
And falling waters we distinctly hear;
When through the gloom more venerable shows
Some ancient fabric, awful in repose,
While sunburnt hills their swarthy looks conceal,
And swelling haycocks thicken up the vale;
When the loosed horse now, as his pasture leads,
Comes slowly grazing through th' adjoining meads,
Whose stealing pace and lengthened shade we fear,
Till torn-up forage in his teeth we hear;
When nibbling sheep at large pursue their food,
And unmolested kine rechew the cud;
When curlews cry beneath the village walls,
And to her straggling brood the partridge calls;

Their short-lived jubilee the creatures keep,
Which but endures whilst tyrant man does sleep;
When a sedate content the spirit feels,
And no fierce light disturbs, whilst it reveals,
But silent musings urge the mind to seek
Something too high for syllables to speak;
Till the free soul to a compos'dness charmed,
Finding the elements of rage disarmed,
O'er all below a solemn quiet grown,
Joys in th' inferior world and thinks it like her own:
In such a night let me abroad remain,
Till morning breaks, and all's confused again:
Our cares, our toils, our clamours are renewed,
Or pleasures, seldom reached, again pursued.

ANNE FINCH, COUNTESS OF WINCHILSEA (1713)

from *Windsor Forest*

COUNTRY SPORTS NEAR WINDSOR

Ye vig'rous Swains! while Youth ferments your Blood,
And purer Spirits swell the sprightly Flood,
Now range the Hills, the gameful Woods beset,
Wind the shrill Horn, or spread the waving Net.
When milder Autumn Summer's Heat succeeds,
And in the new-shorn Field the Partridge feeds,
Before his Lord the ready Spaniel bounds,
Panting with Hope, he tries the furrow'd Grounds,
But when the tainted Gales the Game betray,
Couch'd close he lyes, and meditates the Prey;
Secure they trust th'unfaithful Field, beset,
Till hov'ring o'er 'em sweeps the swelling Net.
Thus (if small Things we may with great compare)
When *Albion* sends her eager Sons to War,
Some thoughtless Town, with Ease and Plenty blest,
Near, and more near, the closing Lines invest;
Sudden they seize th'amaz'd, defenceless Prize,
And high in Air *Britannia*'s Standard flies.

See! from the Brake the whirring Pheasant springs,
And mounts exulting on triumphant Wings;
Short is his Joy! he feels the fiery Wound,
Flutters in Blood, and panting beats the Ground.
Ah! what avail his glossie, varying Dyes,
His Purple Crest, and Scarlet-circled Eyes,
The vivid Green his shining Plumes unfold;
His painted Wings, and Breast that flames with Gold?
     Nor yet, when moist *Arcturus* clouds the Sky,
The Woods and Fields their pleasing Toils deny.
To Plains with well-breath'd Beagles we repair,
And trace the Mazes of the circling Hare.
(Beasts, urg'd by us, their Fellow Beasts pursue,
And learn of Man each other to undo.)
With slaught'ring Guns th'unweary'd Fowler roves,
When Frosts have whiten'd all the naked Groves;
Where Doves in Flocks the leafless Trees o'ershade,
And lonely Woodcocks haunt the watry Glade.
He lifts the Tube, and levels with his Eye;
Strait a short Thunder breaks the frozen Sky.
Oft, as in Airy Rings they skim the Heath,
The clam'rous Lapwings feel the Leaden Death:
Oft as the mounting Larks their Notes prepare,
They fall, and leave their little Lives in Air.
     In genial Spring, beneath the quiv'ring Shade
Where cooling Vapours breathe along the Mead,
The patient Fisher takes his silent Stand
Intent, his Angle trembling in his Hand;
With Looks unmov'd, he hopes the Scaly Breed,
And eyes the dancing Cork and bending Reed.
Our plenteous Streams a various Race supply;
The bright-ey'd Perch with Fins of *Tyrian* Dye,
The silver Eel, in shining Volumes roll'd,
The yellow Carp, in Scales bedrop'd with Gold,
Swift Trouts, diversify'd with Crimson Stains,
And Pykes, the Tyrants of the watry Plains.
     Now *Cancer* glows with *Phœbus*' fiery Car;
The Youth rush eager to the Sylvan War;
Swarm o'er the Lawns, the Forest Walks surround,
Rowze the fleet Hart, and chear the opening Hound.

Th'impatient Courser pants in ev'ry Vein,
And pawing, seems to beat the distant Plain,
Hills, Vales, and Floods appear already crost,
And ere he starts, a thousand Steps are lost.
See! the bold Youth strain up the threatning Steep,
Rush thro' the Thickets, down the Vallies sweep,
Hang o'er their Coursers Heads with eager Speed,
And Earth rolls back beneath the flying Steed.

ALEXANDER POPE (1713)

from *The Seasons – Summer*

A THUNDERSTORM AND A TRAGEDY

Behold, slow-settling o'er the lurid grove
Unusual darkness broods, and, growing, gains
The full possession of the sky, surcharged
With wrathful vapour, from the secret beds
Where sleep the mineral generations drawn.
Thence nitre, sulphur, and the fiery spume
Of fat bitumen, steaming on the day,
With various-tinctured trains of latent flame,
Pollute the sky, and in yon baleful cloud,
A reddening gloom, a magazine of fate,
Ferment; till, by the touch ethereal roused,
The dash of clouds, or irritating war
Of fighting winds, while all is calm below,
They furious spring. A boding silence reigns
Dread through the dun expanse – save the dull sound
That from the mountain, previous to the storm,
Rolls o'er the muttering earth, disturbs the flood,
And shakes the forest-leaf without a breath
Prone to the lowest vale the aerial tribes
Descend: the tempest-loving raven scarce
Dares wing the dubious dusk. In rueful gaze
The cattle stand, and on the scowling heavens
Cast a deploring eye – by man forsook,
Who to the crowded cottage hies him fast,

Or seeks the shelter of the downward cave.
   'Tis listening fear and dumb amazement all:
When to the startled eye the sudden glance
Appears far south, eruptive through the cloud,
And, following slower, in explosion vast
The thunder raises his tremendous voice.
At first, heard solemn o'er the verge of heaven,
The tempest growls; but as it nearer comes,
And rolls its awful burden on the wind,
The lightnings flash a larger curve, and more
The noise astounds, till overhead a sheet
Of livid flame discloses wide, then shuts
And opens wider, shuts and opens still
Expansive, wrapping ether in blaze.
Follows the loosened aggravated roar,
Enlarging, deepening, mingling, peal on peal
Crushed horrible, convulsing heaven and earth.
   Down comes a deluge of sonorous hail,
Or prone-descending rain. Wide-rent, the clouds
Pour a whole flood; and yet, its flame unquenched,
The unconquerable lightning struggles through,
Ragged and fierce, or in red whirling balls,
And fires the mountains with redoubled rage.
Black from the stroke, above, the smouldering pine
Stands a sad shattered trunk; and, stretched below,
A lifeless group the blasted cattle lie:
Here the soft flocks, with that same harmless look
They wore alive, and ruminating still
In fancy's eye; and there the frowning bull,
And ox half-raised. Struck on the castled cliff,
The venerable tower and spiry fane
Resign their aged pride. The gloomy woods
Start at the flash, and from their deep recess
Wide-flaming out, their trembling inmates shake.
Amid Carnarvon's mountains rages loud
The repercussive roar: with mighty crush,
Into the flashing deep, from the rude rocks
Of Penmanmaur heaped hideous to the sky,
Tumble the smitten cliffs: and Snowdon's peak,
Dissolving, instant yields his wintry load.

Far seen, the heights of heathy Cheviot blaze,
And Thulè bellows through her utmost isles.
    Guilt hears appalled, with deeply troubled thought;
And yet not always on the guilty head
Descends the fated flash. Young Celadon
And his Amelia were a matchless pair,
With equal virtue formed and equal grace
The same, distinguished by their sex alone:
Hers the mild lustre of the blooming morn,
And his the radiance of the risen day.
    They loved: but such their guileless passion was
As in the dawn of time informed the heart
Of innocence and undissembling truth.
'Twas friendship heightened by the mutual wish,
The enchanting hope and sympathetic glow
Beamed from the mutual eye. Devoting all
To love, each was to each a dearer self,
Supremely happy in the awakened power
Of giving joy. Alone amid the shades,
Still in harmonious intercourse they lived
The rural day, and talked the flowing heart,
Or sighed and looked unutterable things.
So passed their life, a clear united stream,
By care unruffled; till, in evil hour,
The tempest caught them on the tender walk,
Heedless how far and where its mazes strayed,
While with each other blest, creative Love
Still bade eternal Eden smile around.
Heavy with instant fate, her bosom heaved
Unwonted sighs, and, stealing oft a look
Of the big gloom, on Celadon her eye
Fell tearful, wetting her disordered cheek.
In vain assuring love and confidence
In Heaven repressed her fear; it grew and shook
Her frame near dissolution. He perceived
The unequal conflict, and, as angels look
On dying saints, his eyes compassion shed,
With love illumined high. 'Fear not,' he said,
'Sweet innocence! thou stranger to offence
And inward storm! he who yon skies involves

In frowns of darkness, ever smiles on thee
With kind regard. O'er thee the secret shaft
That wastes at midnight, or the undreaded hour
Of noon, flies harmless: and that very voice,
Which thunders terror through the guilty heart,
With tongues of seraphs whispers peace to thine.
'Tis safety to be near thee sure, and thus
To clasp perfection!' From his void embrace,
Mysterious Heaven! that moment to the ground,
A blackened corse, was struck the beauteous maid.
But who can paint the lover, as he stood
Pierced by severe amazement, hating life.
Speechless, and fixed in all the death of woe?
So, faint resemblance! on the marble tomb
The well-dissembled mourner stooping stands,
For ever silent and for ever sad.

JAMES THOMSON (1726–30)

Grongar Hill

Silent nymph, with curious eye!
Who, the purple evening, lie
On the mountain's lonely van,
Beyond the noise of busy man;
Painting fair the form of things,
While the yellow linnet sings;
Or the tuneful nightingale
Charms the forest with her tale;
Come with all thy various hues,
Come, and aid thy sister muse;
Now, while Phoebus riding high
Gives lustre to the land and sky!
Grongar Hill invites my song,
Draw the landskip bright and strong;
Grongar, in whose mossy cells
Sweetly-musing quiet dwells;
Grongar, in whose silent shade,

For the modest Muses made,
So oft, I have the evening still,
At the fountain of a rill,
Sate upon a flowery bed,
With my hand beneath my head;
And strayed my eyes o'er Towy's flood,
Over mead, and over wood,
From house to house, from hill to hill,
'Till contemplation had her fill.
About his chequered sides I wind,
And leave his brooks and meads behind,
And groves, and grottoes where I lay,
And vistas shooting beams of day:
Wide and wider spreads the vale,
As circles on a smooth canal:
The mountains round, unhappy fate,
Sooner or later, of all height,
Withdraw their summits from the skies,
And lessen as the others rise:
Still the prospect wider spreads,
Adds a thousand woods and meads,
Still it widens, widens still,
And sinks the newly-risen hill.

   Now, I gain the mountain's brow,
What a landskip lies below!
No clouds, no vapours intervene,
But the gay, the open scene
Does the face of nature show,
In all the hues of heaven's bow;
And, swelling to embrace the light,
Spreads around beneath the sight.

   Old castles on the cliffs arise,
Proudly towering in the skies!
Rushing from the woods, the spires
Seem from hence ascending fires!
Half his beams Apollo sheds
On the yellow mountain-heads!
Gilds the fleeces of the flocks,
And glitters on the broken rocks!

   Below me, trees unnumbered rise,

Beautiful in various dyes:
The gloomy pine, the poplar blue,
The yellow beech, the sable yew,
The slender fir that taper grows,
The sturdy oak with broad-spread boughs.
And beyond the purple grove,
Haunt of Phillis, queen of love!
Gaudy as the opening dawn,
Lies a long and level lawn,
On which a dark hill, steep and high,
Holds and charms the wandering eye!
Deep are his feet in Towy's flood,
His sides are clothed with waving wood,
And ancient towers crown his brow,
That cast an aweful look below;
Whose ragged walls the ivy creeps,
And with her arms from falling keeps.
So both a safety from the wind
On mutual dependence find.
    'Tis now the raven's bleak abode;
'Tis now th' apartment of the toad;
And there the fox securely feeds;
And there the poisonous adder breeds,
Concealed in ruins, moss, and weeds:
While, ever and anon, there falls
Huge heaps of hoary mouldered walls.
Yet time has seen that lifts the low,
And level lays the lofty brow,
Has seen this broken pile complete,
Big with the vanity of state;
But transient is the smile of fate!
A little rule, a little sway,
A sunbeam in a winter's day,
Is all the proud and mighty have,
Between the cradle and the grave.
    And see the rivers how they run
Through woods and meads, in shade and sun,
Sometimes swift, and sometimes slow,
Wave succeeding wave, they go
A various journey to the deep,

Like human life, to endless sleep!
Thus is nature's vesture wrought,
To instruct our wandering thought;
Thus she dresses green and gay,
To disperse our cares away.
 Ever charming, ever new,
When will the landskip tire the view!
The fountain's fall, the river's flow,
The woody valleys, warm and low;
The windy summit, wild and high,
Roughly rushing on the sky!
The pleasant seat, the ruined tower,
The naked rock, the shady bower;
The town and village, dome and farm,
Each give each a double charm,
As pearls upon an Aethiop's arm.
 See, on the mountain's southern side,
Where the prospect opens wide,
Where the evening gilds the tide;
How close and small the hedges lie!
What streaks of meadows cross the eye!
A step methinks may pass the stream,
So little distant dangers seem;
So we mistake the future's face,
Eyed through hope's deluding glass;
As yon summits soft and fair,
Clad in colours of the air,
Which, to those who journey near,
Barren and brown, and rough appear.
Still we tread tired the same coarse way,
The present's still a cloudy day.
 O may I with myself agree,
And never covet what I see;
Content me with an humble shade,
My passions tamed, my wishes laid;
For while our wishes wildly roll,
We banish quiet from the soul:
'Tis thus the busy beat the air,
And misers gather wealth and care.
Now, even now, my joy runs high,

As on the mountain-turf I lie;
While the wanton Zephyr sings,
And in the vale perfumes his wings;
While the waters murmur deep,
While the shepherd charms his sheep;
While the birds unbounded fly,
And with music fill the sky.
Now, even now, my joys run high.
   Be full, ye courts; be great who will;
Search for peace, with all your skill:
Open wide the lofty door,
Seek her on the marble floor,
In vain ye search, she is not there;
In vain ye search the domes of care!
Grass and flowers Quiet treads,
On the meads, and mountain-heads,
Along with Pleasure, close allied,
Ever by each other's side:
And often, by the murmuring rill,
Hears the thrush, while all is still,
Within the groves of Grongar Hill.

JOHN DYER (1726)

Ode to Evening

If aught of oaten stop, or pastoral song,
May hope, chaste eve, to soothe thy modest ear,
    Like thy own solemn springs,
    Thy springs and dying gales;

O nymph reserved, while now the bright-haired sun
Sits in yon western tent, whose cloudy skirts,
    With brede ethereal wove,
    O'erhang his wavy bed:

Now air is hushed, save where the weak-eyed bat
With short shrill shriek flits by on leathern wing,
    Or where the beetle winds
    His small but sullen horn,

As oft he rises, 'midst the twilight path
Against the pilgrim borne in heedless hum:
    Now teach me, maid composed,
    To breathe some softened strain,

Whose numbers, stealing through thy darkening vale,
May not unseemly with its stillness suit,
    As, musing slow, I hail
    Thy genial loved return!

For when thy folding-star arising shows
His paly circlet, at his warning lamp
    The fragrant hours, and elves
    Who slept in buds the day,

And many a nymph who wreathes her brows with sedge,
And sheds the freshening dew, and, lovelier still,
    The pensive pleasures sweet,
    Prepare thy shadowy car:

Then lead, calm votaress, where some sheety lake
Cheers the lone heath, or some time-hallowed pile,
    Or upland fallows grey
    Reflect its last cool gleam.

Or if chill blustering winds, or driving rain,
Prevent my willing feet, be mine the hut
    That from the mountain's side
    Views wilds and swelling floods,

And hamlets brown, and dim-discovered spires,
And hears their simple bell, and marks o'er all
    Thy dewy fingers draw
    The gradual dusky veil.

While spring shall pour his show'rs, as oft he wont,
And bathe thy breathing tresses, meekest eve!
  While summer loves to sport
  Beneath thy lingering light;

While sallow autumn fills thy lap with leaves,
Or winter, yelling through the troublous air,
  Affrights thy shrinking train,
  And rudely rends thy robes:

So long, regardful of thy quiet rule,
Shall fancy, friendship, science, rose-lipped health
  Thy gentlest influence own,
  And hymn thy favourite name!

WILLIAM COLLINS (1746)

The poems of William Collins, who was an acquaintance of Samuel Johnson's, were admired by the Romantics, and this personification of Evening probably inspired Keats's later great *Ode to Autumn* (see *The Wordsworth Book of Nineteenth-Century Verse*). Like William Cowper later, Collins suffered from a recurrent mental disorder. He died relatively young and is buried in Chichester Cathedral.

from *The Task*

THE WINTER MORNING WALK

'Tis morning; and the sun, with ruddy orb
Ascending, fires th' horizon: while the clouds,
That crowd away before the driving wind,
More ardent as the disk emerges more,
Resemble most some city in a blaze,
Seen through the leafless wood. His slanting ray
Slides ineffectual down the snowy vale,
And, tinging all with his own rosy hue,
From ev'ry herb and ev'ry spiry blade
Stretches a length of shadow o'er the field.
Mine, spindling into longitude immense,

In spite of gravity, and sage remark
That I myself am but a fleeting shade,
Provokes me to a smile. With eye askance
I view the muscular proportion'd limb
Transform'd to a lean shank. The shapeless pair,
As they design'd to mock me, at my side
Take step for Step; and, as I near approach
The cottage, walk along the plaster'd wall,
Prepost'rous sight! the legs without the man.
The verdure of the plain lies buried deep
Beneath the dazzling deluge; and the bents,
And coarser grass, upspearing o'er the rest,
Of late unsightly and unseen, now shine
Conspicuous, and, in bright apparel clad
And fledg'd with icy feathers, nod superb.
The cattle mourn in corners where the fence
Screens them, and seem half petrified to sleep
In unrecumbent sadness. There they wait
Their wonted fodder; not like hung'ring man,
Fretful if unsupply'd; but silent, meek,
And patient of the slow-pac'd swain's delay.
He from the stack carves out th' accustom'd load,
Deep-plunging, and again deep-plunging oft,
His broad keen knife into the solid mass:
Smooth as a wall the upright remnant stands,
With such undeviating and even force
He severs it away: no needless care,
Lest storms should overset the leaning pile
Deciduous, or its own unbalanc'd weight.
Forth goes the woodman, leaving unconcern'd
The cheerful haunts of man; to wield the axe
And drive the wedge, in yonder forest drear,
From morn to eve his solitary task.
Shaggy, and lean, and shrewd, with pointed ears
And tail cropp'd short, half lurcher and half cur –
His dog attends him. Close behind his heel
Now creeps he slow; and now, with many a frisk
Wide-scamp'ring, snatches up the drifted snow
With iv'ry teeth, or ploughs it with his snout;
Then shakes his powder'd coat, and barks for joy.

Heedless of all his pranks, the sturdy churl
Moves right toward the mark; nor stops for aught,
But now and then with pressure of his thumb
T' adjust the fragrant charge of a short tube
That fumes beneath his nose: the trailing cloud
Streams far behind him, scenting all the air.
Now from the roost, or from the neighb'ring pale,
Where, diligent to catch the first faint gleam
Of smiling day, they gossip'd side by side,
Come trooping at the housewife's well-known call
The feather'd tribes domestic. Half on wing,
And half on foot, they brush the fleecy flood,
Conscious, and fearful of too deep a plunge.
The sparrows peep, and quit the shelt'ring eaves
To seize the fair occasion. Well they eye
The scatter'd grain; and, thievishly resolv'd
T' escape th' impending famine, often scar'd,
As oft return – a pert voracious kind.
Clean riddance quickly made, one only care
Remains to each – the search of sunny nook,
Or shed impervious to the blast. Resign'd
To sad necessity, the cock foregoes
His wonted strut; and, wading at their head
With well-consider'd steps, seems to resent
His alter'd gait and stateliness retrench'd.
How find the myriads, that in summer cheer
The hills and vallies with their ceaseless songs,
Due sustenance, or where subsist they now?
Earth yields them nought: th' imprison'd worm is safe
Beneath the frozen clod; all seeds of herbs
Lie cover'd close; and berry-bearing thorns,
That feed the thrush, (whatever some suppose)
Afford the smaller minstrels no supply.
The long protracted rigour of the year
Thins all their num'rous flocks. In chinks and holes
Ten thousand seek an unmolested end,
As instinct prompts; self-buried ere they die.
The very rooks and daws forsake the fields,
Where neither grub, nor root, nor earth-nut, now
Repays their labour more; and, perch'd aloft

By the way-side, or stalking in the path,
Lean pensioners upon the trav'ler's track,
Pick up their nauseaous dole, though sweet to them,
Of voided pulse or half-digested grain.
The streams are lost amid the splendid blank,
O'erwhelming all distinction. On the flood,
Indurated and fixt, the snowy weight
Lies undissolv'd; while silently beneath,
And unperceiv'd, the current steals away.
Not so where, scornful of a check, it leaps
The mill-dam, dashes on the restless wheel,
And wantons in the pebbly gulph below:
No frost can bind it there; its utmost force
Can but arrest the light and smoky mist
That in its fall the liquid sheet throws wide.
And see where it has hung th' embroider'd banks
With forms so various, that no pow'rs of art,
The pencil or the pen, may trace the scene!
Here glitt'ring turrets rise, upbearing high
(Fantastic misarrangement!) on the roof
Large growth of what may seem the sparkling trees
And shrubs of fairy land. The crystal drops
That trickle down the branches, fast congeal'd,
Shoot into pillars of pellucid length,
And prop the pile they but adorn'd before.
Here grotto within grotto safe defies
The sun-beam; there, emboss'd and fretted wild,
The growing wonder takes a thousand shapes
Capricious, in which fancy seeks in vain
The Likeness of some object seen before.
Thus nature works as if to mock at art,
And in defiance of her rival pow'rs;
By these fortuitous and random strokes
Performing such inimitable feats
As she with all her rules can never reach.

WILLIAM COWPER (published 1785)

SONNET IV

To the Moon

Queen of the silver bow! by thy pale beam
    Alone and pensive I delight to stray
And watch thy shadow trembling in the stream
    Or mark the floating clouds that cross thy way.
And, while I gaze, thy mild and placid light
    Sheds a soft calm upon my troubled breast;
And oft I think, fair planet of the night,
    That in thy orb the wretched may have rest.
The sufferers of the earth perhaps may go,
    Releas'd by death, to thy benignant sphere,
And the sad children of despair and woe
    Forget in thee their cup of sorrow here.
O! that I soon may reach thy world serene,
Poor wearied pilgrim in this toiling scene.

CHARLOTTE SMITH (c.1782)

SONNET XII

Written on the Sea Shore, October 1784

On some rude fragment of the rocky shore,
    Where on the fractur'd cliff the billows break
    Musing, my solitary seat I take
And listen to the deep and solemn roar.
O'er the dark waves, the wind's tempestuous howl,
    The screaming sea-bird quits the troubled sea,
    But the wild gloomy scene has charms for me
And suits the mournful temper of my soul.
Already shipwrecked by the storms of Fate,
    Like the poor mariner methinks I stand,
    Cast on a rock; who sees the distant land
From whence no succour comes – or comes too late.
    Faint and more faint are heard his feeble cries
    'Till in the rising sun th'exhausted sufferer dies.

CHARLOTTE SMITH (1784)

Lines Composed a Few Miles above Tintern Abbey,

ON REVISITING THE BANKS OF THE WYE DURING A TOUR. JULY 13th, 1798

Five years have past; five summers, with the length
Of five long winters! and again I hear
These waters, rolling from their mountain-springs
With a soft inland murmur. Once again
Do I behold these steep and lofty cliffs,
That on a wild secluded scene impress
Thoughts of more deep seclusion; and connect
The landscape with the quiet of the sky.
The day is come when I again repose
Here, under this dark sycamore, and view
These plots of cottage-ground, these orchard-tufts,
Which at this season, with their unripe fruits,
Are clad in one green hue, and lose themselves
'Mid groves and copses. Once again I see
These hedge-rows, hardly hedge-rows, little lines
Of sportive wood run wild: these pastoral farms,
Green to the very door; and wreaths of smoke
Sent up, in silence, from among the trees!
With some uncertain notice, as might seem
Of vagrant dwellers in the houseless woods,
Or of some Hermit's cave, where by his fire
The Hermit sits alone.
                              These beauteous forms,
Through a long absence, have not been to me
As is a landscape to a blind man's eye:
But oft, in lonely rooms, and 'mid the din
Of towns and cities, I have owed to them,
In hours of weariness, sensations sweet,
Felt in the blood, and felt along the heart;
And passing even into my purer mind,
With tranquil restoration: feelings too
Of unremembered pleasure: such, perhaps,

As have no slight or trivial influence
On that best portion of a good man's life,
His little, nameless, unremembered, acts
Of kindness and of love. Nor less, I trust,
To them I may have owed another gift,
Of aspect more sublime; that blessed mood,
In which the burthen of the mystery,
In which the heavy and the weary weight
Of all this unintelligible world,
Is lightened: that serene and blessed mood,
In which the affections gently lead us on,
Until, the breath of this corporeal frame
And even the motion of our human blood
Almost suspended, we are laid asleep
In body, and become a living soul:
While with an eye made quiet by the power
Of harmony, and the deep power of joy,
We see into the life of things.
                                        If this
Be but a vain belief, yet, oh! how oft –
In darkness and amid the many shapes
Of joyless daylight; when the fretful stir
Unprofitable, and the fever of the world,
Have hung upon the beatings of my heart –
How oft, in spirit, have I turned to thee,
O sylvan Wye! thou wanderer through the woods,
How often has my spirit turned to thee!

    And now, with gleams of half-extinguished thought,
With many recognitions dim and faint,
And somewhat of a sad perplexity,
The picture of the mind revives again:
While here I stand, not only with the sense
Of present pleasure, but with pleasing thoughts
That in this moment there is life and food
For future years. And so I dare to hope,
Though changed, no doubt, from what I was when first
I came among these hills; when like a roe
I bounded o'er the mountains, by the sides
Of the deep rivers, and the lonely streams,

Wherever nature led: more like a man
Flying from something that he dreads than one
Who sought the thing he loved. For nature then
(The coarser pleasures of my boyish days,
And their glad animal movements all gone by)
To me was all in all. I cannot paint
What then I was. The sounding cataract
Haunted me like a passion: the tall rock,
The mountain, and the deep and gloomy wood,
Their colours and their forms, were then to me
An appetite; a feeling and a love,
That had no need of a remoter charm,
By thought supplied, nor any interest
Unborrowed from the eye. That time is past,
And all its aching joys are now no more,
And all its dizzy raptures. Not for this
Faint I, nor mourn nor murmur; other gifts
Have followed; for such loss, I would believe,
Abundant recompense. For I have learned
To look on nature, not as in the hour
Of thoughtless youth; but hearing oftentimes
The still, sad music of humanity,
Nor harsh nor grating, though of ample power
To chasten and subdue. And I have felt
A presence that disturbs me with the joy
Of elevated thoughts; a sense sublime
Of something far more deeply interfused,
Whose dwelling is the light of setting suns,
And the round ocean and the living air,
And the blue sky, and in the mind of man:
A motion and a spirit, that impels
All thinking things, all objects of all thought,
And rolls through all things. Therefore am I still
A lover of the meadows and the woods,
And mountains; and of all that we behold
From this green earth; of all the mighty world
Of eye, and ear, both what they half create,
And what perceive; well pleased to recognize
In nature and the language of the sense
The anchor of my purest thoughts, the nurse,

The guide, the guardian of my heart, and soul
Of all my moral being.
                              Nor perchance,
If I were not thus taught, should I the more
Suffer my genial spirits to decay:
For thou art with me here upon the banks
Of this fair river; thou my dearest Friend,
My dear, dear Friend; and in thy voice I catch
The language of my former heart, and read
My former pleasures in the shooting lights
Of thy wild eyes. Oh! yet a little while
May I behold in thee what I was once,
My dear, dear Sister! and this prayer I make,
Knowing that Nature never did betray
The heart that loved her; 'tis her privilege,
Through all the years of this our life, to lead
From joy to joy: for she can so inform
The mind that is within us, so impress
With quietness and beauty, and so feed
With lofty thoughts, that neither evil tongues,
Rash judgments, nor the sneers of selfish men,
Nor greetings where no kindness is, nor all
The dreary intercourse of daily life,
Shall e'er prevail against us, or disturb
Our cheerful faith, that all which we behold
Is full of blessings. Therefore let the moon
Shine on thee in thy solitary walk;
And let the misty mountain-winds be free
To blow against thee: and, in after years,
When these wild ecstasies shall be matured
Into a sober pleasure; when thy mind
Shall be a mansion for all lovely forms,
Thy memory be as a dwelling-place
For all sweet sounds and harmonies; oh! then,
If solitude, or fear, or pain, or grief,
Should be thy portion, with what healing thoughts
Of tender joy wilt thou remember me,
And these my exhortations! Nor, perchance –
If I should be where I no more can hear
Thy voice, nor catch from thy wild eyes these gleams

Of past existence – wilt thou then forget
That on the banks of this delightful stream
We stood together; and that I, so long
A worshipper of Nature, hither came
Unwearied in that service: rather say
With warmer love – oh! with far deeper zeal
Of holier love. Nor wilt thou then forget
That after many wanderings, many years
Of absence, these steep woods and lofty cliffs,
And this green pastoral landscape, were to me
More dear, both for themselves and for thy sake!

WILLIAM WORDSWORTH (1798)

5
RESPONSES TO NATURE
Part Two: Trees, Flowers, Animals and Birds

To the Nightingale

Exert thy voice, sweet harbinger of Spring!
    This moment is thy time to sing,
    This moment I attend to praise,
And set my numbers to thy lays.
    Free as thine shall be my song;
    As thy music, short, or long.
Poets, wild as thee, were born,
    Pleasing best where unconfin'd,
    When to please is least design'd,
Soothing but their cares to rest;
    Cares do still their thoughts molest,
    And still th' unhappy poet's breast,
Like thine, when best he sings, is plac'd against a thorn.

    She begins, let all be still!
      Muse, thy promise now fulfill!
    Sweet, oh! sweet, still sweeter yet
    Can thy words such accents fit,
    Canst thou syllables refine,
    Melt a sense that shall retain
    Still some spirit of the brain,
    Till with sounds like these it join.
      'Twill not be! then change thy note;
      Let division shake thy throat.
    Hark! division now she tries;
    Yet as far the Muse outflies.
      Cease then, prithee, cease thy tune;
      Trifler, wilt thou sing till *June*?
    Till thy bus'ness all lies waste,
    And the time of building's past!
      Thus we poets that have speech,
    Unlike what thy forests teach,
      If a fluent vein be shown
      That's transcendent to our own,
    Criticize, reform, or preach,
    Or censure what we cannot reach.

ANNE FINCH, COUNTESS OF WINCHILSEA (1702)

The Tree

Fair Tree! for thy delightful Shade
'Tis just that some Return be made.
Sure, some Return is due from me
To thy cool Shadows, and to thee.
When thou to Birds dost Shelter give
Thou Musick dost from them receive;
If Travellers beneath thee stay,
Till Storms have worn themselves away,
That Time in praising thee they spend
And thy protecting Pow'r commend:
The Shepherd here from Scorching freed
Tunes to thy dancing Leaves his Reed,
Whilst his lov'd Nymph in Thanks bestows
Her flow'ring Chaplet on thy Boughs.
Shall I then only silent be,
And no Return be made by me?
No; let this Wish upon thee wait,
And still to flourish be they Fate.
To future Ages may'st thou stand
Untouch'd by the rash Workman's hand
Till that large stock of Sap is spent
Which gives thy Summer's Ornament;
Till the fierce Winds, that vainly strive
To shock thy Greatness whilst alive,
Shall on thy lifeless Hour attend,
Prevent the Axe and grace thine End,
Their scatter'd Strength together call
And to the Clouds proclaim thy Fall,
Who then their Ev'ning-Dews may spare
When Thou no longer art their Care;
But shalt, like ancient Heroes, burn,
And some bright Hearth become thine Urn.

ANNE FINCH, COUNTESS OF WINCHILSEA
(published 1713)

from *The Seasons – Spring*

BIRDS IN THE MATING SEASON

When first the soul of love is sent abroad
Warm through the vital air, and on the heart
Harmonious seizes, the gay troops begin
In gallant thought to plume the painted wing;
And try again the long-forgotten strain,
At first faint-warbled. But no sooner grows
The soft infusion prevalent and wide
Than all alive at once their joy o'erflows
In music unconfined. Up springs the lark,
Shrill-voiced and loud, the messenger of morn:
Ere yet the shadows fly, he mounted sings
Amid the dawning clouds, and from their haunts
Calls up the tuneful nations. Every copse
Deep-tangled, tree irregular, and bush
Bending with dewy moisture o'er the heads
Of the coy quiristers that lodge within,
Are prodigal of harmony. The thrush
And wood-lark, o'er the kind-contending throng
Superior heard, run through the sweetest length
Of notes, when listening Philomela[1] deigns
To let them joy, and purposes, in thought
Elate, to make her night excel their day.
The blackbird whistles from the thorny brake,
The mellow bullfinch answers from the grove;
Nor are the linnets, o'er the flowering furze
Poured out profusely, silent. Joined to these
Innumerous songsters, in the freshening shade
Of new-sprung leaves, their modulations mix
Mellifluous. The jay, the rook, the daw,
And each harsh pipet discordant heard alone,
Aid the full concert; while the stock-dove breathes
A melancholy murmur through the whole.
    'Tis love creates their melody, and all

---

[1] the nightingale

This waste of music is the voice of love,
That even to birds and beasts the tender arts
Of pleasing teaches. Hence the glossy kind
Try every winning way inventive love
Can dictate, and in courtship to their mates
Pour forth their little souls. First, wide around,
With distant awe, in airy rings they rove,
Endeavouring by a thousand tricks to catch
The cunning, conscious, half-averted glance
Of their regardless charmer. Should she seem
Softening the least approvance to bestow,
Their colours burnish, and, by hope inspired,
They brisk advance; then, on a sudden struck,
Retire disordered; then again approach,
In fond rotation spread the spotted wing,
And shiver every feather with desire.
  Connubial leagues agreed, to the deep woods
They haste away, all as their fancy leads,
Pleasure, or food, or secret safety prompts;
That Nature's great command may be obeyed,
Nor all the sweet sensations they perceive
Indulged in vain. Some to the holly-hedge
Nestling repair, and to the thicket some;
Some to the rude protection of the thorn
Commit their feeble offspring. The cleft tree
Offers its kind concealment to a few,
Their food its insects, and its moss their nests.
Others apart far in the grassy dale,
Or roughening waste, their humble texture weave
But most in woodland solitudes delight,
In unfrequented glooms, or shaggy banks,
Steep, and divided by a babbling brook
Whose murmurs soothe them all the live-long day
When by kind duty fixed. Among the roots
Of hazel, pendent o'er the plaintive stream,
They frame the first foundation of their domes –
Dry sprigs of trees, in artful fabric laid,
And bound with clay together. Now 'tis nought
But restless hurry through the busy air,
Beat by unnumbered wings. The swallow sweeps

The slimy pool, to build his hanging house
Intent. And often, from the careless back
Of herds and flocks, a thousand tugging bills
Pluck hair and wool; and oft, when unobserved,
Steal from the barn a straw – till soft and warm,
Clean and complete, their habitation grows.
　　As thus the patient dam assiduous sits,
Not to be tempted from her tender task
Or by sharp hunger or by smooth delight,
Though the whole loosened Spring around her blows,
Her sympathizing lover takes his stand
High on the opponent bank, and ceaseless sings
The tedious time away; or else supplies
Her place a moment, while she sudden flits
To pick the scanty meal. The appointed time
With pious toil fulfilled, the callow young,
Warmed and expanded into perfect life,
Their brittle bondage break, and come to light,
A helpless family demanding food
With constant clamour. Oh, what passions then,
What melting sentiments of kindly care,
on the new parents seize! Away they fly
Affectionate, and undesiring bear
The most delicious morsel to their young;
Which equally distributed, again
The search begins. Even so a gentle pair,
By fortune sunk, but formed of generous mould,
And charmed with cares beyond the vulgar breast,
In some lone cot amid the distant woods,
Sustain'd alone by providential Heaven,
Oft, as they weeping eye their infant train,
Check their own appetites, and give them all.

JAMES THOMSON (published 1728)

from *Jubilate Agno*

MY CAT JEOFFRY

For I will consider my Cat Jeoffry.

For he is the servant of the Living God duly and daily serving him.

For at the first glance of the glory of God in the East he worships in his way.

For is this done by wreathing his body seven times round with elegant quickness.

For then he leaps up to catch the musk, which is the blessing of God upon this prayer.

For he rolls upon prank to work it in.

For having done duty and received blessing he begins to consider himself.

For this he performs in ten degrees.

For first he looks upon his fore-paws to see if they are clean.

For secondly he kicks up behind to clear away there.

For thirdly he works it upon stretch with the fore-paws extended.

For fourthly he sharpens his paws by wood.

For fifthly he washes himself.

For sixthly he rolls upon wash.

For seventhly he fleas himself, that he may not be interrupted upon the beat.

For eighthly he rubs himself against a post.

For ninthly he looks up for his instructions.

For tenthly he goes in quest of food.

For having consider'd God and himself he will consider his neighbour.

For if he meets another cat he will kiss her in kindness.

For when he takes his prey he plays with it to give it a chance.

For one mouse in seven escapes by his dallying.

For when his day's work is done his business more properly begins.

For he keeps the Lord's watch in the night against the
    adversary.

For he counteracts the powers of darkness by his electrical
    skin and glaring eyes.

For he counteracts the Devil, who is death, by brisking
    about the life.

For in his morning orisons he loves the sun and the sun
    loves him.

For he is of the tribe of Tiger.

For the Cherub Cat is a term of the Angel Tiger.

For he has the subtlety and hissing of a serpent, which in
    goodness he suppresses.

For he will not do destruction if he is well-fed, neither will
    he spit without provocation.

For he purrs in thankfulness, when God tells him he's a
    good Cat.

For he is an instrument for the children to learn
    benevolence upon.

For every house is incomplete without him and a blessing is
    lacking in the spitit.

For the Lord commanded Moses concerning the cats at the
    departure of the Children of Israel from Egypt.

For every family had one cat at least in the bag.

For the English Cats are the best in Europe.

For he is the cleanest in the use of his fore-paws of any
    quadrupede.

For the dexterity of his defence is an instance of the love of
    God to him exceedingly.

For he is the quickest to his mark of any creature.

For he is tenacious of his point.

For he is a mixture of gravity and waggery.

For he knows that God is his Saviour.

For there is nothing sweeter than his peace when at rest.

For there is nothing brisker than his life when in motion.

For he is of the Lord's poor and so indeed is he called by
    benevolence perpetually –

Poor Jeoffry! poor Jeoffry! the rat has bit thy throat.

For I bless the name of the Lord Jesus that Jeoffry is better.

For the divine spirit comes about his body to sustain it in
    complete cat.

For his tongue is exceeding pure so that it has in purity
  what it wants in music.
For he is docile and can learn certain things.
For he can set up with gravity which is patience upon
  approbation.
For he can fetch and carry, which is patience in
  employment.
For he can jump over a stick which is patience upon proof
  positive.
For he can spraggle upon waggle at the word of command.
For he can jump from an eminence into his master's
  bosom.
For he can catch the cork and toss it again.
For he is hated by the hypocrite and miser.
For the former is afraid of detection.
For the latter refuses the charge.
For he camels his back to bear the first notion of business.
For he is good to think on, if a man would express himself
  neatly.
For he made a great figure in Egypt for his signal services.
For he killed the Icneumon-rat very pernicious by land.
For his ears are so acute that they sting again.
For from this proceeds the passing quickness of his
  attention.
For by stroking of him I have found out electricity.
For I perceived God's light about him both wax and fire.
For the Electrical fire is the spiritual substance, which God
  sends from heaven to sustain the bodies both of man
  and beast.
For God has blessed him in the variety of his movements.
For, though he cannot fly, he is an excellent clamberer.
For his motions upon the face of the earth are more than
  any other quadrupede.
For he can tread to all the measures upon the music.
For he can swim for life.
For he can creep.

CHRISTOPHER SMART (by 1763)

SONNET 58

The Glow Worm

When on some balmy-breathing night of Spring
   The happy child, to whom the world is new
Pursues the evening moth, of mealy wing,
   Or from the heath-bell beats the sparkling dew;
He sees before his inexperienc'd eyes
   The brilliant Glow Worm, like a meteor, shine
On the turf bank; amaz'd and pleas'd he cries
   'Star of the dewy grass! – I make thee mine!'
Then, ere he sleep, collects the moistened flower
   And bids soft leaves his glittering prize enfold,
And dreams that fairy lamps illume his bower.
   Yet, with the morning, shudders to behold
His lucid treasure, rayless as the dust;
So turn the World's bright joys, to cold and blank disgust.

                  CHARLOTTE SMITH (c.1784)

The Poplar-Field

The poplars are fell'd, farewell to the shade
And the whispering sound of the cool colonnade,
The winds play no longer, and sing in the leaves,
Nor Ouse on his bosom their image receives.

Twelve years have elaps'd since I last took a view
Of my favourite field and the bank where they grew,
And now in the grass behold they are laid,
And the tree is my seat that once lent me a shade.

The blackbird has fled to another retreat
Where the hazels afford him a screen from the heat,
And the scene where his melody charm'd me before,
Resounds with his sweet-flowing ditty no more.

My fugitive years are all hasting away,
And I must ere long lie as lowly as they,

With a turf on my breast, and a stone at my head,
Ere another such grove shall arise in its stead.

'Tis a sight to engage me, if any thing can,
To muse on the perishing pleasures of man;
Though his life be a dream, his enjoyments, I see,
Have a being less durable even than he.

WILLIAM COWPER (1784)

The Wild Honeysuckle

Fair flower, that dost so comely grow,
 Hid in this silent, dull retreat,
Untouched thy honied blossoms blow,
 Unseen thy little branches greet:
  No roving foot shall crush thee here,
  No busy hand provoke a tear.

By Nature's self in white arrayed,
 She bade thee shun the vulgar eye,
And planted here the guardian shade,
 And sent soft waters murmuring by;
  Thus quietly thy summer goes,
  Thy days declining to repose.

Smit with those charms, that must decay,
 I grieve to see your future doom;
They died – nor were those flowers more gay,
 The flowers that did in Eden bloom;
  Unpitying frosts and Autumn's power
  Shall leave no vestige of this flower.

From morning suns and evening dews
 At first thy little being came;
If nothing once, you nothing lose,
 For when you die you are the same;
  The space between is but an hour,
  The frail duration of a flower.

PHILIP FRENEAU (1786)

To a Mouse,

ON TURNING HER UP IN HER NEST
WITH THE PLOUGH, NOVEMBER 1785

Wee, sleekit, cow'rin', tim'rous beastie,
O what a panic 's in thy breastie!
Thou need na start awa sae hasty,
    Wi' bickering[1] brattle![2]
I wad be laith to rin an' chase thee
    Wi' murd'ring pattle![3]

I'm truly sorry man's dominion
Has broken Nature's social union,
An' justifies that ill opinion
    Which makes thee startle
At me, thy poor earth-born companion,
    An' fellow-mortal!

I doubt na, whiles, but thou may thieve;
What then? poor beastie, thou maun live!
A daimen-icker[4] in a thrave[5]
    'S a sma' request:
I'll get a blessin' wi' the lave,[6]
    And never miss 't!

Thy wee bit housie, too, in ruin!
Its silly wa's the win's are strewin'!
An' naething, now, to big[7] a new ane,
    O' foggage[8] green!
An' bleak December's winds ensuin',
    Baith snell[9] an' keen!

---

[1] hurried   [2] scuttling   [3] plough spade   [4] an occasional ear of corn
[5] group of sheaves   [6] the rest   [7] build   [8] coarse grass   [9] bitter

Thou saw the fields laid bare and waste,
An' weary winter comin' fast,
An' cozie here, beneath the blast,
              Thou thought to dwell,
Till crash! the cruel coulter[10] past
              Out-thro' thy cell.

That wee bit heap o' leaves an' stibble
Has cost thee mony a weary nibble!
Now thou's turned out, for a' thy trouble,
              But house or hald,[11]
To thole[12] the winter's sleety dribble,
              An' cranreuch[13] cauld!

But, Mousie, thou art no thy lane,[14]
In proving foresight may be vain:
The best laid schemes o' mice an' men
              Gang aft a-gley,[15]
An' lea'e us nought but grief an' pain
              For promised joy.

Still thou art blest compared wi' me!
The present only toucheth thee:
But oh! I backward cast my e'e
              On prospects drear!
An' forward tho' I canna see,
              I guess an' fear!

                       ROBERT BURNS (1785)

---

[10] ploughshare   [11] without house or property   [12] endure   [13] hoarfrost
[14] not alone   [15] awry

To a Mountain Daisy

ON TURNING ONE DOWN WITH THE PLOUGH IN APRIL 1786

Wee modest crimson-tippèd flow'r,
Thou 's met me in an evil hour;
For I maun crush amang the stoure
   Thy slender stem:
To spare thee now is past my pow'r,
   Thou bonnie gem.

Alas! it 's no thy neibor sweet,
The bonnie lark, companion meet,
Bending thee 'mang the dewy weet
   Wi' spreckled breast,
When upward springing, blythe to greet
   The purpling east.

Cauld blew the bitter-biting north
Upon thy early humble birth;
Yet cheerfully thou glinted forth
   Amid the storm,
Scarce reared above the parent-earth
   Thy tender form.

The flaunting flow'rs our gardens yield
High shelt'ring woods and wa's[1] maun shield,
But thou, beneath the random bield
   O' clod or stane,
Adorns the histie stibble-field,
   Unseen, alane.

There, in thy scanty mantle clad,
Thy snawy bosom sun-ward spread,
Thou lifts thy unassuming head
   In humble guise;
But now the share uptears thy bed,
   And low thou lies!

[1] walls

Such is the fate of artless maid,
Sweet flow'ret of the rural shade,
By love's simplicity betrayed,
          And guileless trust,
Till she like thee, all soiled, is laid
          Low i' the dust.

Such is the fate of simple bard,
On life's rough ocean luckless starred:
Unskilful he to note the card
          Of prudent lore,
Till billows rage, and gales blow hard,
          And whelm him o'er!

Such fate to suffering worth is giv'n,
Who long with wants and woes has striv'n,
By human pride or cunning driv'n
          To mis'ry's brink,
Till wrenched of ev'ry stay but Heaven,
          He, ruined, sink!

Ev'n thou who mourn'st the Daisy's fate,
That fate is thine – no distant date;
Stern Ruin's ploughshare drives elate
          Full on thy bloom,
Till crushed beneath the furrow's weight
          Shall be thy doom!

ROBERT BURNS (1786)

Ode to the Poppy

Not for the promise of the laboured field,
Not for the good the yellow harvests yield,
    I bend at Ceres'[1] shrine;
For dull, to humid eyes, appear
The golden glories of the year,
    Alas! – a melancholy worship's mine.

I hail the goddess for her scarlet flower!
    Thou brilliant weed,
    That does so far exceed
The richest gifts gay Flora can bestow:
Heedless I passed thee, in life's morning hour,
    Thou comforter of woe,
Till sorrow taught me to confess thy power.

In early days, when Fancy cheats,
    A varied wreath I wove
Of laughing Spring's luxuriant sweets,
    To deck ungrateful Love:
The rose, or thorn, my labours crowned,
As Venus smiled, or Venus frowned;
But Love, and Joy, and all their train, are flown;
    E'en languid Hope no more is mine,
And I will sing of thee alone,
Unless, perchance, the attributes of Grief,
The cypress bud, and willow leaf,
    Their pale funereal foliage blend with thine.

Hail, lovely blossom! – thou canst ease
The wretched victims of Disease;
Canst close those weary eyes in gentle sleep,
Which never open but to weep;
For, oh! thy potent charm
Can agonizing Pain disarm;
Expel imperious Memory from her seat,
And bid the throbbing heart forget to beat.

---

[1] goddess of agriculture

Soul-soothing plant! that can such blessings give,
By thee the mourner bears to live!
  By thee the hopeless die!
Oh! ever 'friendly to despair,'
Might Sorrow's pallid votary dare,
Without a crime, that remedy implore,
    Which bids the spirit from its bondage fly,
I'd court thy palliative aid no more;

    No more I'd sue that thou shouldst spread
    Thy spell around my aching head,
    But would conjure thee to impart
    Thy balsam for a broken heart;
  And by thy soft Lethean power,
      Inestimable flower,
Burst these terrestrial bonds, and other regions try.

                    HENRIETTA O'NEILL (1792)

The Tiger

Tiger, tiger, burning bright
In the forests of the night,
What immortal hand or eye
Could frame thy fearful symmetry?

In what distant deeps or skies
Burnt the fire of thine eyes?
On what wings dare he aspire?
What the hand dare seize the fire?

And what shoulder and what art
Could twist the sinews of thy heart?
And when thy heart began to beat,
What dread hand? And what dread feet?

What the hammer? What the chain?
In what furnace was thy brain?

What the anvil? What dread grasp
Dare its deadly terrors grasp?

When the stars threw down their spears
And watered Heaven with their tears,
Did he smile his work to see?
Did he who made the Lamb make thee?

Tiger, tiger, burning bright
In the forests of the night,
What immortal hand or eye
Dare frame thy fearful symmetry?

WILLIAM BLAKE (by 1794)

The Sick Rose

O rose, thou art sick:
The invisible worm
That flies in the night,
In the howling storm,

Has found out thy bed
Of crimson joy;
And his dark secret love
Does thy life destroy.

WILLIAM BLAKE (1794 version)

Ah, Sunflower

Ah, sunflower, weary of time,
Who countest the steps of the sun,
Seeking after that sweet golden clime
Where the traveller's journey is done;

Where the youth pined away with desire
And the pale virgin shrouded with snow
Arise from their graves and aspire
Where my sunflower wishes to go.

WILLIAM BLAKE (1794)

The Snowdrop

The snowdrop, Winter's timid child,
    Awakes to life, bedew'd with tears;
And flings around its fragrance mild,
And where no rival flowerets bloom,
Amid the bare and chilling gloom,
    A beauteous gem appears.

All weak and wan, with head inclin'd,
    Its parent breast the drifted snow;
It trembles while the ruthless wind
Bends its slim form; the tempest lowers,
Its emerald eye drops crystal showers
    On its cold bed below.

Poor flower! on thee the sunny beam
    No touch of genial warmth bestows;
Except to thaw the icy stream
Whose little current purls along,
Thy fair and glossy charms among,
    And whelms thee as it flows.

The night-breeze tears thy silky dress,
    Which deck'd with silvery lustre shone:
The morn returns, not thee to bless;
The gaudy crocus flaunts its pride,
And triumphs where its rival died,
    Unshelter'd and unknown!

No sunny beams shall gild thy grave,
    No bird of pity thee deplore;
There shall no spreading branches wave;
For Spring shall all her gems unfold,
And revel 'mid her buds of gold,
    When thou art seen no more.

Where'er I find thee, gentle flower,
    Thou still art sweet and dear to me!
For I have known the cheerless hour,
Have seen the sunbeams cold and pale,
Have felt the chilling wintry gale,
    And wept, and shrunk like thee!

MARY ROBINSON (1797)

To a Spider

1

Spider! thou need'st not run in fear about
    To shun my curious eyes;
I won't humanely crush thy bowels out
    Lest thou should'st eat the flies;
Nor will I roast thee with a damn'd delight
    Thy strange instinctive fortitude to see,
        For there is One who might
        One day roast me.

2

Thou art welcome to a Rhymer sore-perplext,
    The subject of his verse;
There's many a one who on a better text
    Perhaps might comment worse.
Then shrink not, old Free-Mason, from my view,
    But quietly like me spin out the line;
        Do thou thy work pursue
        As I will mine.

3

Weaver of snares, thou emblemest the ways
    Of Satan, Sire of lies;
Hell's huge black Spider, for mankind he lays
    His toils, as thou for flies.
When Betty's busy eye runs round the room,

Woe to that nice geometry, if seen!
But where is he whose broom
The earth shall clean?

4

Spider! of old thy flimsy webs were thought,
And 'twas a likeness true,
To emblem laws in which the weak are caught,
But which the strong break through:
And if a victim in thy toils is ta'en,
Like some poor client is that wretched fly;
I'll warrant thee thou'lt drain
His life-blood dry.

5

And is not thy weak work like human schemes
And care on earth employ'd?
Such are young hopes and Love's delightful dreams
So easily destroy'd!
So does the Statesman, whilst the Avengers sleep,
Self-deem'd secure, his wiles in secret lay,
Soon shall destruction sweep
His work away.

6

Thou busy labourer! one resemblance more
May yet the verse prolong,
For, Spider, thou art like the Poet poor,
Whom thou hast help'd in song.
Both busily our needful food to win.
We work, as Nature taught, with ceaseless pains;
Thy bowels thou dost spin,
I spin my brains.

ROBERT SOUTHEY (1798)

6
CITY LIFE

A Description of the Morning

Now hardly here and there a Hackney-Coach
Appearing, show'd the Ruddy Morn's Approach.
Now *Betty* from her Master's Bed had flown,
And softly stole to discompose her own.
The Slipshod Prentice from his Master's Door,
Had par'd the Dirt, and Sprinkled round the Floor.
Now *Moll* had whirl'd her Mop with dext'rous Airs,
Prepar'd to Scrub the Entry and the Stairs.
The Youth with Broomy Stumps began to trace
The Kennel-Edge, where Wheels had worn the Place.
The Smallcoal-Man was heard with Cadence deep,
'Till drown'd in Shriller Notes of *Chimney-Sweep*.
Duns at his Lordship's Gate began to meet,
And Brickdust *Moll* had Scream'd through half a Street.
The Turnkey now his Flock returning sees,
Duly let out a' Nights to Steal for Fees.
The watchful Bailiffs take their silent Stands,
And School-Boys lag with Satchels in their Hands.

JONATHAN SWIFT (1709)

from *Trivia, or The Art of Walking the Streets in London*

SOME HAZARDS OF WALKING IN LONDON

What Trades prejudicial to Walkers

If cloath'd in black you tread the busy town,
Or if distinguish'd by the rev'rend gown,
Three trades avoid; oft in the mingling press
The barber's apron soils the sable dress;
Shun the perfumer's touch with cautious eye,
Nor let the baker's step advance too nigh.
Ye walkers too that youthful colours wear,
Three sullying trades avoid with equal care;
The little chimney-sweeper skulks along,
And marks with sooty stains the heedless throng;

When small-coal murmurs in the hoarser throat,
From smutty dangers guard thy threaten'd coat:
The dust-man's cart offends thy cloaths and eyes,
When through the street a cloud of ashes flies;
But whether black or lighter dyes are worn,
The chandler's basket, on his shoulder born,
With tallow spots thy coat; resign the way,
To shun the surly butcher's greasy tray,
Butchers, whose hands are dy'd with blood's foul stain,
And always foremost in the hangman's train.

To whom to give the Wall

    Let due civilities be strictly paid.
The wall surrender to the hooded maid;
Nor let thy sturdy elbow's hasty rage
Jostle the feeble steps of trembling age:
And when the porter bends beneath his load,
And pants for breath; clear thou the crouded road.
But, above all, the groping blind direct,
And from the pressing throng the lame protect.
You'll sometimes meet a fop, of nicest tread,
Whose mantling peruke veils his empty head,
At ev'ry step he dreads the wall to lose,
And risques, to save a coach, his red-heel'd shoes;
Him, like the miller, pass with caution by,
Lest from his shoulder clouds of powder fly.

To whom to refuse the Wall

But when the bully, with assuming pace,
Cocks his broad hat, edg'd round with tarnish'd lace,
Yield not the way; defie his strutting pride,
And thrust him to the muddy kennel's side;
He never turns again, nor dares oppose,
But mutters coward curses as he goes.

Of whom to enquire the Way

    If drawn by bus'ness to a street unknown,
Let the sworn porter point thee through the town;
Be sure observe the signs, for signs remain,
Like faithful land-marks to the walking train.
Seek not from prentices to learn the way,
Those fabling boys will turn thy steps astray;
Ask the grave tradesman to direct thee right,
He ne'er deceives, but when he profits by't.

    Where famed *St Giles's* ancient limits spread,
An inrail'd column rears its lofty head,

Here to sev'n streets sev'n dials count the day,
And from each other catch the circling ray.
Here oft the peasant, with enquiring face,
Bewilder'd, trudges on from place to place;
He dwells on ev'ry sign with stupid gaze,
Enters the narrow alley's doubtful maze,
Tries ev'ry winding court and street in vain,
And doubles o'er his weary steps again.
Thus hardy *Theseus*, with intrepid feet,
Travers'd the dang'rous labyrinth of *Crete*;
But still the wandring passes forc'd his stay,
Till *Ariadne*'s clue unwinds the way.
But do not thou, like that bold chief, confide
Thy ventrous footsteps to a female guide;
She'll lead thee with delusive smiles along,
Dive in thy fob, and drop thee in the throng.

* * *

Where elevated o'er the gaping croud,
Clasp'd in the board the perjur'd head is bow'd,
Betimes retreat; here, thick as hailstones pour
Turnips, and half-hatch'd eggs, (a mingled show'r)
Among the rabble rain: Some random throw
May with the trickling yolk thy cheek o'erflow.

Of narrow Streets   Though expedition bids, yet never stray
Where no rang'd posts defend the rugged way.
Here laden carts with thundring waggons meet,
Wheels clash with wheels, and bar the narrow street;
The lashing whip resounds, the horses strain,
And blood in anguish bursts the swelling vein.
O barb'rous men, your cruel breasts asswage,
Why vent ye on the gen'rous steed your rage?
Does not his service earn your daily bread?
Your wives, your children by his labours fed!
If, as the *Samian* taught, the soul revives,
And, shifting seats, in other bodies lives;
Severe shall be the brutal coachman's change,
Doom'd in a hackney horse the town to range:
Carmen, transform'd, the groaning load shall draw,
Whom other tyrants with the lash shall awe.

*The most
inconvenient
Streets to
Walkers*

Who would of *Watling-street* the dangers share,
When the broad pavement of *Cheap-side* is near?
Or who that rugged street would traverse o'er,
That stretches, O *Fleet-ditch*, from thy black shore
To the *Tow'r's* moated walls? Here steams ascend
That, in mix'd fumes, the wrinkled nose offend.
Where chandlers cauldrons boil; where fishy prey
Hide the wet stall, long absent from the sea;
And where the cleaver chops the heifer's spoil,
And where huge hogsheads sweat with trainy oil,
Thy breathing nostril hold; but how shall I
Pass, where in piles *Cornavian* cheeses lye;
Cheese, that the table's closing rites denies,
And bids me with th' unwilling chaplain rise.

*The Pell-mell
celebrated*

O bear me to the paths of fair *Pell-mell*,
Safe are thy pavements, grateful is thy smell!
At distance rolls along the gilded coach,
Nor sturdy carmen on thy walks encroach;
No lets would bar thy ways were chairs deny'd
The soft supports of laziness and pride;
Shops breathe perfumes, thro' sashes ribbons glow,
The mutual arms of ladies, and the beau.
Yet still ev'n here, when rains the passage hide,
Oft' the loose stone spirts up a muddy tide
Beneath thy careless foot; and from on high,
Where masons mount the ladder, fragments fly;
Mortar, and crumbled lime in show'rs descend,
And o'er thy head destructive tiles impend.

*The Pleasure
of walking
through an
Alley*

But sometimes let me leave the noisie roads,
And silent wander in the close abodes
Where wheels ne'er shake the ground; there pensive
      stray,
In studious thought, the long uncrouded way.
Here I remark each walker's diff'rent face,
And in their look their various bus'ness trace.
The broker here his spacious beaver wears,
Upon his brow sit jealousies and cares;
Bent on some mortgage (to avoid reproach)
He seeks bye streets, and saves th' expensive coach.
Soft, at low doors, old letchers tap their cane,

For fair recluse, who travels *Drury-lane*;
Here roams uncomb'd the lavish rake, to shun
His *Fleet-street* draper's everlasting dun.

JOHN GAY (1716)

Ariadne was the daughter of Minos, King of Crete. She helped
Theseus slay the monstrous Minotaur by giving him a thread to
guide him through the original labyrinth. The 'perjur'd head' is that
of a minor criminal, possibly a slanderer, placed as a punishment in
the pillory. Cornavian cheeses are Cheshire cheeses.

from *London*

THE POOR MAN LEAVES THE CITY
FOR A BETTER LIFE

By Numbers here from Shame or Censure free,
All Crimes are safe, but hated Poverty.
This, only this, the rigid Law persues,
This, only this, provokes the snarling Muse;
The sober Trader at a tatter'd Cloak,
Wakes from his Dream, and labours for a Joke;
With brisker Air the silken Courtiers gaze,
And turn the varied Taunt a thousand Ways.
Of all the Griefs that harrass the Distrest,
Sure the most bitter is a scornful Jest;
Fate never wounds more deep the gen'rous Heart,
Than when a Blockhead's Insult points the Dart.

Has Heaven reserv'd, in Pity to the Poor,
No pathless Waste, or undiscover'd Shore?
No secret Island in the boundless Main?
No peaceful Desart yet unclaim'd by Spain?
Quick let us rise, the happy Seats explore,
And bear Oppression's Insolence no more.
This mournful Truth is ev'ry where confest,
Slow rises Worth, by Poverty deprest:

But here more slow, where all are Slaves to Gold,
Where Looks are Merchandise, and Smiles are sold,
Where won by Bribes, by Flatteries implor'd,
The Groom retails the Favours of his Lord.

But hark! th'affrighted Crowd's tumultuous Cries
Roll thro' the Streets, and thunder to the Skies;
Rais'd from some pleasing Dream of Wealth and Pow'r,
Some pompous Palace, or some blissful Bow'r,
Aghast you start, and scarce with aking Sight
Sustain th'approaching Fire's tremendous Light;
Swift from pursuing Horrors take your Way,
And Leave your little *All* to Flames a Prey;
Then thro' the World a wretched Vagrant roam,
For where can starving Merit find a Home?
In vain your mournful Narrative disclose,
While all neglect, and most insult your Woes.

Should Heaven's just Bolts *Orgilio*'s Wealth confound,
And spread his flaming Palace on the Ground,
Swift o'er the Land the dismal Rumour flies,
And publick Mournings pacify the Skies;
The Laureat Tribe in servile Verse relate,
How Virtue wars with persecuting Fate;
With well-feign'd Gratitude the pension'd Band
Refund the Plunder of the begger'd Land.
See! while he builds, the gaudy Vassals come,
And crowd with sudden Wealth the rising Dome;
The Price of Boroughs and of Souls restore,
And raise his Treasures higher than before.
Now bless'd with all the Baubles of the Great,
The polish'd Marble, and the shining Plate,
Orgilio sees the golden Pile aspire,
And hopes from angry Heav'n another Fire.
Could'st thou resign the Park and Play content,
For the fair Banks of *Severn* or of *Trent*;
There might'st thou find some elegant Retreat,
Some hireling Senator's deserted Seat;
And stretch thy Prospects o'er the smiling Land,
For less than rent the Dungeons of the *Strand*;

There prune thy Walks, support thy drooping Flow'rs,
Direct thy Rivulets, and twine thy Bow'rs;
And, while thy grounds a cheap Repast afford,
Despise the Dainties of a venal Lord:
There ev'ry Bush with Nature's Music rings,
There ev'ry Breeze bears Health upon its Wings;
On all thy Hours Security shall smile,
And bless thine Evening Walk and Morning Toil.

Prepare for Death, if here at Night you roam,
And sign your Will before you sup from Home.
Some fiery Fop, with new Commission vain,
Who sleeps on Brambles till he kills his Man;
Some frolick Drunkard, reeling from a Feast,
Provokes a Broil, and stabs you for a Jest.
Yet ev'n these Heroes, mischievously gay,
Lords of the Street, and Terrors of the Way;
Flush'd as they are with Folly, Youth and Wine,
Their prudent Insults to the Poor confine;
Afar they mark the Flambeau's bright Approach,
And shun the shining Train, and golden Coach.

In vain, these Dangers past, your Doors you close,
And hope the balmy Blessings of Repose:
Cruel with Guilt, and daring with Despair,
The midnight Murd'rer bursts the faithless Bar;
Invades the sacred Hour of silent Rest
And leaves, unseen, a Dagger in your Breast.

Scarce can our Fields, such Crowds at *Tyburn* die,
With Hemp the Gallows and the Fleet supply.
Propose your Schemes, ye Senatorian Band,
Whose *Ways and Means* support the sinking Land;

Lest Ropes be wanting in the tempting Spring,
To rig another Convoy for the King.

A single Jail, in Alfred's golden Reign,
Could half the Nation's Criminals contain;
Fair Justice then, without Constraint ador'd

Held high the steady Scale, but sheath'd the sword;
No Spies were paid, no *Special Juries* known,
Blest Age! but ah! how diff'rent from our own!

Much could I add, but see the Boat at hand,
The Tide retiring, calls me from the Land:
Farewell — When Youth, and Health, and Fortune spent,
Thou fly'st for Refuge to the Wilds of *Kent*:
And tir'd like me with Follies and with Crimes,
In angry Numbers warn'st succeeding Times;
Then shall thy Friend, nor thou refuse his Aid,
Still Foe to Vice forsake his *Cambrian* Shade;
In Virtue's Cause once more exert his Rage,
Thy Satire point, and animate thy Page.

SAMUEL JOHNSON (published 1738)

from *The Task*

                    Rank abundance breeds
In gross and pamper'd cities sloth and lust,
And wantonness and gluttonous excess.
In cities vice is hidden with most ease,
Or seen with least reproach; and virtue, taught
By frequent lapse, can hope no triumph there
Beyond th' achievement of successful flight.
I do confess them nurs'ries of the arts,
In which they flourish most; where, in the beams
Of warm encouragement, and in the eye
Of public note, they reach their perfect size.
Such London is, by taste and wealth proclaim'd
The fairest capital of all the world,
By riot and incontinence the worst.
There, touch'd by Reynolds, a dull blank becomes
A lucid mirror, in which Nature sees
All her reflected features. Bacon there
Gives more than female beauty to a stone,

And Chatham's eloquence to marble lips.
Nor does the chissel occupy alone
The pow'rs of sculpture, but the style as much;
Each province of her art her equal care.
With nice incision of her guided steel
She ploughs a brazen field, and clothes a soil
So sterile with what charms soe'er she will,
The richest scen'ry and the loveliest forms.
Where finds philosophy her eagle eye,
With which she gazes at yon burning disk
Undazzled, and detects and counts his spots?
In London: where her implements exact,
With which she calculates, computes, and scans,
All distance, motion, magnitude, and now
Measures an atom, and now girds a world?
In London. Where has commerce such a mart,
So rich, so throng'd, so drain'd, and so supplied,
As London – opulent, enlarged, and still
Increasing, London? Babylon of old
Not more the glory of the earth than she,
A more accomplish'd world's chief glory now.
      She has her praise. Now mark a spot or two,
That so much beauty would do well to purge;
And show this queen of cities, that so fair
May yet be foul; so witty, yet not wise.
It is not seemly, nor of good report,
That she is slack in discipline; more prompt
T' avenge than to prevent the breach of law:
That she is rigid in denouncing death
On petty robbers, and indulges life
And liberty, and oft-times honour too,
To peculators of the public gold:
That thieves at home must hang; but he, that puts
Into his overgorg'd and bloated purse
The wealth of Indian provinces, escapes.
Nor is it well, nor can it come to good,
That, through profane and infidel contempt
Of holy writ, she has presum'd t' annul
And abrogate, as roundly as she may,
The total ordinance and will of God;

Advancing fashion to the post of truth,
And cent'ring all authority in modes
And customs of her own, till sabbath rites
Have dwindled into unrespected forms,
And knees and hassocks are well-nigh divorc'd.
   God made the country, and man made the town.
What wonder then that health and virtue, gifts
That can alone make sweet the bitter draught
That life holds out to all, should most abound
And least be threatened in the fields and groves?
Possess ye, therefore, ye, who, borne about
In chariots and sedans, know no fatigue
But that of idleness, and taste no scenes
But such as art contrives, possess ye still
Your element; there only can ye shine,
There only minds like your's can do no harm.
Our groves were planted to console at noon
The pensive wand'rer in their shades. At eve
The moon-beam, sliding softly in between
The sleeping leaves, is all the light they wish,
Birds warbling all the music. We can spare
The splendour of your lamps; they but eclipse
Our softer satellite. Your songs confound
Our more harmonious notes: the thrush departs
Scar'd, and th' offended nightingale is mute.
There is a public mischief in your' mirth;
It plagues your country. Folly such as your's,
Grac'd with a sword, and worthier of a fan,
Has made, what enemies could ne'er have done,
Our arch of empire, stedfast but for you,
A mutilated structure, soon to fall.

WILLIAM COWPER (1785)

London

It is a goodly sight through the clean air,
From Hampstead's heathy height to see at once
England's vast capital in fair expanse,
Towers, belfries, lengthen'd streets, and structures fair.
St. Paul's high dome amidst the vassal bands
Of neighb'ring spires, a regal chieftain stands,
And over fields of ridgy roofs appear,
With distance softly tinted, side by side,
In kindred grace, like twain of sisters dear,
The Towers of Westminster, her Abbey's pride;
While, far beyond, the hills of Surrey shine
Through thin soft haze, and show their wavy line.
View'd thus, a goodly sight! but when survey'd
Through denser air when moisten'd winds prevail,
In her grand panoply of smoke array'd,
While clouds aloft in heavy volumes sail,
She is sublime. She seems a curtain'd gloom
Connecting heaven and earth – a threat'ning sign of doom.
With more than natural height, rear'd in the sky
'Tis then St. Paul's arrests the wondering eye;
The lower parts in swathing mist conceal'd,
The higher through some half spent shower reveal'd,
So far from earth removed, that well, I trow,
Did not its form man's artful structure show,
It might some lofty alpine peak be deem'd,
The eagle's haunt, with cave and crevice seam'd.
Stretch'd wide on either hand, a rugged screen,
In lurid dimness, nearer streets are seen
Like shoreward billows of a troubled main,
Arrested in their rage. Through drizzly rain,
Cataracts of tawny sheen pour from the skies.
Of furnace smoke black curling columns rise,
And many tinted vapours, slowly pass
O'er the wide draping of that pictured mass.

So shows by day this grand imperial town,

And, when o'er all the night's black stole is thrown,
The distant traveller doth with wonder mark
Her luminous canopy athwart the dark,
Cast up, from myriads of lamps that shine
Along her streets in many a starry line:
He wondering looks from his yet distant road,
And thinks the northern streamers are abroad.
'What hollow sound is that?' approaching near,
The roar of many wheels breaks on his ear.
It is the flood of human life in motion!
It is the voice of a tempestuous ocean!
With sad but pleasing awe his soul is fill'd,
Scarce heaves his breast, and all within is still'd,
As many thoughts and feelings cross his mind,
Thoughts, mingled, melancholy, undefined,
Of restless, reckless man, and years gone by,
And Time fast wending to Eternity.

JOANNA BAILLIE (*c.*1790)

January, 1795

Pavement slippery, people sneezing,
Lords in ermine, beggars freezing;
Titled gluttons dainties carving,
Genius in a garret starving.

Lofty mansions, warm and spacious;
Courtiers cringing and voracious;
Misers scarce the wretched heeding;
Gallant soldiers fighting, bleeding.

Wives who laugh at passive spouses;
Theatres, and meeting-houses;
Balls, where simpering misses languish;
Hospitals, and groans of anguish.

Arts and sciences bewailing;
Commerce drooping, credit failing;
Placemen mocking subjects loyal;
Separations, weddings royal.

Authors who can't earn a dinner;
Many a subtle rogue a winner;
Fugitives for shelter seeking;
Misers hoarding, tradesmen breaking.

Taste and talents quite deserted;
All the laws of truth perverted;
Arrogance o'er merit soaring;
Merit silently deploring.

Ladies gambling night and morning;
Fools the works of genius scorning;
Ancient dames for girls mistaken,
Youthful damsels quite forsaken.

Some in luxury delighting;
More in talking than in fighting;
Lovers old, and beaux decrepid;
Lordlings empty and insipid.

Poets, painters, and musicians;
Lawyers, doctors, politicians:
Pamphlets, newspapers, and odes,
Seeking fame by different roads.

Gallant souls with empty purses,
Generals only fit for nurses;
School-boys, smit with martial spirit,
Taking place of veteran merit.

Honest men who can't get places,
Knaves who show unblushing faces;
Ruin hastened, peace retarded;
Candour spurned, and art[1] rewarded.

MARY ROBINSON (1795)

[1] cunning

7
VIEWS OF CHILDHOOD
& PARENTHOOD

Shadows in the Water

In unexperienc'd infancy
Many a sweet mistake doth lie;
Mistake though false intending true.
A *seeming* somewhat more than *view*;
      That doth instruct the mind
      In things that lie behind
And many secrets to us doth show
Which afterwards we come to know.

Thus did I by the water's brink
Another world beneath me think;
And, while the lofty spacious skies
Reversed there abused mine eyes,
      I fancied other feet
      Came, mine to touch and meet;
As by some puddle I did play,
Another world within it lay.

Beneath the water people drown'd.
Yet, with another Heaven crown'd,
In spacious regions seemed to go
Freely moving to and fro;
      In bright and open space
      I saw their very face;
Eyes, hands and feet they had like mine;
Another sun did with them shine.

'Twas strange that people there should walk,
And yet I could not hear them talk:
And through a little watery chink,
Which one dry ox or horse might drink,
      We other worlds should see,
      Yet not admitted be:
And other confines there behold
Of light and darkness, heat and cold.

I call'd them oft, but call'd in vain:
No speeches we could entertain:
Yet I did there expect to find
Another world to please my mind.
     I plainly saw by these
      A new Antipodes,
Whom, though they were so plainly seen,
A film, kept off that stood between.

By walking men's reversed feet
I chanc'd another world to meet;
Though it did not to view exceed
A phantasm, 'tis a world indeed,
     Where skies beneath us shine,
      And Earth, by art divine,
Another face presents below,
Where people's feet against ours go.

Within the regions of the air,
Compass'd about with heavens fair.
Great tracts of land may there be found
Enricht with fields and fertile ground;
     Where many num'rous hosts,
      In those far distant coasts,
For other great and glorious ends,
Inhabit, my yet unknown friends.

O ye that stand upon the brink,
Whom I so near me, through the chink,
With wonder see: what faces there,
Whose feet, whose bodies, do ye wear?
     I my companions see
      In you, another me,
They seemed others, but are we;
Our second selves those shadows be.

Look how far off those lower skies
Extend themselves! Scarce with mine eyes
I can them reach. O ye, my friends,
What secret border's on those ends?

Are lofty heavens hurl'd
   'Bout your inferior world?
Are ye the representatives
   Of other people's distant lives ?

Of all the playmates which I knew
That here I did the image view
In other selves; what can it mean?
But that below the purling stream
     Some unknown joys there be
     Laid up in store for me;
To which I shall, when that thin skin
Is broken, be admitted in.

THOMAS TRAHERNE (*d.*1674)

Traherne's remarkable late metaphysical poems were only discovered early this century.

To a Child of Quality

FIVE YEARS OLD; THE AUTHOR FORTY

Lords, knights and squires, the num'rous band,
   That wear the fair Miss Mary's fetters,
Were summoned by her high command
   To show their passions by their letters.

My pen amongst the best I took,
   Lest those bright eyes that cannot read
Shou'd dart their kindling fires, and look,
   The power they have to be obey'd.

Nor quality, nor reputation,
   Forbid me yet my flame to tell,
Dear five-years old befriends my passion,
   And I may write till she can spell.

For while she makes her silk-worms beds
  With all the tender things I swear,
Whilst all the house my passion reads,
  In papers round her baby's hair,

She may receive and own my flame,
  For tho' the strictest prudes should know it,
She'll pass for a most virtuous dame,
  And I for an unhappy poet.

Then, too, alas! when she shall tear
  The lines some younger rival sends,
She'll give me leave to write I fear,
  And we shall still continue friends;

For, as our diff'rent ages move,
  'Tis so ordain'd, wou'd fate but mend it,
That I shall be past making love
  When she begins to comprehend it.

                                MATTHEW PRIOR (c.1704)

Written for My Son, and Spoken by Him at His First Putting on Breeches

What is it our mammas bewitches,
To plague us little boys with breeches?
To tyrant Custom we must yield
Whilst vanquished Reason flies the field.
Our legs must suffer by ligation,
To keep the blood from circulation;
And then our feet, though young and tender,
We to the shoemaker surrender,
Who often makes our shoes so strait
Our growing feet they cramp and fret;
Whilst, with contrivance most profound,

Across our insteps we are bound;
Which is the cause, I make no doubt,
Why thousands suffer in the gout.
Our wiser ancestors wore brogues,
Before the surgeons bribed these rogues,
With narrow toes, and heels like pegs,
To help to make us break our legs.

    Then, ere we know to use our fists,
Our mothers closely bind our wrists;
And never think our clothes are neat,
Till they're so tight we cannot eat.
And, to increase our other pains,
The hat-band helps to cramp our brains.
The cravat finishes the work,
Like bowstring sent from the Grand Turk.

    Thus dress, that should prolong our date,
Is made to hasten on our fate.
Fair privilege of nobler natures,
To be more plagued than other creatures!
The wild inhabitants of air
Are clothed by heaven with wondrous care:
The beauteous, well-compacted feathers
Are coats of mail against all weathers;
Enamelled, to delight the eye,
Gay as the bow that decks the sky.
The beasts are clothed with beauteous skins;
The fishes armed with scales and fins,
Whose lustre lends the sailor light,
When all the stars are hid in night.

    O were our dress contrived like these,
For use, for ornament and ease!
Man only seems to sorrow born,
Naked, defenceless and forlorn.

    Yet we have Reason, to supply
What nature did to man deny:
Weak viceroy! Who thy power will own,

When Custom has usurped thy throne?
In vain did I appeal to thee,
Ere I would wear his livery;
Who, in defiance to thy rules,
Delights to make us act like fools.
O'er human race the tyrant reigns,
And binds them in eternal chains.
We yield to his despotic sway,
The only monarch all obey.

MARY BARBER (1731)

Ode on a Distant Prospect of Eton College

Being a man is sufficient reason to be unfortunate.

MENANDER

Ye distant spires, ye antique towers,
    That crown the watery glade,
Where grateful Science' still adores
    Her Henry's[1] holy shade;
And ye, that from the stately brow
Of Windsor's heights the expanse below
    Of grove, of lawn, of mead survey,
Whose turf, whose shade, whose flowers among
Wanders the hoary Thames along
    His silver-winding way.

Ah happy hills, ah pleasing shade,
    Ah fields beloved in vain,
Where once my careless childhood strayed,
    A stranger yet to pain!
I feel the gales, that from ye blow,
A momentary bliss bestow,
    As waving fresh their gladsome wing,
My weary soul they seem to soothe,
And redolent of joy and youth
    To breathe a second spring.

[1] Henry VI, founder of Eton

Say, Father Thames, for thou hast seen
  Full many a sprightly race
Disporting on thy margent green
  The paths of pleasure trace,
Who foremost now delight to cleave
With pliant arm thy glassy wave?
  The captive linnet which enthrall?[2]
What idle progeny succeed
To chase the rolling circle's speed,
  Or urge the flying ball?

While some on earnest business bent
  Their murmuring labors ply
'Gainst graver hours, that bring constraint
  To sweeten liberty:
Some bold adventurers disdain
The limits of their little reign,
  And unknown regions dare descry:
Still as they run they look behind,
They hear a voice in every wind,
  And snatch a fearful joy.

Gay hope is theirs by fancy fed,
  Less pleasing when possessed;
The tear forgot as soon as shed,
  The sunshine of the breast:
Theirs buxom health of rosy hue,
Wild wit, invention ever new,
  And lively cheer of vigor born;
The thoughtless day, the easy night,
The spirits pure, the slumbers light,
  That fly the approach of morn.

Alas, regardless of their doom,
  The little victims play!
No sense have they of ills to come,
  Nor care beyond today.
Yet see how all around 'em wait

---

[2] cage

The ministers of human fate,
  And black Misfortune's baleful train!
Ah, show them where in ambush stand
To seize their prey the murderous band!
  Ah, tell them they are men!

These shall the fury Passions tear,
  The vultures of the mind,
Disdainful Anger, pallid Fear,
  And Shame that skulks behind;
Or pining Love shall waste their youth,
Or Jealousy with rankling tooth,
  That inly gnaws the secret heart,
And Envy wan, and faded Care,
Grim-visaged comfortless Despair,
  And Sorrow's piercing dart.

Ambition this shall tempt to rise,
  Then whirl the wretch from high,
To bitter Scorn a sacrifice,
  And grinning Infamy.
The stings of Falsehood those shall try,
And hard Unkindness' altered eye,
  That mocks the tear it forced to flow;
And keen Remorse with blood defiled,
And moody Madness laughing wild
  Amid severest woe.

Lo, in the vale of years beneath
  A grisly troop are seen,
The painful family of Death,
  More hideous than their queen:
This racks the joints, this fires the veins,
That every laboring sinew strains,
  Those in the deeper vitals rage:
Lo, Poverty, to fill the band,
That numbs the soul with icy hand,
  And slow-consuming Age.

To each his sufferings: all are men,
   Condemned alike to groan;
The tender for another's pain,
   The unfeeling for his own.
Yet ah! why should they know their fate?
Since sorrow never comes too late,
   And happiness too swiftly flies.
Thought would destroy their paradise.
No more; where ignorance is bliss,
   'Tis folly to be wise.

THOMAS GRAY (1742)

from *Tirocinium, or A Review of Schools*

EDUCATION IN THE PUBLIC SCHOOLS

Say, muse (for, education made the song,
No muse can hesitate or linger long)
What causes move us, knowing, as we must,
That these *menageries* all fail their trust,
To send our sons to scout and scamper there,
While colts and puppies cost us so much care?
   Be it a weakness, it deserves some praise;
We love the play-place of our early days –
The scene is touching, and the heart is stone
That feels not at that sight, and feels at none.
The wall on which we tried our graving skill,
The very name we carv'd subsisting still;
The bench on which we sat while deep employ'd,
Tho' mangled, hack'd, and hew'd, not yet destroy'd:
The little ones, unbutton'd, glowing hot,
Playing our games, and on the very spot;
As happy as we once, to kneel and draw
The chalky ring, and knuckle down at taw;
To pitch the ball in to the grounded hat,
Or drive it devious with a dext'rous pat –
The pleasing spectacle at once excites
Such recollection of our own delights,
That, viewing it, we seem almost t' obtain

Our innocent sweet simple years again.
This fond attachment to the well-known place,
Whence first we started into life's long race,
Maintains its hold with such unfailing sway,
We feel it ev'n in age, and at our latest day.
Hark! how the sire of chits, whose future share
Of classic food begins to be his care,
With his own likeness plac'd on either knee,
Indulges all a father's heart-felt glee;
And tells them, as he strokes their silver locks,
That they must soon learn Latin, and to box;
Then, turning, he regales his list'ning wife
With all th' adventures of his early life;
His skill in coachmanship, or driving chaise,
In bilking tavern bills, and spouting plays;
What shifts he us'd, detected in a scrape,
How he was flogg'd, or had the luck t' escape;
What sums he lost at play, and how he sold
Watch, seals, and all – till all his pranks are told.
Retracing thus his *frolics*, ('tis a name
That palliates deeds of folly and of shame)
He gives the local bias all its sway;
Resolves that where he play'd his sons shall play,
And destines their bright genius to be shown
Just in the scene where he display'd his own.
The meek and bashful boy will soon be taught
To be as bold and forward as he ought;
The rude will scuffle through with ease enough,
Great schools suit best the sturdy and the rough.
Ah, happy designation, prudent choice,
Th' event is sure; expect it, and rejoice!
Soon see your wish fulfill'd in either child –
The pert made perter, and the tame made wild.
The great indeed by titles, riches, birth,
Excus'd th' incumbrance of more solid worth,
Are best dispos'd of where with most success
They may acquire that confident address,
Those habits of profuse and lewd expense,
That scorn of all delights but those of sense,
Which, though in plain plebeians we condemn,

With so much reason all expect from them.
But families of less illustrious fame,
Whose chief distinction is their spotless name,
Whose heirs, their honours none, their income small,
Must shine by true desert, or not at all –
What dream they of, that with so little care
They risk their hopes, their dearest treasure, there?
They dream of little Charles or William grac'd
With wig prolix, down-flowing to his waist;
They see th' attentive crowds his talents draw,
They hear him speak – the oracle of law!
The father, who designs his babe a priest,
Dreams him episcopally such at least;
And, while the playful jockey scours the room
Briskly, astride upon the parlour broom,
In fancy sees him more superbly ride
In coach with purple lin'd, and mitres on its side.
Events improbable and strange as these,
Which only a parental eye forsees,
A public school shall bring to pass with ease.
But how! resides such virtue in that air
As must create an appetite for pray'r?
And will it breathe into him all the zeal
That candidates for such a prize should feel,
To take the lead and be the foremost still
In all true worth and literary skill?
  'Ah, blind to bright futurity, untaught
The knowledge of the world, and dull of thought!
Church-ladders are not always mounted best
By learned clerks and Latinists profess'd.
Th' exalted prize demands an upward look,
Not to be found by poring on a book.
Small skill in Latin, and still less in Greek,
Is more than adequate to all I seek.
His intercourse with peers, and sons of peers –
There dawns the splendour of his future years;
In that bright quarter his propitious skies
Shall blush betimes, and there his glory rise.
Your Lordship and *Your Grace!* what school can teach
A rhet'ric equal to those parts of speech?

What need of Homer's verse or Tully's prose,
Sweet interjections! if he learn but those?
Let rev'rend churls his ignorance rebuke,
Who starve upon a dog's-ear'd Pentateuch,
The parson knows enough who knows a duke.' –
Egregious purpose! worthily begun
In barb'rous prostitution of your son;
Press'd on *his* part by means that would disgrace
A scriv'ner's clerk or footman out of place,
And ending, if at last its end be gain'd,
In sacrilege, in God's own house profan'd!
It may succeed, and, if his sins should call
For more than common punishment, it shall;
The wretch shall rise, and be the thing on earth
Least qualified in honour, learning, worth,
To occupy a sacred, awful post,
In which the best and worthiest tremble most.

WILLIAM COWPER (*c*.1785)

'Public' as used of schools in England means, of course,
'private and expensive'.

A Mother to Her Waking Infant

Now in thy dazzling half-oped eye,
Thy curlèd nose and lip awry,
Thy up-hoist arms and noddling head,
And little chin with chrystal spread,
Poor helpless thing! what do I see,
  That I should sing of thee?

From thy poor tongue no accents come,
Which can but rub thy toothless gum;
Small understanding boasts thy face,
Thy shapeless limbs nor step nor grace;
A few short words thy feats may tell,
  And yet I love thee well.

When sudden wakes the bitter shriek,
And redder swells thy little cheek;
When rattled keys thy woes beguile,
And through the wet eye gleams the smile,
Still for thy weakly self is spent
   Thy little silly plaint.

But when thy friends are in distress,
Thou'lt laugh and chuckle ne'er the less;
Nor e'en with sympathy be smitten,
Though all are sad but thee and kitten;
Yet little varlet that thou art,
   Thou twitchest at the heart.

Thy rosy cheek so soft and warm;
Thy pinky hand and dimpled arm;
Thy silken locks that scantly peep,
With gold-tipped ends, where circles deep
Around thy neck in harmless grace
So soft and sleekly hold their place,
Might harder hearts with kindness fill,
   And gain our right good will.

Each passing clown bestows his blessing,
Thy mouth is worn with old wives' kissing:
E'en lighter looks the gloomy eye
Of surly sense, when thou art by;
And yet I think whoe'er they be,
   They love thee not like me.

Perhaps when time shall add a few
Short years to thee, thou'lt love me too.
Then wilt thou through life's weary way
Become my sure and cheering stay:
Wilt care for me, and be my hold,
   When I am weak and old.

Thou'lt listen to my lengthened tale,
And pity me when I am frail –
But see, the sweepy spinning fly
Upon the window takes thine eye.
Go to thy little senseless play –
   Thou dost not heed my lay.

JOANNA BAILLIE (1790)

The Schoolboy

I love to rise in a summer morn,
When the birds sing in every tree;
The distant huntsman winds his horn,
And the skylark sings with me.
O what sweet company!

But to go to school on a summer morn —
O it drives all joy away!
Under a cruel eye outworn
The little ones spend the day
In sighing and dismay.

And then at times I drooping sit
And spend many an anxious hour;
Nor in my book can take delight,
Nor sit in learning's bower,
Worn through with the dreary shower.

How can the bird that is born for joy
Sit in a cage and sing?
How can a child, when fears annoy,
But droop his tender wing,
And forget his youthful spring?

Oh, father and mother, if buds are nipped,
And blossoms blown away,
And if the tender plants are stripped
Of their joy in the springing day
By sorrow, and care's dismay,

How shall the summer arise in joy,
Or the summer fruits appear?
Or how shall we gather what griefs destroy,
Or bless the mellowing year
When the blasts of winter appear?

WILLIAM BLAKE (by 1789)

A Poet's Welcome to His Love-begotten Daughter

THE FIRST INSTANCE THAT ENTITLED HIM TO THE VENERABLE APPELLATION OF FATHER

Thou's welcome, wean; mishanter fa' me,[1]
If thoughts o' thee, or yet they mammie,
Shall ever daunton me or awe me,
   My sweet wee lady,
Or if I blush when thou shalt ca' me
   Tyta or daddie.

Tho' now they ca' me fornicator,
An' tease my name in countra clatter,
The mair they talk, I'm kend the better,
   E'en let them clash;
An auld wife's tongue's a feckless[2] matter
   To gie ane fash.

Welcome! my bonie, sweet, wee dochter,
Tho' ye come here a wee unsought for,
And tho' your comin' I hae fought for,
   Baith kirk and queir;
Yet, by my faith, ye're no unwrought for,
   That I shall swear!

Sweet fruit o' monie a merry dint,[3]
My funny toil is no a' tint,[4]
Tho' thou cam to the warl' asklent,[5]
   Which fools may scoff at;
In my last plack[6] thy part's be in't
   The better ha'f o't.

---

[1] disaster befall me   [2] powerless to cause any vexation   [3] attack   [4] all wasted
[5] irregularly   [6] small coin

Tho' I should be the waur bestead,[7]
Thou's be as braw and bienly clad,[8]
And thy young years as nicely bred
            Wi' education,
As onie brat o' wedlock's bed,
               In a' thy station.

Wee image o' my bonnie Betty,
As fatherly I kiss and daut[9] thee,
As dear and near my heart I set thee
            Wi' as gude will
As a' the priests had seen me get thee,
              That's out o' hell.

Lord grant that thou may aye inherit
Thy mither's person, grace, an' merit,
An' thy poor, worthless daddy's spirit,
              Without his failins,
'Twill please me mair to see thee heir[10] it,
              Than stockit mailens.[11]

For if thou be what I wad hae thee,
And tak the counsel I shall gie thee,
I'll never rue my trouble wi' thee –
              The cost nor shame o't.
But be a loving father to thee.
              And brag the name o't.

              ROBERT BURNS (by 1790)

---

[7] worse off   [8] finely and comfortably clad   [9] fondle   [10] inherit
[11] well-stocked farms

To a Little Invisible Being Who Is Expected Soon to Become Visible

Germ of new life, whose powers expanding slow
For many a moon their full perfection wait,
Haste, precious pledge of happy love, to go
Auspicious born through life's mysterious gate.

What powers lie folded in thy curious frame,
Senses from objects locked, and mind from thought!
How little canst thou guess thy lofty claim
To grasp at all the worlds the Almighty wrought!

And see, the genial season's warmth to share,
Fresh younglings shoot, and opening roses glow!
Swarms of new life exulting fill the air,
Haste, infant bud of being, haste to blow!

For thee the nurse prepares her lulling songs,
The eager matrons count the lingering day;
But far the most thy anxious parent longs
On thy soft cheek a mother's kiss to lay.

She only asks to lay her burden down,
That her glad arms that burden may resume;
And nature's sharpest pangs her wishes crown,
That free thee living from thy living tomb.

She longs to fold to her maternal breast
Part of herself, yet to herself unknown;
To see and to salute the stranger guest,
Fed with her life through many a tedious moon.

Come, reap thy rich inheritance of love!
Bask in the fondness of a Mother's eye!
Nor wit nor eloquence her heart shall move
Like the first accents of thy feeble cry.

Haste, little captive, burst thy prison doors!
Launch on the living world, and spring to light!
Nature for thee displays her various stores,
Opens her thousand inlets of delight.

If charmed verse or muttered prayers had power,
With favouring spells to speed thee on thy way,
Anxious I'd bid my beads each passing hour,
Till thy wished smile thy mother's pangs o'erpay.

ANNA LAETITIA BARBAULD (1790s)

We Are Seven

A simple Child
That lightly draws its breath,
And feels its life in every limb,
What should it know of death?

I met a little cottage Girl:
She was eight years old, she said;
Her hair was thick with many a curl
That clustered round her head.

She had a rustic woodland air,
And she was wildly clad:
Her eyes were fair, and very fair;
Her beauty made me glad.

'Sisters and brothers, little Maid,
How many may you be?'
'How many? Seven in all,' she said,
And wondering looked at me.

'And where are they? I pray you tell.'
She answered, 'Seven are we;
And two of us at Conway dwell,
And two are gone to sea.

'Two of us in the church-yard lie,
My sister and my brother;
And, in the church-yard cottage, I
Dwell near them with my mother.'

'You say that two at Conway dwell,
And two are gone to sea,
Yet ye are seven! I pray you tell,
Sweet Maid, how may this be?'

Then did the little Maid reply,
'Seven boys and girls are we;
Two of us in the church-yard lie,
Beneath the church-yard tree.'

'You run about, my little Maid,
Your limbs they are alive;
If two are in the church-yard laid,
Then ye are only five.'

'Their graves are green, they may be seen,'
The little Maid replied,
'Twelve steps or more from my mother's door,
And they are side by side.

'My stockings there I often knit,
My kerchief there I hem;
And there upon the ground I sit
And sing a song to them.

'And often after sunset, Sir,
When it is light and fair,
I take my little porringer,
And eat my supper there.

'The first that died was sister Jane;
In bed she moaning lay,
Till God released her of her pain;
And then she went away.

'So in the church-yard she was laid;
And, when the grass was dry,
Together round her grave we played,
My brother John and I.

'And when the ground was white with snow,
And I could run and slide,
My brother John was forced to go,
And he lies by her side.'

'How many are you, then,' said I,
'If they two are in Heaven?'
Quick was the little Maid's reply,
'O, Master, we are seven.'

'But they are dead; those two are dead!
Their spirits are in Heaven!'
'Twas throwing words away; for still
The little Maid would have her will,
And said, 'Nay, we are seven!'

WILLIAM WORDSWORTH (published 1798)

This poem written in the almost too transparent style for which
Wordsworth was sometimes mocked, shows a genuine,
compassionate interest, which is shared by Blake, in the difference
between childhood and adult experience. An intense interest of this
kind is characteristic of the Romantics, as opposed to their
eighteenth-century predecessors.

8
THOUGHTS &
MEMORIES OF DEATH

On the Death of Mr Purcell

1

Mark how the Lark and Linnet sing,
　　With rival Notes
　They strain their warbling Throats
　　To welcome in the Spring.
　　But in the close of night,
When *Philomel* begins her Heav'nly Lay,
　　They cease their mutual spight,
　　Drink in her Musick with delight,
And list'ning and silent, and silent and list'ning, and
　　list'ning and silent obey.

2

So ceas'd the rival Crew, when Purcell came,
They Sung no more, or only Sung his Fame.
　　Struck dumb, they all admir'd
　　　The godlike man,
　　Alas, too soon retir'd,
　　　As He too late began.
We beg not Hell our *Orpheus* to restore;
　　Had He been there,
　　Their Sovereigns fear
　Had sent Him back before.
The pow'r of Harmony too well they knew;
He long e'er this had Tun'd their jarring Sphere,
　　And left no Hell below.

3

The Heav'nly Quire, who heard his Notes from high,
Let down the Scale of Musick from the Sky:
　　　They handed him along,
And all the way He taught, and all the way they Sung.
Ye Brethren of the *Lyre* and tunefull Voice
Lament his lott: but at your own rejoyce.
Now live secure, and linger out your days,
The Gods are pleas'd alone with *Purcell's* Layes,
　　Nor know to mend their Choice.

JOHN DRYDEN (1696)

To the Memory of Mr Oldham

Farewell, too little, and too lately known,
Whom I began to think and call my own:
For sure our souls were near allied, and thine
Cast in the same poetic mold with mine.
One common note on either lyre did strike,
And knaves and fools we both abhorred alike.
To the same goal did both our studies drive;
The last set out the soonest did arrive.
Thus Nisus fell upon the slippery place,
While his young friend performed and won the race.
O early ripe! to thy abundant store
What could advancing age have added more?
It might (what nature never gives the young)
Have taught the numbers of thy native tongue.
But satire needs not those, and wit will shine
Through the harsh cadence of a rugged line.
A noble error, and but seldom made,
When poets are by too much force betrayed.
Thy generous fruits, though gathered ere their prime }
Still showed a quickness; and maturing time }
But mellows what we write to the dull sweets of rhyme. }
Once more, hail and farewell; farewell, thou young,
But ah too short, Marcellus of our tongue;
Thy brows with ivy, and with laurels bound;
But fate and gloomy night encompass thee around.

JOHN DRYDEN (1684)

John Oldham (1653–83) was a poet who had made an impact with
his translations and aggressive satires. The reference to Nisus is to
an incident in the *Aeneid* of Virgil when he and his friend Euryalus
(who was later to die with him in battle) were taking part in games.
Marcellus, mentioned in Book VI of the same poem, was one of
several heirs to the Emperor Augustus who died prematurely.

Death

Oh the sad day
When friends shall shake their heads and say
Of miserable me,
Hark how he groans, look how he pants for breath,
See how he struggles with the pangs of Death!
When they shall say of these poor eyes,
How hollow, and how dim they be!
Mark how his breast does swell and rise,
Against his potent Enemy!
When some old friend shall step to my bedside,
Touch my chill face, and thence shall gently slide,
And when his next companions say,
How does he do? what hopes? shall turn away,
Answering only with a lift up hand,
Who can his fate withstand?
Then shall a gasp or two do more
Than e'er my Rhetorick could before,
Persuade the peevish world to trouble me no more.

THOMAS FLATMAN (d. 1688)

To Death

O King of Terrors, whose unbounded sway
All that have life, must certainly obey,
The King, the Priest, the Prophet, all are thine,
Nor would even God (in flesh) thy stroke decline.
My name is on thy roll, and sure I must
Encrease thy gloomy kingdom in the dust.
My soul at this no apprehension feels,
But trembles at thy swords, thy racks, thy wheels;
Thy scorching fevers, which distract the sense,
And snatch us raving, unprepar'd from hence;
At thy contagious darts, that wound the heads

Of weeping friends, who wait at dying beds.
Spare these, and let thy time be when it will;
My business is to die, and thine to kill.
Gently thy fatal sceptre on me lay,
And take to thy cold arms, insensibly, thy prey.

ANNE FINCH, COUNTESS OF WINCHILSEA
(published 1713)

Elegy to the Memory of an Unfortunate Lady

What beck'ning ghost, along the moonlight shade
Invites my step, and points to yonder glade?
'Tis she! – but why that bleeding bosom gor'd,
Why dimly gleams the visionary sword?
Oh ever beauteous, ever friendly! tell,
Is it, in heav'n, a crime to love too well?
To bear too tender, or too firm a heart,
To act a Lover's or a *Roman*'s part?
Is there no bright reversion in the sky,
For those who greatly think, or bravely die?
    Why bade ye else, ye Pow'rs! her soul aspire
Above the vulgar flight of low desire?
Ambition first sprung from your blest abodes;
The glorious fault of Angels and of Gods:
Thence to their Images on earth it flows,
And in the breasts of Kings and Heroes glows!
Most souls, 'tis true, but peep out once an age,
Dull sullen pris'ners in the body's cage:
Dim lights of life that burn a length of years,
Useless, unseen, as lamps in sepulchres;
Like Eastern Kings a lazy state they keep,
And close confin'd to their own palace sleep.
    From these perhaps (ere nature bade her die)
Fate snatch'd her early to the pitying sky.
As into air the purer spirits flow,
And sep'rate from their kindred dregs below;
So flew the soul to its congenial place,

Nor left one virtue to redeem her Race.
    But thou, false guardian of a charge too good,
Thou, mean deserter of thy brother's blood!
See on these ruby lips the trembling breath,
These cheeks, now fading at the blast of death:
Cold is that breast which warm'd the world before,
And those love-darting eyes must roll no more.
Thus, if eternal justice rules the ball,
Thus shall your wives, and thus your children fall:
On all the line a sudden vengeance waits,
And frequent herses shall besiege your gates.
There passengers shall stand, and pointing say,
While the long fun'rals blacken all the way)
Lo these were they, whose souls the Furies steel'd,
And curs'd with hearts unknowing how to yield.
Thus unlamented pass the proud away,
The gaze of fools, and pageant of a day!
So perish all, whose breast ne'er learn'd to glow
For others' good, or melt at others' woe.
    What can atone (oh ever-injur'd shade!)
Thy fate unpity'd, and thy rites unpaid?
No friend's complaint, no kind domestic tear
Pleas'd thy pale ghost, or grac'd thy mournful bier;
By foreign hands thy dying eyes were clos'd,
By foreign hands thy decent limbs compos'd,
By foreign hands thy humble grave adorn'd,
By strangers honour'd, and by strangers mourn'd!
What tho' no friends in sable weeds appear,
Grieve for an hour, perhaps, then mourn a year,
And bear about the mockery of woe
To midnight dances, and the publick show?
What tho' no weeping Loves thy ashes grace,
Nor polish'd marble emulate thy face?
What tho' no sacred earth allow thee room,
Nor hallow'd dirge be mutter'd o'er thy tomb?
Yet shall thy grave with rising flow'rs be drest,
And the green turf lie lightly on thy breast:
There shall the morn her earliest tears bestow,
There the first roses of the year shall blow;
While Angels with their silver wings o'ershade

The ground, now sacred by thy reliques made.
  So peaceful rests, without a stone, a name,
What once had beauty, titles, wealth, and fame.
How lov'd, how honour'd once, avails thee not,
To whom related, or by whom begot;
A heap of dust alone remains of thee;
'Tis all thou art, and all the proud shall be!
  Poets themselves must fall, like those they sung;
Deaf the prais'd ear, and mute the tuneful tongue.
Ev'n he, whose soul now melts in mournful lays,
Shall shortly want the gen'rous tear he pays;
Then from his closing eyes thy form shall part,
And the last pang shall tear thee from his heart,
Life's idle business at one gasp be o'er,
The Muse forgot, and thou belov'd no more!

ALEXANDER POPE (1717)

No one has yet discovered the identity of this mysterious woman of
high birth apparently driven abroad and to suicide by rich relatives
who rejected her.

A Satirical Elegy on the Death of a Late Famous General

His Grace! impossible! what, dead!
of old age too, and in his bed!
And could that Mighty Warrior fall?
And so inglorious, after all!
Well, since he's gone, no matter how,
The last loud trump must wake him now:
And, trust me, as the noise grows stronger,
He'd wish to sleep a little longer.
And could he be indeed so old
As by the newspapers we're told?
Threescore, I think, is pretty high;
'Twas time in conscience he should die.
This world he cumbered long enough;
He burnt his candle to the snuff;
And that's the reason, some folks think,
He left behind *so great a stink*.
Behold his funeral appears,
Nor widow's sighs, nor orphan's tears,
Wont at such times each heart to pierce,
Attend the progress of his hearse.
But what of that, his friends may say,
He had those honours in his day.
True to his profit and his pride,
He made them weep before he died.

Come hither, all ye empty things,
Ye bubbles raised by breath of kings;
Who float upon the tide of state,
Come hither, and behold your fate.
Let pride be taught by this rebuke,
How very mean a thing's a Duke;
From all his ill-got honours flung,
Turned to that dirt from whence he sprung.

JONATHAN SWIFT (1722)

The general concerned was Marlborough, who was seen as corrupt
and was disliked by Swift and his circle.

Swift Foresees His Own Death

The time is not remote, when I
Must by the course of nature die:
When I foresee my special friends,
Will try to find their private ends:
Though it is hardly understood,
Which way my death can do them good;
Yet, thus methinks, I hear 'em speak;
'See, how the Dean begins to break:
Poor gentleman, he droops apace,
You plainly find it in his face:
That old vertigo in his head,
Will never leave him, till he's dead:
Besides, his memory decays,
He recollects not what he says;
He cannot call his friends to mind;
Forgets the place where last he dined:
Plies you with stories o'er and o'er,
He told them fifty times before.
How does he fancy we can sit,
To hear his out-of-fashioned wit?
But he takes up with younger folks,
Who for his wine will bear his jokes:
Faith, he must make his stories shorter,
Or change his comrades once a quarter:
In half the time, he talks them round;
There must another set be found.

'For poetry, he's past his prime,
He takes an hour to find a rhyme:
His fire is out, his wit decayed,
His fancy sunk, his muse a jade.
I'd have him throw away his pen;
But there's no talking to some men.'

And, then their tenderness appears,
By adding largely to my years:

'He's older than he would be reckoned,
And well remembers Charles the Second.

  'He hardly drinks a pint of wine;
And that, I doubt, is no good sign.
His stomach too begins to fail:
Last Year we thought him strong and hale;
But now, he's quite another thing;
I wish he may hold out till spring.'

  Then hug themselves, and reason thus:
'It is not yet so bad with us.'

  In such a case they talk in tropes,
And, by their fears express their hopes:
Some great misfortune to portend,
No enemy can match a friend;
With all the kindness they profess,
The merit of a lucky guess,
(When daily 'Howd'y's' come of course,
And servants answer: 'Worse and worse')
Would please 'em better than to tell,
That, God be praised, the Dean is well.
Then he who prophesied the best,
Approves his foresight to the rest:
'You know, I always feared the worst,
And often told you so at first':
He'd rather choose that I should die,
Than his prediction prove a lie.
No one foretells I shall recover;
But, all agree, to give me over.

  Yet should some neighbour feel a pain,
Just in the parts, where I complain;
How many a message would he send?
What hearty prayers that I should mend?
Enquire what regimen I kept;
What gave me ease, and how I slept?
And more lament, when I was dead,
Than all the snivellers round my bed.

My good companions, never fear,
For though you may mistake a year;
Though your prognostics run too fast,
They must be verified at last.

   'Behold the fatal day arrive!
How is the Dean? He's just alive.
Now the departing prayer is read.
He hardly breathes. The Dean is dead.
Before the passing-bell begun,
The news through half the town has run.
O, may we all for death prepare!
What has he left? And who's his heir?
I know no more than what the news is,
'Tis all bequeathed to public uses.
To public use! A perfect whim!
What had the public done for him?
Mere envy, avarice, and pride!
He gave it all — But first he died.
And had the Dean, in all the nation,
No worthy friend, no poor relation?
So ready to do strangers good,
Forgetting his own flesh and blood?'

   Now Grub Street wits are all employed;
With elegies, the town is cloyed:
Some paragraph in every paper,
To curse the Dean, or bless the Drapier.
   The doctors tender of their fame,
Wisely on me lay all the blame:
'We must confess his case was nice;
But he would never take advice;
Had he been ruled, for aught appears,
He might have lived these twenty years:
For when we opened him we found,
That all his vital parts were sound.'

   From Dublin soon to London spread,
'Tis told at court, the Dean is dead.

Kind Lady Suffolk in the spleen,
Runs laughing up to tell the Queen.
The Queen, so gracious, mild, and good,
Cries, 'Is he? 'Tis time he should.
He's dead you say, why let him rot;
I'm glad the medals were forgot.
I promised them, I own; but when?
I only was a princess then;
But now as consort of the King,
You know 'tis quite a different thing.'

Now, Chartres at Sir Robert's levee,
Tells, with a sneer, the tidings heavy:
'Why, is he dead without his shoes?'
(Cries Bob) 'I'm sorry for the news;
Oh, were the wretch but living still,
And in his place my good friend Will;
Or had a mitre on his head
Provided Bolingbroke were dead.'

Now Curll[1] his shop from rubbish drains;
Three genuine tomes of Swift's remains.
And then to make them pass the glibber,
Revised by Tibbalds, Moore, and Cibber.[2]
He'll treat me as he does my betters.
Publish my will, my life, my letters.
Revive the libels born to die;
Which Pope must bear, as well as I.

Here shift the scene, to represent
How those I love, my death lament.
Poor Pope will grieve a month; and Gay
A week; and Arbuthnot a day.

St John himself will scarce forbear,
To bite his pen, and drop a tear.
The rest will give a shrug and cry
'I'm sorry; but we all must die.'

[1] a bookseller and publisher   [2] three inferior writers

Indifference clad in wisdom's guise,
All fortitude of mind supplies:
For how can stony bowels melt,
In those who never pity felt;
When *we* are lashed, *they* kiss the rod;
Resigning to the will of God.

The fools, my juniors by a year,
Are tortured with suspense and fear.
Who wisely thought my age a screen,
When death approached, to stand between:
The screen removed, their hearts are trembling,
They mourn for me without dissembling.

My female friends, whose tender hearts
Have better learnt to act their parts,
Receive the news in doleful dumps,
'The Dean is dead, (*and what is trumps?*)
Then Lord have mercy on his soul.
(*Ladies, I'll venture for the vole.*)
Six deans they say must bear the pall.
(*I wish I knew which king to call.*)'
'Madam, your husband will attend
The funeral of so good a friend.'
'No madam, 'tis a shocking sight,
And he's engaged tomorrow night!
My Lady Club would take it ill,
If he should fail her at quadrille.
He loved the Dean. (*I lead a heart.*)
But dearest friends, they say, must part.
His time was come, he ran his race;
We hope he's in a better place.'

JONATHAN SWIFT (1731)

Sonnet on the Death of Richard West

In vain to me the smiling mornings shine,
And reddening Phoebus lifts his golden fire:
The birds in vain their amorous descant join,
Or cheerful fields resume their green attire:
These ears, alas! for other notes repine,
A different object do these eyes require.
My lonely anguish melts no heart but mine;
And in my breast the imperfect joys expire.
Yet morning smiles, the busy race to cheer,
And new-born pleasure brings to happier men:
The fields to all their wonted tribute bear;
To warm their little loves the birds complain.
I fruitless mourn to him that cannot hear,
And weep the more because I weep in vain.

THOMAS GRAY (1742)

This deeply felt reaction to the death of a close friend was later criticised by Wordsworth for the artificiality of its diction, but Coleridge and others, such as Gerard Manley Hopkins, have praised it highly. Phoebus (Apollo) is the sun-god.

from Night Thoughts on Life, Death, and Immortality

DEATH'S PLEASURES AND DISGUISES

Like other tyrants, death delights to smite
What, smitten, most proclaims the pride of power
And arbitrary nod. His joy supreme,
To bid the wretch survive the fortunate;
The feeble wrap th' athletic in his shroud;
And weeping fathers build their children's tomb:
Me thine, Narcissa! – What tho' short thy date?

Virtue, not rolling suns, the mind matures.
That life is long which answers life's great end.
The time that bears no fruit, deserves no name;
The man of wisdom is the man of years.
In hoary youth Methusalems may die;
O how misdated on their flatt'ring tombs.
    Narcissa's youth has lectur'd me thus far
And can her gaiety give counsel too?
That, like the Jews fam'd oracle of gems,
Sparkles instruction; such as throws new light,
And opens more the character of death;
Ill known to thee Lorenzo! This thy vaunt:
'Give death his due, the wretched and the old;
Ev'n let him sweep his rubbish to the grave;
Let him not violate kind nature's laws,
But own man born to live as well as die.'
Wretched and old thou giv'st him; young and gay
He takes; and plunder is a tyrant's joy.
What if I prove, 'The farthest from the fear,
Are often nearest to the stroke of Fate?'
    All, more than common, menaces an end.
A blaze betokens brevity of life:
As if bright embers should emit a flame,
Glad spirits sparkled from Narcissa's eye,
And made youth younger, and taught life to live,
As natures' opposites wage endless war,
For this offence, as treason to the deep
Inviolable stupor of his reign,
Where lust, and turbulent ambition sleep,
Death took swift vengeance. As he life detests,
More life is still more odious; and, reduc'd
By conquest, aggrandizes more his power,
But wherefore aggrandiz'd? By heaven's decree,
To plant the soul on her eternal guard,
In awful expectation of our end.
Thus runs death's dread commission: 'Strike, but so
As most alarms the living by the dead.'
Hence stratagem delights him, and surprise,
And cruel sport with man's securities.
Not simple conquest, triumph is his aim;

And where least fear'd, there conquest triumphs most.
This proves my bold assertion not too bold.
    What are his arts to lay our fears asleep?
Tiberian arts his purposes wrap up
In deep dissimulation's darkest night.
Like princes unconfest in foreign courts,
Who travel under cover, death assumes
The name and look of life, and dwells among us.
He takes all shapes that serve his black designs:
Tho' master of a wider empire far
Than that, o'er which the Roman eagle flew.
Like Nero, he's a fiddler, charioteer,
Or drives his phaeton, in female guise;
Quite unsuspected, till, the wheel beneath,
His disarray'd oblation he devours.
    He most affects the forms least like himself,
His slender self. Hence, burly corpulence
Is his familiar wear, and sleek disguise.
Behind the rosy bloom he loves to lurk,
Or ambush in a smile; or wanton dive
In dimples deep; love's eddies, which draw in
Unwary hearts, and sink them in despair.
Such on Narcissa's couch he loiter'd long
Unknown; and when detected still was seen
To smile; such peace has innocence in death!
Most happy they! whom least his arts deceive.
One eye on death, and one full fix'd on heaven,
Becomes a mortal, and immortal man.
Long on his wiles a piqu'd and jealous spy,
I've seen, or dreamt I saw, the tyrant dress,
Lay by his horrors, and put on his smiles.
Say, muse, for thou remember'st, call it back,
And show Lorenzo the surprising scene;
If 'twas a dream, his genius can explain.
    'Twas in a circle of the gay I stood.
Death would have enter'd; Nature push'd him back;
Supported by a doctor of renown,
His point he gain'd. Then artfully dismist
The sage; for death design'd to be conceal'd.
He gave an old vivacious usurer

His meagre aspect, and his naked bones;
In gratitude for plumping up his prey,
A pamper'd spendthrift; whose fantastic air,
Well-fashion'd figure and cockaded brow,
He took in change, and underneath the pride
Of costly linen, tuck'd his filthy shroud.
His crooked bow he straighten'd to a cane;
And hid his deadly shafts in Myra's eye.

    This dreadful masquerader, thus equipt,
Outsallies on adventures. Ask you where?
Where is he not? For his peculiar haunts,
Let this suffice; sure as night follows day,
Death treads in pleasure's footsteps round the world,
When pleasure treads the path which reason shuns,
When, against reason, riot shuts the door,
And gaiety supplies the place of sense,
Then, foremost at the banquet and the ball,
Death leads the dance, or stamps the deadly die;
Nor ever fails the midnight bowl to crown.
Gaily carousing to his gay compeers,
Inly he laughs, to see them laugh at him,
As absent far; and, when the revel burns,
When fear is banisht and triumphant thought,
Calling for all the joys beneath the moon,
Against him turns the key; and bids him sup
With their progenitors – He drops his mask;
Frowns out at full; they start, despair, expire.

    Scarce with more sudden terror and surprise,
From his black masque of nitre, touch'd with fire,
He bursts, expands, roars, blazes, and devours.
And is not this triumphant treachery,
And more than simple conquest, in the fiend?

    And now, Lorenzo, dost thou wrap thy soul
In soft security, because unknown
Which moment is commissioned to destroy?
In death's uncertainty thy danger lies.
Is death uncertain? Therefore thou be fixt;
Fixt as a centinel, all eye, all ear,
All expectation of the coming foe.
Rouse, stand in arms, nor lean against thy spear;

Lest slumber steal one moment o'er thy soul,
And fate surprise thee, nodding. Watch, be strong;
Thus give each day the merit and renown,
Of dying well; though doom'd but once to die.
Nor let life's period, hidden (as from most)
Hide too from thee the precious use of life.

EDWARD YOUNG (by 1745)

Young's *Night Thoughts* were inspired by the deaths of his stepdaughter and wife. The Roman emperors Tiberius and Nero were renowned for their cruelty, and Tiberius for his cunning.

Ode on the Death of Mr Thomson

1

In yonder grave a Druid lies
   Where slowly winds the stealing wave!
The year's best sweets shall duteous rise
   To deck its poet's sylvan grave!

2

In yon deep bed of whispering reeds
   His airy harp shall now be laid.
That he, whose heart in sorrow bleeds,
   May love through life the soothing shade.

3

Then maids and youths shall linger here,
   And while its sounds at distance swell,
Shall sadly seem in pity's ear
   To hear the woodland pilgrim's knell.

4

Remembrance oft shall haunt the shore
    When Thames in summer wreaths is dressed,
And oft suspend the dashing oar
    To bid his gentle spirit rest!

5

And oft as ease and health retire
    To breezy lawn or forest deep,
The friend shall view yon whitening spire,
    And mid the varied landscape weep.

6

But thou, who own'st that earthy bed,
    Ah! what will every dirge avail?
Or tears, which love and pity shed
    That mourn beneath the gliding sail!

7

Yet lives there one, whose heedless eye
    Shall scorn thy pale shrine glimmering near?
With him, sweet bard, may fancy die,
    And joy desert the blooming year.

8

But thou, lorn stream, whose sullen tide
    No sedge-crowned sisters now attend,
Now waft me from the green hill's side,
    Whose cold turf hides the buried friend!

9

And see, the fairy valleys fade,
    Dun night has veiled the solemn view!
– Yet once again, dear parted shade,
    Meek nature's child again adieu!

10

The genial meads, assigned to bless
    Thy life, shall mourn thy early doom,
Their hinds and shepherd girls shall dress
    With simple hands thy rural tomb.

11

Long, long, thy stone and pointed clay
   Shall melt the musing Briton's eyes,
'O! vales and wild woods,' shall he say,
   'In yonder grave your Druid lies!'

WILLIAM COLLINS (published 1749)

Collins is here mourning the death of James Thomson, the Scottish poet, whose work is represented in this anthology.

Elegy Written in a Country Churchyard

The curfew tolls the knell of parting day,
   The lowing herd wind slowly o'er the lea,
The plowman homeward plods his weary way,
   And leaves the world to darkness and to me.

Now fades the glimmering landscape on the sight,
   And all the air a solemn stillness holds,
Save where the beetle wheels his droning flight,
   And drowsy tinklings lull the distant folds;

Save that from yonder ivy-mantled tower
   The moping owl does to the moon complain
Of such as, wand'ring near her secret bower,
   Molest her ancient solitary reign.

Beneath those rugged elms, that yew-tree's shade,
   Where heaves the turf in many a mould'ring heap,
Each in his narrow cell for ever laid,
   The rude forefathers of the hamlet sleep.

The breezy call of incense-breathing morn,
  The swallow twitt'ring from the straw-built shed,
The cock's shrill clarion, or the echoing horn,
  No more shall rouse them from their lowly bed.

For them no more the blazing hearth shall burn,
  Or busy housewife ply her evening care:
No children run to lisp their sire's return,
  Or climb his knees the envied kiss to share.

Oft did the harvest to their sickle yield,
  Their furrow oft the stubborn glebe has broke:
How jocund did they drive their team afield!
  How bowed the woods beneath their sturdy stroke!

Let not Ambition mock their useful toil,
  Their homely joys, and destiny obscure;
For Grandeur hear with a disdainful smile
  The short and simple annals of the poor.

The boast of heraldry, the pomp of power,
  And all that beauty, all that wealth e'er gave,
Awaits alike th' inevitable hour:
  The paths of glory lead but to the grave.

Nor you, ye proud, impute to These the fault,
  If Memory o'er their tomb no trophies raise,
Where through the long-drawn aisle and fretted vault
  The pealing anthem swells the note of praise.

Can storied urn or animated bust
  Back to its mansion call the fleeting breath?
Can Honour's voice provoke the silent dust,
  Or Flatt'ry soothe the dull cold ear of death?

Perhaps in this neglected spot is laid
  Some heart once pregnant with celestial fire;
Hands, that the rod of empire might have swayed,
  Or waked to ecstasy the living lyre.

But knowledge to their eyes her ample page
    Rich with the spoils of time did ne'er unroll;
Chill Penury repressed their noble rage,
    And froze the genial current of the soul.

Full many a gem of purest ray serene
    The dark unfathomed caves of ocean bear:
Full many a flower is born to blush unseen,
    And waste its sweetness on the desert air.

Some village Hampden that with dauntless breast
    The little tyrant of his fields withstood,
Some mute inglorious Milton here may rest,
    Some Cromwell guiltless of his country's blood.

Th' applause of list'ning senates to command,
    The threats of pain and ruin to despise,
To scatter plenty o'er a smiling land,
    And read their history in a nation's eyes,

Their lot forbade: nor circumscribed alone
    Their growing virtues, but their crimes confined;
Forbade to wade through slaughter to a throne.
    And Shut the gates of mercy on mankind.

The struggling pangs of conscious truth to hide,
    To quench the blushes of ingenuous shame,
Or heap the shrine of Luxury and Pride
    With incense kindled at the Muse's flame.

Far from the madding crowd's ignoble strife
    Their sober wishes never learned to stray;
Along the cool sequestered vale of life
    They kept the noiseless tenor of their way.

Yet ev'n these bones from insult to protect
    Some frail memorial still erected nigh,
With uncouth rhymes and shapeless sculpture decked,
    Implores the passing tribute of a sigh.

Their name, their years, spelt by th' unlettered Muse,
   The place of fame and elegy supply:
And many a holy text around she strews,
   That teach the rustic moralist to die.

For who, to dumb Forgetfulness a prey,
   This pleasing anxious being e'er resigned,
Left the warm precincts of the cheerful day,
   Nor cast one longing ling'ring look behind?

On some fond breast the parting soul relies,
   Some pious drops the closing eye requires;
E'en from the tomb the voice of Nature cries,
   E'en in our Ashes live their wonted fires.

For thee, who, mindful of th' unhonoured dead,
   Dost in these lines their artless tale relate;
If chance, by lonely contemplation led,
   Some kindred spirit shall inquire thy fate,

Haply some hoary-headed Swain may say,
   'Oft have we seen him at the peep of dawn
Brushing with hasty steps the dews away
   To meet the sun upon the upland lawn.

'There at the foot of yonder nodding beech
   That wreathes its old fantastic roots so high,
His listless length at noontide would he stretch,
   And pore upon the brook that babbles by.

'Hard by yon wood, now smiling as in scorn,
   Mutt'ring his wayward fancies he would rove,
Now drooping, woeful wan, like one forlorn,
   Or crazed with care, or crossed in hopeless love.

'One morn I missed him on the customed hill,
   Along the heath and near his fav'rite tree;
Another came; nor yet beside the rill,
   Nor up the lawn, nor at the wood was he;

'The next with dirges due in sad array
    Slow through the church-way path we saw him borne.
Approach and read (for thou canst read) the lay
    Graved on the stone beneath yon aged thorn:'

The Epitaph

Here rests his head upon the lap of Earth
    A Youth to Fortune and to Fame unknown.
Fair Science frowned not on his humble birth,
    And Melancholy marked him for her own.

Large was his bounty, and his soul sincere,
    Heaven did a recompense as largely send:
He gave to Mis'ry all he had, a tear,
    He gained from Heaven ('twas all he wished) a friend.

No further seek his merits to disclose,
    Or draw his frailties from their dread abode,
(There they alike in trembling hope repose,)
    The bosom of his Father and his God.

THOMAS GRAY (1750)

Tom Bowling

Here, a sheer hulk, lies poor Tom Bowling,
The darling of our crew;
No more he'll hear the tempest howling,
For death has broached him to.
His form was of the manliest beauty,
His heart was kind and soft;
Faithful below Tom did his duty,
And now he's gone aloft.

Tom never from his word departed,
His virtues were so rare;
His friends were many, and true hearted,
His Poll was kind and fair.
And then he'd sing so blithe and jolly,
Ah! many 's the time and oft;
But mirth is turned to melancholy,
For Tom is gone aloft.

Yet shall poor Tom find pleasant weather,
When He, Who all commands,
Shall give, to call life's crew together,
The word to pipe all hands.
Thus Death, who kings and tars dispatches,
In vain Tom's life has doffed;
For though his body's under hatches,
His soul is gone aloft.

CHARLES DIBDIN (*c.*1780)

Dibdin, who wrote a number of nautical ballads, was said to have been inspired to write this one by the death of his own brother Tom, a naval captain.

On the Death of Dr Robert Levet

Condemned to Hope's delusive mine,
    As on we toil from day to day,
By sudden blasts, or slow decline,
    Our social comforts drop away.

Well tried through many a varying year,
    See Levet to the grave descend;
Officious,[1] innocent, sincere,
    Of every friendless name the friend.

Yet still he fills Affection's eye,
    Obscurely wise, and coarsely kind;
Nor, lettered Arrogance, deny
    Thy praise to merit unrefined.

When fainting Nature called for aid,
    And hovering Death prepared the blow,
His vigorous remedy displayed
    The power of art without the show.

In Misery's darkest cavern known,
    His useful care was ever nigh,
Where hopeless Anguish poured his groan,
    And lonely Want retired to die.

No summons mocked by chill delay,
    No petty gain disdained by pride,
The modest wants of every day
    The toil of every day supplied.

His virtues walked their narrow round,
    Nor made a pause, nor left a void;
And sure the Eternal Master found
    The single talent well employed.

[1] dutiful

The busy day, the peaceful night,
Unfelt, uncounted, glided by;
His frame was firm, his powers were bright,
Though now his eightieth year was nigh.

Then with no throbbing fiery pain,
No cold gradations of decay,
Death broke at once the vital chain,
And freed his soul the nearest way.

SAMUEL JOHNSON (1782)

Johnson is here vigorously defending the memory of his uncouth lodger, an unqualified doctor of whom many of his friends disapproved. The reference in the seventh stanza is to the parable of the talents in the New Testament (Matthew 25).

from *The Deserted Village*

THE PAUPER'S DEATH

'These fruitful fields, these numerous flocks I see,
Are others' gain, but killing cares to me;
To me the children of my youth are lords,
Cool in their looks, but hasty in their words:
Wants of their own demand their care; and who
Feels his own want and succours others too?
A lonely, wretched man, in pain I go,
None need my help, and none relieve my wo;
Then let my bones beneath the turf be laid,
And men forget the wretch they would not aid.'
    Thus groan the old, till, by disease oppress'd,
They taste a final wo, and then they rest.
    Theirs is yon house that holds the parish-poor,
Whose walls of mud scarce bear the broken door;
There, where the putrid vapours, flagging, play,
And the dull wheel hums doleful through the day;

There children dwell who know no parents' care;
Parents, who know no children's love, dwell there!
Heartbroken matrons on their joyless bed,
Forsaken wives, and mothers never wed;
Dejected widows with unheeded tears,
And crippled age with more than childhood fears;
The lame, the blind, and, far the happiest they!
The moping idiot and the madman gay.
Here too sick their final doom receive,
Here brought, amid the scenes of grief, to grieve,
Where the loud groans from some sad chamber flow,
Mix'd with the clamours of the crowd below;
Here, sorrowing, they each kindred sorrow scan,
And the cold charities of man to man:
Whose laws indeed for ruin'd age provide,
And strong compulsion plucks the scrap from pride;
But still that scrap is bought with many a sigh,
And pride embitters what it can't deny.
　　Say ye, oppress'd by some fantastic woes,
Some jarring nerve that baffles your repose;
Who press the downy couch, while slaves advance
With timid eye, to read the distant glance;
Who with sad prayers the weary doctor tease,
To name the nameless ever-new disease;
Who with mock patience dire complaints endure,
Which real pain and that alone can cure;
How would ye bear in real pain to lie,
Despised, neglected, left alone to die?
How would ye bear to draw your latest breath,
Where all that's wretched paves the way for death?
　　Such is that room which one rude beam divides,
And naked rafters form the sloping sides;
Where the vile bands that blind the thatch are seen,
And lath and mud are all that lie between;
Save one dull pane, that, coarsely patch'd, gives way
To the rude tempest, yet excludes the day:
Here, on a matted flock, with dust o'erspread,
The dropping wretch reclines his languid head;
For him no hand the cordial cup applies,

Or wipes the tear that stagnates in his eyes;
No friends with soft discourse his pain beguile,
Or promise hope till sickness wears a smile.

But soon a loud and hasty summons calls,
Shakes the thin roof, and echoes round the walls;
Anon, a figure enters, quaintly neat,
All pride and business, bustle and conceit;
With looks unalter'd by these scenes of wo,
With speed that, entering, speaks his haste to go,
He bids the gazing throng around him fly,
And carries fate and physic in his eye:
A potent quack, long versed in human ills,
Who first insults the victim whom he kills;
Whose murd'rous hand a drowsy Bench protect,
And whose most tender mercy is neglect.

Paid by the parish for attendance here,
He wears contempt upon his sapient sneer;
In haste he seeks the bed where Misery lies,
Impatience mark'd in his averted eyes;
And, some habitual queries hurried o'er,
Without reply, he rushes on the door:
His drooping patient, long inured to pain,
And long unheeded, knows remonstrance vain;
He ceases now the feeble help to crave
Of man; and silent sinks into the grave.

But ere his death some pious doubts arise,
Some simple fears, which 'bold bad' men despise;
Fain would he ask the parish-priest to prove
His title certain to the joys above:
For this he sends the murmuring nurse, who calls
The holy stranger to these dismal walls:
And doth not he, the pious man, appear,
He, 'passing rich with forty pounds a year?'
Ah! no; a shepherd of a different stock,
And far unlike him, feeds this little flock:
A jovial youth, who thinks his Sunday's task
As much as God or man can fairly ask;
The rest he gives to loves and labours light,
To fields the morning, and to feasts the night;
None better skill'd the noisy pack to guide,

To urge their chase, to cheer them or to chide;
A sportsman keen, he shoots through half the day,
And, skill'd at whist, devotes the night to play:
Then, while such honours bloom around his head,
Shall he sit sadly by the sick man's bed,
To raise the hope he feels not, or with zeal
To combat fears that e'en the pious feel?

   Now once again the gloomy scene explore,
Less gloomy now; the bitter hour is o'er,
The man of many sorrows sighs no more.
Up yonder hill, behold how sadly slow
The bier moves winding from the vale below;
There lie the happy dead, from trouble free,
And the glad parish pays the frugal fee:
No more, O Death! thy victim starts to hear
Churchwarden stern, or kingly overseer;
No more the farmer claims his humble bow,
Thou art his lord, the best of tyrants thou!

   Now to the church behold the mourners come,
Sedately torpid and devoutly dumb;
The village children now their games suspend,
To see the bier that bears their ancient friend;
For he was one in all their idle sport,
And like a monarch ruled their little court,
The pliant bow he form'd, the flying ball,
The bat, the wicket, were his labours all;
Him now they follow to his grave, and stand
Silent and sad, and gazing, hand in hand;
While bending low, their eager eyes explore
The mingled relics of the parish poor:
The bell tolls late, the moping owl flies round,
Fear marks the flight and magnifies the sound;
The busy priest, detain'd by weightier care,
Defers his duty till the day of prayer;
And, waiting long, the crowd retire distress'd,
To think a poor man's bones should lie unbless'd.

GEORGE CRABBE (1783)

The Indian Burying Ground

In spite of all the learn'd have said,
   I still my old opinion keep;
The posture that we give the dead
   Points out the soul's eternal sleep.

Not so the ancients of these lands:
   The Indian, when from life released,
Again is seated with his friends,
   And shares again the joyous feast.

His imaged birds, and painted bowl,
   And venison for a journey dressed,
Bespeak the nature of the soul,
   Activity, that wants no rest.

His bow for action ready bent,
   And arrows with a head of stone,
Can only mean that life is spent,
   And not the old ideas gone.

Thou, stranger, that shalt come this way,
   No fraud upon the dead commit,
Observe the swelling turf, and say,
   They do not lie, but here they sit.

Here still a lofty rock remains,
   On which the curious eye may trace
(Now wasted half by wearing rains)
   The fancies of a ruder race.

Here still an aged elm aspires,
   Beneath whose far projecting shade
(And which the shepherd still admires)
   The children of the forest played.

There oft a restless Indian queen
   (Pale Shebah with her braided hair),
And many a barbarous form is seen
   To chide the man that lingers there.

By midnight moons, o'er moistening dews,
   In habit for the chase arrayed,
The hunter still the deer pursues,
   The hunter and the deer – a shade!

And long shall timorous fancy see
   The painted chief, and pointed spear,
And Reason's self shall bow the knee
   To shadows and delusions here.

PHILIP FRENEAU (published 1788)

Highland Mary

Ye banks and braes and streams around
   The castle o' Montgomery,
Green be your woods, and fair your flowers,
   Your waters never drumlie!
There simmer first unfauld her robes,
   And there the langest tarry;
For there I took the last fareweel
   O' my sweet Highland Mary.

How sweetly bloomed the gay green birk,
   How rich the hawthorn's blossom,
As underneath their fragrant shade
   I clasped her to my bosom!
The golden hours on angel wings
   Flew o'er me and my dearie;
For dear to me as light and life
   Was my sweet Highland Mary.

Wi' monie a vow and locked embrace
 Our parting was fu' tender;
And, pledging aft to meet again,
 We tore oursels asunder;
But oh! fell Death's untimely frost,
 That nipt my flower sae early!
Now green's the sod, and cauld's the clay,
 That wraps my Highland Mary!

O pale, pale now, those rosy lips
 I aft hae kissed sae fondly!
And closed for aye the sparkling glance
 That dwelt on me sae kindly!
And mouldering now in silent dust
 That heart that lo'ed me dearly!
But still within my bosom's core
 Shall live my Highland Mary.

ROBERT BURNS (1792)

9
MEN & WOMEN,
LOVE & MARRIAGE

from *Paradise Lost*

EVE EXPRESSES HER LOVE FOR ADAM

Sweet is the breath of morn, her rising sweet,
With charm of earliest birds, pleasant the sun
When first on this delightful land he spreads
His orient beams on herb, tree, fruit and flower
Glistering with dew; fragrant the fertile earth
After soft showers; and sweet the coming on
Of grateful evening mild, then silent night
With this her solemn bird and this fair moon
And these the gems of heaven, her starry train.
But neither breath of morn when she ascends
With charm of earliest birds, nor rising sun
On this delightful land, nor herb, fruit, flower
Glistering with dew, nor fragrance after showers,
Nor grateful evening mild, nor silent night
With this her solemn bird, nor walk by moon
Or glittering starlight without thee is sweet.

JOHN MILTON (1667)

from *Paradise Lost*

MILTON'S PRAISE OF LOVE WITHIN MARRIAGE

Hail wedded love, mysterious law, true source
Of human offspring, sole propriety
In Paradise of all things common else.
By thee adulterous lust was driven from men
Among the bestial herds to range, by thee
Founded in reason, loyal, just and pure,
Relations dear and all the charities
Of father, son and brother first were known.
Far be it that I should write thee sin or blame,
O think thee unbefitting holiest place,
Perpetual fountain of domestic sweets,

Whose bed is undefiled and chaste pronounced,
Present or past, as saints and patriarchs used.
Here Love his golden shafts employs, here lights
His constant lamp and waves his purple wings,
Reigns here and revels; not in the bought smile
Of harlots, loveless, joyless, unendeared,
Casual fruition, nor in court amours,
Mixed dance or wanton masque or midnight ball
Or serenade which the starved lover sings
To his proud fair, best quitted with disdain.
These, lulled by nightingales, embracing slept,
And on their naked limbs the flowery roof
Showered roses, which the morn repaired.

JOHN MILTON (1667)

A Song of a Young Lady to Her Ancient Lover

1

Ancient Person, for whom I,
All the flatt'ring Youth defy;
Long be it e're thou grow Old,
Aking, shaking, Crazy Cold.
But still continue as thou art,
Ancient Person of My Heart.

2

On thy wither'd Lips and dry,
Which like barren Furrows lye,
Brooding Kisses I will pour,
Shall thy youthful Heart restore.
Such kind Show'rs in Autumn fall,
And a second Spring recall:
Nor from thee will ever part,
Ancient Person of my Heart.

3

Thy Nobler Part[s], which but to name,
In our Sex wou'd be counted shame,
By Ages frozen grasp possest,
From their Ice shall be releast:
And, sooth'd by my reviving Hand,
In former Warmth and Vigor stand.
All a Lover's Wish can reach,
For thy Joy my Love shall teach:
And for thy Pleasure shall improve,
All that Art can add to Love.
Yet still I love thee without Art,
Ancient Person of my Heart.

JOHN WILMOT, EARL OF ROCHESTER
(*c*.1676)

The Mistress

An Age in her Embraces past,
    Would seem a Winter's day;
Where Life and Light, with envious hast,
    Are torn and snatch'd away.

But, oh how slowly Minutes rowl,
    When absent from her Eyes,
That feed my Love, which is my Soul,
    It languishes and dyes.

For then no more a Soul but shade,
    It mournfully does move;
And haunts my Breast, by absence made
    The living Tomb of Love.

You Wiser men despise me not,
    Whose Love-sick Fancy raves
On Shades of Souls, and Heaven knows what;
    Short Ages live in Graves.

When e're those wounding Eyes, so full
  Of Sweetness, you did see;
Had you not been profoundly dull,
  You had gone mad like me.

Nor Censure us you who perceive
  My best belov'd and me,
Sigh and lament, complain and grieve,
  You think we disagree.

Alas! 'tis Sacred Jealousie,
  Love rais'd to an Extream;
The only Proof 'twixt her and me,
  We love, and do not dream.

Fantastick Fancies fondly move,
  And in frail Joys believe,
Taking false Pleasure for true Love;
  But Pain can ne'er deceive.

Kind Jealous Doubts, tormenting Fears,
  And Anxious Cares, when past;
Prove our Hearts' Treasure fixt and dear,
  And make us blest at last.

JOHN WILMOT, EARL OF ROCHESTER
(c. 1676)

Song from *Marriage à-la-Mode*

Why should a foolish Marriage Vow
  Which long ago was made,
Oblige us to each other now
  When Passion is decay'd?
We lov'd, and we lov'd, as long as we cou'd,
  Till our Love was lov'd out in us both:
But our Marriage is dead, when the Pleasure is fled:
  'Twas Pleasure first made it an Oath.
If I have Pleasures for a Friend,

And farther love in store,
What wrong has he whose joys did end,
    And who cou'd give no more?
'Tis a madness that he should be jealous of me,
    Or that I shou'd bar him of another:
For all we can gain, is to give our selves pain,
    When neither can hinder the other.

                                    JOHN DRYDEN (1673)

Song

As wretched, vain, and indiscreet,
Those matches I deplore,
Whose bartering friends in council meet
To huddle in a wedding sheet
Some miserable pair that never met before.

Poor love of no account must be,
Tho' ne'er so fix'd and true:
No merit but in gold they see;
So portion and estate agree,
No matter what the bride and bridegroom do.

Curs'd may all covetous husbands be,
That wed with such design,
And curs'd they are; for while they ply
Their wealth, some lover by the by
Reaps the true bliss, and digs the richer mine.

                                    APHRA BEHN (by 1689)

The Willing Mistress

Amyntas led me to a Grove
    Where all the Trees did shade us.
The Sun itself, though it had strove
    It could not have betray'd us.
The place secur'd from humane Eyes
    No other Fear allows,
But when the Winds that gently rise
    Do Kiss the yielding Boughs

Down there we satt upon the Moss
    And did begin to play
A Thousand Amorous Tricks, to pass
    The heat of all the day.
A many Kisses he did give
    And I return'd the same,
Which made me willing to receive
    That which I dare not name.

His charming Eyes no Aid requir'd
    To tell their soft'ning Tale.
On her that was already Fir'd
    'Twas Easy to prevaile.
He did but Kiss and Clasp me round
    Whilst those his Thoughts Exprest:
And lay'd me gently on the Ground;
    Ah who can guess the rest?

APHRA BEHN (by 1689)

Millamant's Song

Love's but the frailty of the mind,
　　When 'tis not with ambition join'd;
A sickly flame, which if not fed expires;
And, feeding, wastes in self-consuming fires.

　　'Tis not to wound a wanton boy
　　Or amorous youth, that gives the joy;
But 'tis the glory to have pierced a swain,
For whom inferior beauties sighed in vain.

　　Then I alone the conquest prize,
　　When I insult a rival's eyes:
If there's delight in love, 'tis when I see
That heart which others bleed for, bleed for me.

WILLIAM CONGREVE (1700)

'Tis strange this Heart . . .

'Tis strange this Heart within my Breast,
Reason opposing and the Pow'rs
Cannot one gentle Moment rest,
Unless it knows what's done in Yours.

In vain I ask it of your Eyes
Which subtly would my Fears controul;
For Art has taught them to disguise
Which Nature made t'explain the Soul.

In vain that Sound, your voice affords
Flatters sometimes my easy Mind;
But of too vast Extent are Words
In them the Jewel Truth to find.

Then let my fond Enquiries cease
And so let all my Troubles end
For sure that Heart shall ne'er know Peace
Which on Another's do's depend.

ANNE FINCH, COUNTESS OF WINCHILSEA
(by 1701)

A Better Answer (to Cloe Jealous)

Dear Cloe, how blubber'd is that pretty Face?
    Thy Cheek all on Fire, and thy Hair all uncurl'd:
Prythee quit this Caprice, and (as old Falstaff says)
    Let us e'en talk a little like folks of This world.

How can'st Thou presume, Thou hast leave to destroy
    The Beauties which Venus but Lent to thy keeping?
Those Looks were design'd to inspire Love and Joy:
    More ord'nary Eyes may serve People for weeping.

To be vext at a Trifle or two that I writ,
    Your Judgement at once, and my Passion You wrong;
You take that for Fact, which will scarce be found Wit:
    Od's Life, must one swear to the Truth of a Song?

What I speak, my fair Cloe, and what I write, shews
    The Diff'rence there is betwixt Nature and Art:
I court others in Verse; but I love Thee in Prose;
    And They have my Whimsies; but Thou hast my Heart.

The God of us Verse-men (You know, Child) the Sun,
    How after his Journeys he sets up his Rest:
If at Morning o'er Earth 'tis his Fancy to run;
    At Night he reclines on his Thetis's Breast.

So when I am weary'd with wand'ring all Day;
    To Thee my Delight in the Evening I come;
No matter what Beauties I saw in my Way:
    They were but my Visits; but thou art my Home.

Then finish, dear Cloe this Pastoral War;
   And let us like Horace and Lydia agree:
For Thou art a Girl as much brighter than her,
   As He was a Poet sublimer than Me.

MATTHEW PRIOR (published 1709)

from *Eloisa to Abelard*

Pope's poem is based on a famous medieval love affair between the young Heloise and Abelard, a poet, theologian and scholar, who was punished by castration. Pope imagines Heloise's thought's after their painful separation and withdrawal to a monastery and nunnery.

Come thou, my father, brother, husband, friend!
Ah let thy handmaid, sister, daughter, move,
And, all those tender names in one, thy love!
The darksom pines that o'er yon' rocks reclin'd
Wave high, and murmur to the hollow wind,
The wandring streams that shine between the hills,
The grots that eccho to the tinkling rills,
The dying gales that pant upon the trees,
The lakes that quiver to the curling breeze;
No more these scenes my meditation aid,
Or lull to rest the visionary maid:
But o'er the twilight groves, and dusky caves,
Long-sounding isles, and intermingled graves,
Black Melancholy sits, and round her throws
A death-like silence, and a dread repose:
Her gloomy presence saddens all the scene,
Shades ev'ry flow'r, and darkens ev'ry green,
Deepens the murmur of the falling floods,
And breathes a browner horror on the woods.
   Yet here for ever, ever must I stay;
Sad proof how well a lover can obey!
Death, only death, can break the lasting chain;

And here ev'n then, shall my cold dust remain,
Here all its frailties, all its flames resign,
And wait, till 'tis no sin to mix with thine.
    Ah wretch! believ'd the spouse of God in vain,
Confess'd within the slave of love and man.
Assist me heav'n! but whence arose that pray'r?
Sprung it from piety, or from despair?
Ev'n here, where frozen chastity retires,
Love finds an altar for forbidden fires.
I ought to grieve, but cannot what I ought;
I mourn the lover, not lament the fault;
I view my crime, but kindle at the view,
Repent old pleasures, and sollicit new:
Now turn'd to heav'n, I weep my past offence,
Now think of thee, and curse my innocence.
Of all affliction taught a lover yet,
'Tis sure the hardest science to forget!
How shall I lose the sin, yet keep the sense,
And love th' offender, yet detest th' offence?
How the dear object from the crime remove,
Or how distinguish penitence from love?
Unequal task! a passion to resign,
For hearts so touch'd, so pierc'd, so lost as mine.
Ere such a soul regains its peaceful state,
How often must it love, how often hate!
How often, hope, despair, resent, regret,
Conceal, disdain – do all things but forget.
But let heav'n seize it, all at once 'tis fir'd,
Not touch'd, but rapt, not waken'd, but inspir'd!
Oh come! oh teach me nature to subdue,
Renounce my love, my life, my self – and you.
Fill my fond heart with God alone, for he
Alone can rival, can succeed to thee.
    How happy is the blameless Vestal's lot!
The world forgetting, by the world forgot.
Eternal sun-shine of the spotless mind!
Each pray'r accepted, and each wish resign'd;
Labour and rest, that equal periods keep;
'Obedient slumbers that can wake and weep';
Desires compos'd, affections ever ev'n,

Tears that delight, and sighs that waft to heav'n.
Grace shines around her with serenest beams,
And whisp'ring Angels prompt her golden dreams.
For her th' unfading rose of *Eden* blooms,
And wings of Seraphs shed divine perfumes;
For her the Spouse prepares the bridal ring,
For her white virgins *Hymenæals* sing;
To sounds of heav'nly harps, she dies away,
And melts in visions of eternal day.

    Far other dreams my erring soul employ,
Far other raptures, of unholy joy:
When at the close of each sad, sorrowing day,
Fancy restores what vengeance snatch'd away,
Then conscience sleeps, and leaving nature free,
All my loose soul unbounded springs to thee.
O curst, dear horrors of all-conscious night!
How glowing guilt exalts the keen delight!
Provoking Dæmons all restraint remove,
And stir within me ev'ry source of love.
I hear thee, view thee, gaze o'er all thy charms,
And round thy phantom glue my clasping arms.
I wake – no more I hear, no more I view,
The phantom flies me, as unkind as you,
I call aloud; it hears not what I say;
I stretch my empty arms; it glides away:
To dream once more I close my willing eyes;
Ye soft illusions, dear deceits, arise!
Alas no more! – methinks we wandring go
Thro' dreary wastes, and weep each other's woe;
Where round some mould'ring tow'r pale ivy creeps,
And low-brow'd rocks hang nodding o'er the deeps.
Sudden you mount! you becken from the skies;
Clouds interpose, waves roar, and winds arise.
I shriek, start up, the same sad prospect find,
And wake to all the griefs I left behind.

ALEXANDER POPE (1717)

from *Cadenus and Vanessa*

Cupid, though all his darts were lost,
Yet still resolved to spare no cost;
He could not answer to his fame
The triumphs of that stubborn dame;
A nymph so hard to be subdued,
Who neither was coquette nor prude.
'I find,' says he, 'she wants a doctor,
Both to adore her and instruct her;
I'll give her what she most admires,
Among those venerable sires.
Cadenus is a subject fit,
Grown old in politics and wit;
Caressed by ministers of state,
Of half mankind the dread and hate.
Whate'er vexations love attend,
She need no rivals apprehend.
Her sex, with universal voice,
Must laugh at her capricious choice.'

Cadenus many things had writ;
Vanessa much esteemed his wit;
And called for his poetic works;
Meantime the boy in secret lurks,
And while the book was in her hand,
The urchin from his private stand
Took aim, and shot with all his strength
A dart of such prodigious length,
It pierced the feeble volume through,
And deep transfixed her bosom too.
Some lines more moving than the rest,
Stuck to the point that pierced her breast;
And born directly to the heart,
With pains unknown increased her smart.

Vanessa, not in years a score,
Dreams of a gown of forty-four;

Imaginary charms can find,
In eyes with reading almost blind;
Cadenus now no more appears
Declined in health, advanced in years.
She fancies music in his tongue,
Nor further looks, but thinks him young.
What mariner is not afraid,
To venture in a ship decayed?
What planter will attempt to yoke
A sapling with a fallen oak?
As years increase, she brighter shines,
Cadenus with each day declines,
And he must fall a prey to time,
While she continues in her prime.

Cadenus, common forms apart,
In every scene had kept his heart;
Had sighed and languished, vowed and writ,
For pastime, or to show his wit;
But time, and books, and state affairs,
Had spoiled his fashionable airs;
He now could praise, esteem, approve,
But understood not what was love:
His conduct might have made him styled
A father, and the nymph his child.
That innocent delight he took
To see the virgin mind her book,
Was but the master's secret joy
In school to hear the finest boy.
Her knowledge with her fancy grew;
She hourly pressed for something new:
Ideas came into her mind
So fast, his lessons lagged behind:
She reasoned, without plodding long,
Nor ever gave her judgement wrong.
But now a sudden change was wrought,
She minds no longer what he taught.
She wished her tutor were her lover;
Resolved she would her flame discover:
And when Cadenus would expound

Some notion subtle or profound,
The nymph would gently press his hand,
As if she seemed to understand;
Or dextrously dissembling chance,
Would sigh, and steal a secret glance.
Cadenus was amazed to find
Such marks of a distracted mind;
For though she seemed to listen more
To all he spoke, than e'er before;
He found her thoughts would absent range,
Yet guessed not whence could spring the change.
And first he modestly conjectures
His pupil might be tired with lectures;
Which helped to mortify his pride,
Yet gave him not the heart to chide;
But in a mild dejected strain,
At last he ventured to complain:
Said, she should be no longer teased;
Might have her freedom when she pleased:
Was now convinced he acted wrong,
To hide her from the world so long;
And in dull studies to engage,
One of her tender sex and age.
That every nymph with envy owned,
How she might shine in the *grand monde*,
And every shepherd was undone
To see her cloistered like a nun.
This was a visionary scheme,
He waked, and found it but a dream;
A project far above his skill,
For nature must be nature still.
If he was bolder than became
A scholar to a courtly dame,
She might excuse a man of letters;
Thus tutors often treat their betters.
And since his talk offensive grew,
He came to take his last adieu.

    Vanessa, filled with just disdain,
Would still her dignity maintain,

Instructed from her early years
To scorn the art of female tears.

Had he employed his time so long,
To teach her what was right or wrong,
Yet could such notions entertain,
That all his lectures were in vain?
She owned the wandering of her thoughts,
But he must answer for her faults.
She well remembered to her cost,
That all his lessons were not lost.
Two maxims she could still produce,
And sad experience taught their use:
That virtue, pleased by being shown,
Knows nothing which it dare not own;
Can make us without fear disclose
Our inmost secrets to our foes:
That common forms were not designed
Directors to a noble mind.
'Now,' said the nymph, 'to let you see
My actions with your rules agree,
That I can vulgar forms despise,
And have no secrets to disguise:
I knew by what you said and writ,
How dangerous things were men of wit,
You cautioned me against their charms,
But never gave me equal arms:
Your lessons found the weakest part,
Aimed at the head, but reached the heart.'

Cadenus felt within him rise
Shame, disappointment, guilt, surprise.
He knew not how to reconcile
Such language, with her usual style:
And yet her words were so expressed
He could not hope she spoke in jest.
His thoughts had wholly been confined
To form and cultivate her mind.
He hardly knew, till he was told,
Whether the nymph were young or old;

Had met her in a public place,
Without distinguishing her face.
Much less could his declining age
Vanessa's earliest thoughts engage.
And if her youth indifference met,
His person must contempt beget.
Or grant her passion be sincere,
How shall his innocence be clear?
Appearances were all so strong,
The world must think him in the wrong;
Would say, he made a treacherous use
Of wit, to flatter and seduce:
The town would swear he had betrayed,
By magic spells, the harmless maid;
And every beau would have his jokes,
That scholars were like other folks:
That when platonic flights were over,
The tutor turned a mortal lover.
So tender of the young and fair?
It showed a true paternal care –
'Five thousand guineas in her purse:
The doctor might have fancied worse . . . '

    But not to dwell on things minute;
Vanessa finished the dispute,
Brought weighty arguments to prove
That reason was her guide in love.
She thought he had himself described,
His doctrines when she first imbibed;
What he had planted, now was grown;
His virtues she might call her own;
As he approves, as he dislikes,
Love or contempt, her fancy strikes.
Self-love, in nature rooted fast,
Attends us first, and leaves us last:
Why she likes him, admire not at her,
She loves herself, and that's the matter.
How was her tutor wont to praise
The geniuses of ancient days!
(Those authors he so oft had named

For learning, wit, and wisdom famed);
Was struck with love, esteem and awe,
For persons whom he never saw.
Suppose Cadenus flourished then,
He must adore such godlike men.
If one short volume could comprise
All that was witty, learned, and wise,
How would it be esteemed, and read,
Although the writer long were dead?
If such an author were alive,
How would all for his friendship strive;
And come in crowds to see his face:
And this she takes to be her case:
Cadenus answers every end,
The book, the author, and the friend.
The utmost her desires will reach,
Is but to learn what he can teach;
His converse is a system, fit
Alone to fill up all her wit;
While every passion of her mind
In him is centred and confined.

'Tis an old maxim in the schools,
That vanity's the food of fools;
Yet now and then your men of wit
Will condescend to take a bit.
So when Cadenus could not hide,
He chose to justify his pride;
Construing the passion she had shown,
Much to her praise, more to his own.
Nature in him had merit placed,
In her, a most judicious taste.
Love, hitherto a transient guest,
Ne'er held possession of his breast;
So, long attending at the gate,
Disdained to enter in so late.
Love, why do we one passion call?
When 'tis a compound of them all;
Where hot and cold, where sharp and sweet,
In all their equipages meet;

Where pleasures mixed with pains appear,
Sorrow with joy, and hope with fear;
Wherein his dignity and age
Forbid Cadenus to engage.
But friendship in its greatest height,
A constant, rational delight,
On virtue's basis fixed to last,
When love's allurements long are past;
Which gently warms, but cannot burn;
He gladly offers in return:
His want of passion will redeem,
With gratitude, respect, esteem:
With that devotion we bestow,
When goddesses appear below.

While thus Cadenus entertains
Vanessa in exalted strains,
The nymph in sober words entreats
A truce with all sublime conceits.
For why such raptures, flights, and fancies,
To her, who durst not read romances;
In lofty style to make replies,
Which he had taught her to despise.
But when her tutor will affect
Devotion, duty, and respect,
He fairly abdicates his throne,
The government is now her own;
He has a forfeiture incurred:
She vows to take him at his word,
And hopes he will not think it strange
If both should now their stations change.
The nymph will have her turn, to be
The tutor; and the pupil, he:
Though she already can discern,
Her scholar is not apt to learn;
Or wants capacity to reach
The science she designs to teach:
Wherein his genius was below
The skill of every common beau;
Who though he cannot spell, is wise

Enough to read a lady's eyes;
And will each accidental glance
Interpret for a kind advance.

But what success Vanessa met,
Is to the world a secret yet:
Whether the nymph, to please her swain,
Talks in a high romantic strain;
Or whether he at last descends
To like with less seraphic ends;
Or, to compound the business, whether
They temper love and books together;
Must never to mankind be told,
Nor shall the conscious muse unfold.

JONATHAN SWIFT (1713)

This describes the development of the relationship between Dean
Swift ('Decanus', of which Cadenus is an anagram, means 'Dean' in
Latin) and his much younger admirer Esther Van Homrigh.

Sally in Our Alley

Of all the girls that are so smart
    There's none like pretty Sally;
She is the darling of my heart,
    And she lives in our alley.
There is no lady in the land
    Is half so sweet as Sally;
She is the darling of my heart,
    And she lives in our alley.

Her father he makes cabbage-nets,
    And through the streets does cry 'em;
Her mother she sells laces long

To such as please to buy 'em:
But sure such folks could ne'er beget
　　So sweet a girl as Sally!
She is the darling of my heart,
　　And she lives in our alley.

When she is by, I leave my work,
　　I love her so sincerely;
My master comes like any Turk,
　　And bangs me most severely:
But let him bang his bellyful,
　　I'll bear it all for Sally;
She is the darling of my heart,
　　And she lives in our alley.

Of all the days that's in the week
　　I dearly love but one day –
And that's the day that comes betwixt
　　A Saturday and Monday;
For then I'm dressed all in my best
　　To walk abroad with Sally;
She is the darling of my heart,
　　And she lives in our alley.

My master carries me to church,
　　And often am I blamèd
Because I leave him in the lurch
　　As soon as text is namèd;
I leave the church in sermon-time
And slink away to Sally;
　　She is the darling of my heart,
And she lives in our alley.

When Christmas comes about again,
　　O, then I shall have money;
I'll hoard it up, and box it all,
　　I'll give it to my honey:
I would it were ten thousand pound,
　　I'd give it all to Sally;
She is the darling of my heart,
　　And she lives in our alley.

My master and the neighbours all
    Make game of me and Sally,
And, but for her, I'd better be
    A slave and row a galley;
But when my seven long years are out,
    O, then I'll marry Sally;
O, then we'll wed, and then we'll bed –
    But not in our alley!

HENRY CAREY (*c.*1713)

Stella's Birthday, 13 March 1726

This Day, whate'er the Fates decree,
Shall still be kept with Joy by me:
This Day then, let us not be told,
That you are sick, and I grown old,
Nor think on our approaching Ills,
And talk of Spectacles and Pills;
To morrow will be Time enough
To hear such mortifying Stuff.
Yet, since from Reason may be brought
A better and more pleasing Thought,
Which can in spite of all Decays,
Support a few remaining Days:
From not the gravest of Divines,
Accept for once some serious Lines.

Although we now can form no more
Long Schemes of Life, as heretofore;
Yet you, while Time is running fast,
Can look with Joy on what is past.

Were future Happiness and Pain,
A mere Contrivance of the Brain,
As Atheists argue, to entice,
And fit their Proselytes for Vice;

(The only Comfort they propose,
To have Companions in their Woes.)
Grant this the Case, yet sure 'tis hard,
That Virtue, stil'd its own Reward,
And by all Sages understood
To be the chief of human Good,
Should acting, die, nor leave behind
Some lasting Pleasure in the Mind,
Which by Remembrance will assuage,
Grief, Sickness, Poverty, and Age;
And strongly shoot a radiant Dart,
To shine through Life's declining Part.

    Say, *Stella*, feel you no Content,
Reflecting on a Life well spent?
Your skilful Hand employ'd to save
Despairing Wretches from the Grave;
And then supporting with your Store,
Those whom you dragg'd from Death before:
(So Providence on Mortals waits,
Preserving what it first creates)
Your gen'rous Boldness to defend
An innocent and absent Friend;
That Courage which can make you just,
To Merit humbled in the Dust:
The Detestation you express
For Vice in all its glitt'ring Dress:
That Patience under tort'ring Pain,
Where stubborn Stoicks would complain.

    Shall these like empty Shadows pass,
Or Forms reflected from a Glass?
Or mere Chimæra's in the Mind,
That fly and leave no Marks behind?
Does not the Body thrive and grow
By Food of twenty Years ago?
And, had it not been still supply'd,
It must a thousand Times have dy'd.
Then, who with Reason can maintain,
That no Effects of Food remain?

And, is not Virtue in Mankind
The Nutriment that feeds the Mind?
Upheld by each good Action past,
And still continued by the last:
Then, who with Reason can pretend,
That all Effects of Virtue end?

Believe me *Stella*, when you show
That true Contempt for Things below,
Nor prize your Life for other Ends
Than merely to oblige your Friends;
Your former Actions claim their Part,
And join to fortify your Heart.
For Virtue in her daily Race,
Like *Janus*, bears a double Face;
Looks back with Joy where she has gone,
And therefore goes with Courage on.
She at your sickly Couch will wait,
And guide you to a better State.

O then, whatever Heav'n intends,
Take Pity on your pitying Friends;
Nor let your Ills affect your Mind,
To fancy they can be unkind.
Me, surely me, you ought to spare,
Who gladly would your Suff'rings share;
Or give my Scrap of Life to you,
And think it far beneath your Due;
You, to whose Care so oft I owe,
That I'm alive to tell you so.

JONATHAN SWIFT (1726)

This affectionate poem was written only two years before Esther Johnson's (Stella's) death, after a friendship of more than twenty years' standing. Neither of them ever married.

Song

To fix her, 'twere a task as vain
To combat April drops of rain
To sow in Afric's barren soil
Or tempests hold within a toil.

I know it, friend, she's light as air,
False as the fowler's artful snare;
Inconstant as the passing wind,
As winter's dreary frost unkind.

She's such a miser, too, for love
Its joys she'll neither share, nor prove,
Though hundreds of gallants await
From her victorious eyes their fate.

Blushing at such inglorious reign,
I sometimes strive to break her chain;
My reason summon to my aid,
Resolv'd no more to be betray'd.

Ah, friend, 'tis but a short-liv'd trance,
Dispell'd by one entrancing glance;
She needs but look and I confess
Those looks completely curse, or bless.

So soft, so elegant, so fair,
Sure something more than human's there;
I must submit, for strife is vain.
Twas destiny that forg'd the chain.

TOBIAS SMOLLETT (*c.*1745)

The Lover: A Ballad

At length, by so much importunity pressed,
Take, (Molly), at once, the inside of my breast;[1]
This stupid indifference so often you blame
Is not owing to nature, to fear, or to shame;
I am not as cold as a Virgin in lead,
Nor is Sunday's sermon so strong in my head;
I know but too well how time flies along,
That we live but few years and yet fewer are young.

But I hate to be cheated, and never will buy
Long years of repentance for moments of joy.
Oh was there a man (but where shall I find
Good sense and good nature so equally joined?)
Would value his pleasure, contribute to mine,
Not meanly would boast, nor lewdly design,
Not over severe, yet not stupidly vain,
For I would have the power though not give the pain;

No pedant yet learnèd, not rakehelly gay
Or laughing because he has nothing to say,
To all my whole sex obliging and free,
Yet never be fond of any but me;
In public preserve the decorums are just,
And show in his eyes he is true to his trust,
Then rarely approach, and respectfully bow,
Yet not fulsomely pert, nor yet foppishly low.

But when the long hours of public are past
And we meet with champagne and a chicken at last,
May every fond pleasure that hour endear,
Be banished afar both discretion and fear,
Forgetting or scorning the airs of the crowd
He may cease to be formal, and I to be proud,
Till lost in the joy we confess that we live,
And he may be rude, and yet I may forgive.

[1] i.e. learn what I feel

And that my delight may be solidly fixed,
Let the friend and the lover be handsomely mixed,
In whose tender bosom my soul might confide,
Whose kindness can sooth me, whose counsel could guide.
From such a dear lover as here I describe
No danger should fright me, no millions should bribe;
But till this astonishing creature I know,
As I long have lived chaste, I will keep myself so.

I never will share with the wanton coquette,
Or be caught by a vain affectation of wit.
The toasters and songsters may try all their art
But never shall enter the pass of my heart.
I loathe the lewd rake, the dressed fopling despise;
Before such pursuers the nice virgin flies;
And as Ovid has sweetly in parables told
We harden like trees, and like rivers are cold.

LADY MARY WORTLEY MONTAGU
(published 1747, written much earlier)

from The Duenna

SONG

Give Isaac the nymph who no beauty can boast,
But health and good humour to make her his toast;
If straight, I don't mind whether slender or fat,
And six feet or four – we'll ne'er quarrel for that.

Whate'er her complexion, I vow I don't care;
If brown, it is lasting – more pleasing, if fair:
And though in her face I no dimples should see,
Let her smile – and each dell is a dimple to me.

Let her locks be the reddest that ever were seen,
And her eyes may be e'en any colour but green;
For in eyes, though so various in lustre and hue,
I swear I've no choice – only let her have two.

'Tis true I'd dispense with a throne on her back,
And white teeth, I own, are genteeler than black;
A little round chin too's a beauty, I've heard;
But I only desire she mayn't have a beard.

SONG

Oh, had my love ne'er smiled on me,
    I ne'er had known such anguish;
But think how false, how cruel she,
    To bid me cease to languish;

To bid me hope her hand to gain,
    Breathe on a flame half perish'd;
And then with cold and fixed disdain,
    To kill the hope she cherish'd.

Not worse his fate, who on a wreck,
    That drove as winds did blow it,
Silent had left the shatter'd deck,
    To find a grave below it.
Then land was cried – no more resign'd,
    He glow'd with joy to hear it;
Not worse his fate, his woe, to find
    The wreck must sink ere near it!

RICHARD BRINSLEY SHERIDAN (1775)

On Cessnock Banks

On Cessnock banks a lassie dwells;
    Could I describe her shape and mien;
Our lasses a' she far excels,
    An' she has twa sparkling rogueish een.

She's sweeter than the morning dawn
    When rising Phœbus first is seen,
And dew-drops twinkle o'er the lawn;
    An' she has twa sparkling rogueish een.

She's stately like yon youthful ash
    That grows the cowslip braes between,
And drinks the stream with vigour fresh;
    An' she has twa sparkling rogueish een.

She's spotless like the flow'ring thorn
    With flow'rs so white and leaves so green
When purest in the dewy morn;
    An' she has twa sparkling rogueish een.

Her looks are like the vernal May,
    When ev'ning Phœbus shines serene,
While birds rejoice on every spray;
    An' she has twa sparkling rogueish een.

Her hair is like the curling mist
    That climbs the mountain-sides at een,
When flow'r-reviving rains are past;
    An' she has twa sparkling rogueish een.

Her forehead's like the show'ry bow,
    When gleaming sunbeams intervene
And gild the distant mountain's brow;
    An' she has twa sparkling rogueish een.

Her cheeks are like yon crimson gem,
    The pride of all the flowery scene,
Just opening on its thorny stem;
    An' she has twa sparkling rogueish een.

Her bosom's like the nightly snow
    When pale the morning rises keen,
While hid the murmuring streamlets flow;
    An' she has twa sparkling rogueish een.

Her lips are like yon cherries ripe,
    That sunny walls from Boreas screen;
They tempt the taste and charm the Sight;
    An' she has twa sparkling rogueish een.

Her teeth are like a flock of sheep,
    With fleeces newly washen clean,
That slowly mount the rising steep;
    An' she has twa sparkling rogueish een.

Her breath is like the fragrant breeze
   That gently stirs the blossom'd bean,
When Phœbus sinks behind the seas;
   An' she has twa sparkling rogueish een.

Her voice is like the ev'ning thrush
   That sings on Cessnock banks unseen,
While his mate sits nestling in the bush;
   An' she has twa sparkling rogueish een.

But it's not her air, her form, her face,
   Tho' matching beauty's fabled queen;
'Tis the mind that shines in ev'ry grace,
   An' chiefly in her rogueish een.

ROBERT BURNS (1780)

John Anderson My Jo

John Anderson my jo, John,
   When we were first acquent,
Your locks were like the raven,
   Your bonnie brow was brent;
But now your brow is beld, John,
   Your locks are like the snow;
But blessings on your frosty pow,
   John Anderson, my jo.

John Anderson my jo, John,
   We clamb the hill thegither;
And mony a canty day, John,
   We've had wi' ane anither:
Now we maun totter down, John,
   And hand in hand we'll go,
And sleep thegither at the foot,
   John Anderson, my jo.

ROBERT BURNS (1788)

My Mary

The twentieth year is wellnigh past
Since first our sky was overcast;
Ah, would that this might be the last!
                 My Mary!

Thy spirits have a fainter flow,
I see thee daily weaker grow;
'Twas my distress that brought thee low,
                 My Mary!

Thy needles, once a shining store,
For my sake restless heretofore,
Now rust disused, and shine no more;
                 My Mary!

For though thou gladly wouldst fulfil
The same kind office for me still,
Thy sight now seconds not thy will,
                 My Mary!

But well thou play'dst the housewife's part,
And all thy threads with magic art
Have wound themselves about this heart,
                 My Mary!

Thy indistinct expressions seem
Like language uttered in a dream;
Yet me they charm, whate'er the theme,
                 My Mary!

Thy silver locks, once auburn bright,
Are still more lovely in my sight
Than golden beams of orient light,
                 My Mary!

For I could view nor them nor thee,
What sight worth seeing could I see?
The sun would rise in vain for me,
                 My Mary!

Partakers of thy sad decline,
Thy hands their little force resign;
Yet, gently pressed, press gently mine,
          My Mary!

Such feebleness of limbs thou prov'st
That now at every step thou mov'st
Upheld by two; yet still thou lov'st,
          My Mary!

And still to love, though pressed with ill,
In wintry age to feel no chill,
With me is to be lovely still,
          My Mary!

But ah! by constant heed I know
How oft the sadness that I show
Transforms thy smiles to looks of woe,
          My Mary!

And should my future lot be cast
With much resemblance of the past,
Thy worn-out heart will break at last –
          My Mary!

           WILLIAM COWPER (1793)

Lines, Written on Seeing My Husband's Picture, Painted when He Was Young

Those are the features, those the smiles
    That first engaged my virgin heart:
I feel the pencil'd image true,
    I feel the mimic pow'r of art.

For ever on my soul engrav'd
    His glowing cheek, his manly mien;
I need not thee, thou painted shade,
    To tell me what my love has been.

O dearer now, though bent with age,
    Than in the pride of blooming youth!
I knew not then his constant heart,
    I knew not then his matchless truth.

Full many a year, at random toss'd,
    The sport of many an adverse gale,
Together, hand in hand, we've strayed
    O'er dreary hill, and lonely vale.

Hope only flattered to betray,
    Her keenest shafts misfortune shot;
In spite of prudence, spite of care,
    Dependence was our bitter lot.

Ill can'st thou bear the sneer of wealth,
    Averted looks, and rustic scorn;
For thou wert born to better hopes,
    And brighter rose thy vernal morn.

Thy evening hours to want expos'd,
    I cannot, cannot bear to see:
Were but thy honest heart at ease,
    I care not what becomes of me.

But tho', my Love, the winds of woe
    Beat cold upon thy silver hairs,
Thy Anna's bosom still is warm;
    Affection still shall soothe thy cares.

And Conscience, with unclouded ray,
    The cottage of our age will chear;
Friendship will lift our humble latch,
    And Pity pour her healing tear.

ANNA SAWYER (1796)

10
WARFARE & WARRIORS

from *Last Instruction to a Painter*

DUTCH WARSHIPS IN ENGLISH RIVERS

Marvell mocks the incompetent English commanders in the
Anglo-Dutch War of 1665–7.

Ruyter the while, that had our ocean curbed,
Sailed now among our rivers undisturbed,
Surveyed their crystal streams and banks so green
And beauties ere this never naked seen.
Through the vain sedge, the bashful nymphs he eyed:
Bosoms, and all which from themselves they hide.
The sun much brighter, and the skies more clear,
He finds the air and all things sweeter here.
The sudden change, and such a tempting sight
Swells his old veins with fresh blood, fresh delight.
Like am'rous victors he begins to shave,
And his new face looks in the English wave.
His sporting navy all about him swim
And witness their complacence in their trim.
Their streaming silks play through the weather fair
And with inveigling colours court the air,
While the red flags breathe on their topmasts high
Terror and war, but want an enemy.
Among the shrouds the seamen sit and sing,
And wanton boys on every rope do cling.
Old Neptune springs the tides and water lent
(The gods themselves do help the provident),
And where the deep keel on the shallow cleaves,
With trident's lever, and great shoulder heaves.
Aeolus their sails inspires with eastern wind,
Puffs them along, and breathes upon them kind.
With pearly shell the Tritons all the while
Sound the sea-march and guide to Sheppey Isle.
So have I seen in April's bud arise
A fleet of clouds, sailing along the skies;
The liquid region with their squadrons filled,
Their airy sterns the sun behind does gild;

And gentle gales them steer, and heaven drives,
When, all on sudden, their calm bosom rives
With thunder and lightning from each armèd cloud;
Shepherds themselves in vain in bushes shroud.
Such up the stream the Belgic navy glides
And at Sheerness unloads its stormy sides.
   Spragge there, though practised in the sea command,
With panting heart lay like a fish on land
And quickly judged the fort was not tenáble –
Which, if a house, yet were not tenantáble –
No man can sit there safe: the cannon pours
Thorough the walls untight and bullet showers,
The neighbourhood ill, and an unwholesome seat,
So at the first salute resolves retreat,
And swore that he would never more dwell there
Until the city put it in repair.
So he in front, his garrison in rear,
March straight to Chatham to increase the fear.
   There our sick ships unrigged in summer lay
Like moulting fowl, a weak and easy prey,
For whose strong bulk earth scarce could timber find,
The ocean water, or the heavens wind –
Those oaken giants of the ancient race,
That ruled all seas and did our Channel grace.
The conscious stag so, once the forest's dread,
Flies to the wood and hides his armless head.
Ruyter forthwith a squadron does untack;
They sail securely through the river's track.
An English pilot too (O shame, O sin!)
Cheated of pay, was he that showed them in.
Our wretched ships within their fate attend,
And all our hopes now on frail chain depend:
(Engine so slight to guard us from the sea,
It fitter seemed to captivate a flea).
A skipper rude shocks it without respect,
Filling his sails more force to re-collect.
Th' English from shore the iron deaf invoke
For its last aid: 'Hold chain, or we are broke.'
But with her sailing, weight, the Holland keel,
Snapping, the brittle links, does thorough reel,

And to the rest the opened passage show;
Monck from the bank the dismal sight does view.
Our feathered gallants, which came down that day
To be spectators safe of the new play,
Leave him alone when first they hear the gun
(Cornb'ry the fleetest) and to London run.
Or seamen, whom no danger's shape could fright,
Unpaid, refuse to mount our ships for spite,
Or to their fellows swim on board the Dutch,
Which show the tempting metal in their clutch.
Oft had he sent of Duncombe and of *Legge*
Cannon and powder, but in vain, to beg;
And Upnor Castle's ill-deserted wall,
Now needful, does for ammunition call.
He finds, wheres'e'er he succor might expect,
Confusion, folly, treach'ry, fear, neglect.
But when the *Royal Charles* (what rage, what grief)
He saw seized, and could give her no relief!
That sacred keel which had, as he, restored
His exiled sovereign on its happy board,
And thence the British Admiral became,
Crowned, for that merit, with their master's name;
That pleasure-boat of war, in whose dear side
Secure so oft he had this foe defied,
Now a cheap spoil, and the mean victor's slave,
Taught the Dutch colours from its top to wave;
Of former glories the reproachful thought,
With present shame compared, his mind distraught.
Such from Euphrates' bank, a tigress fell
After the robber for her whelps doth yell;
But sees enraged the river flow between,
Frustrate revenge and love, by loss more keen,
At her own breast her useless claws does arm:
She tears herself; since him she cannot harm.
  The guards, placed for the chain's and fleet's defence,
Long since were fled on many a feigned pretence.
Daniel had there adventured, man of might,
Sweet Painter, draw his picture while I write.
Paint him of person tall, and big of bone,
Large limbs like ox, not to be killed but shown.

Scarce can burnt ivory feign an hair so black,
Or face so red, thine ochre and thy lac.
Mix a vain terror in his martial look,
And all those lines by which men are mistook;
But when, by shame constrained to go on board,
He heard how the wild cannon nearer roared,
And saw himself confined like sheep in pen,
Daniel then thought he was in lion's den.
And when the frightful fireships he saw,
Pregnant with sulphur, to him nearer draw,
Captain, lieutenant, ensign, all make haste
Ere in the fiery furnace they be cast –
Three children tall, unsinged, away they row,
Like Shadrack, Meschack, and Abednego.

   Not so brave *Douglas*, on whose lovely chin
The early down but newly did begin,
And modest beauty yet his sex did veil,
While envious virgins hope he is a male.
His yellow locks curl back themselves to seek,
Nor other courtship knew but to his cheek.
Oft, as he in chill Esk or Seine by night
Hardened and cooled his limbs, so soft, so white,
Among the reeds, to be espied by him,
The nymphs would rustle; he would forward swim.
They sighed and said, 'Fond boy, why so untame
That fliest love's fires, reserved for other flame?'
Fixed on his ship, he faced that horrid day
And wondered much at those that run away.
Nor other fear himself could comprehend
Then, lest heaven fall ere thither he ascend,
But entertains the while his time too short
With birding at the Dutch, as if in sport,
Or waves his sword, and could he them conjúre
Within its circle, knows himself secure.
The fatal bark him boards with grappling fire,
And safely through its port the Dutch retire.
That precious life he yet disdains to save
Or with known art to try the gentle wave.
Much him the honours of his ancient race
Inspire, nor would he his own deeds deface,

And secret joy in his calm soul does rise
That Monck looks on to see how Douglas dies.
Like a glad lover, the fierce flames he meets,
And tries his first embraces in their sheets.
His shape exact, which the bright flames enfold,
Like the sun's statue stands of burnished gold.
Round the transparent fire about him glows,
As the clear amber on the bee does close,
And, as on angels' heads their glories shine,
His burning locks adorn his face divine.
But when in his immortal mind he felt
His altering form and soldered limbs to melt,
Down on the deck he laid himself and died,
With his dear sword reposing by his side,
And on the flaming plank, so rests his head
As one that's warmed himself and gone to bed.
His ship burns down, and with his relics sinks,
And the sad stream beneath his ashes drinks.
Fortunate boy, if either pencil's fame,
Or if my verse can propagate thy name,
When Oeta and Alcides are forgot,
Our English youth shall sing the valiant Scot.

ANDREW MARVELL (1667)

from *The Campaign*

BLENHEIM

Behold in awful march and dread array
The long-extended squadrons shape their way!
Death, in approaching terrible, imparts
An anxious horror to the bravest hearts;
Yet do their beating breasts demand the strife,
And thirst of glory quells the love of life.
No vulgar fears can British minds control;
Heat of revenge, and noble pride of soul,
O'erlook the foe, advantaged by his post,
Lessen his numbers, and contract his host;

Though fens and floods possest the middle space,
That unprovoked they would have feared to pass;
Nor fens nor floods can stop Britannia's bands,
When her proud foe ranged on her borders stands.
   But O, my Muse, what numbers wilt thou find
To sing the furious troops in battle join'd!
Methinks I hear the drums' tumultuous sound
The victors' shouts and dying groans confound,
The dreadful burst of cannon rend the skies,
And all the thunder of the battle rise.
'Twas then great Marlborough's mighty soul was proved
That, in the shock of charging hosts unmoved,
Amidst confusion, horror and despair,
Examined all the dreadful scenes of war;
In peaceful thought the field of death survey'd,
To fainting squadrons sent the timely aid,
Inspired repulsed battalions to engage,
And taught the doubtful battle where to rage.
So when an angel, by divine command,
With rising tempests shakes a guilty land,
Such as of late o'er pale Britannia past,
Calm and serene he drives the furious blast;
And pleased th' Almighty's orders to perform,
Rides in the whirlwind, and directs the storm.
   But see the haughty household troops advance!
The dread of Europe and the pride of France.
The war's whole art each private soldier knows,
And with a general's love of conquest glows;
Proudly he marches on, and void of fear,
Laughs at the shaking of the British spear:
Vain insolence! with native freedom brave,
The meanest Briton scorns the highest slave;
Contempt and fury fire their souls by turns,
Each nation's glory in each warrior burns;
Each fights, as in his arm th'important day
And all the fate of his great monarch lay:
A thousand glorious actions, that might claim
Triumphant laurels, and immortal fame,
Confused in crowds of glorious actions lie,
And troops of heroes undistinguish'd die.

O Dormer, how can I behold thy fate!
And not the wonders of thy youth relate!
How can I see the gay, the brave, the young,
Fall in the clouds of war, and lie unsung!
In joys of conquest he resigns his breath,
And, fill'd with England's glory, smiles in death.
    The rout begins, the Gallic squadrons run,
Compell'd in crowds to meet the fate they shun;
Thousands of fiery steeds with wounds transfix'd,
Floating in gore, with their dead masters mixt,
'Midst heaps of spears and standards driven round,
Lie in the Danube's bloody whirlpools drown'd.
Troops of bold youths, born on the distant Soane,
Or sounding borders of the rapid Rhone,
Or where the Seine her flowery banks divides,
Or where the Loire through winding vineyards glides,
In heaps the rolling billows sweep away,
And into Scythian seas their bloated corps convey.
From Blenheim's towers the Gaul with wild affright,
Beholds the various havoc of the fight;
His waving banners, that so oft had stood
Planted in fields of death and streams of blood,
So wont the guarded enemy to reach,
And rise triumphant in the fatal breach,
Or pierce the broken foe's remotest lines,
The hardy veteran with tears resigns.
    Unfortunate Tallard! Oh, who can name
The pangs of rage, of sorrow, and of shame,
That with mixt tumult in thy bosom swell'd,
When first thou saw thy bravest troops repell'd;
Thine only son pierced with a deadly wound,
Choked in his blood? and gasping on the ground;
Thyself in bondage by the victor kept!
The chief, the father, and the captive wept.
An English Muse is touch'd with generous woe,
And in th'unhappy man forgets the foe.

JOSEPH ADDISON (1705)

Ode, Written in the Beginning
of the Year 1746

How sleep the brave, who sink to rest
By all their country's wishes blest!
When Spring, with dewy fingers cold,
Returns to deck their hallowed mould,
She there shall dress a sweeter sod
Than Fancy's feet have ever trod.

By fairy hands their knell is rung,
By forms unseen their dirge is sung;
There Honour comes, a pilgrim grey,
To bless the turf that wraps their clay,
And freedom shall awhile repair
To dwell a weeping hermit there!

WILLIAM COLLINS (1746)

The Tears of Scotland

Mourn, hapless Caledonia, mourn
Thy banish'd peace, thy laurels torn!
Thy sons, for valour long renown'd
Lie slaughtered on their native ground;
Thy hospitable roofs no more
Invite the stranger to the door:
In smoky ruins sunk they lie,
The monuments of cruelty.

The wretched owner sees afar
His all become the prey of war,
Bethinks him of his babes and wife,
Then smites his breast and curses life.
Thy swains are famish'd on the rocks

Where once they fed their wanton flocks:
Thy ravish'd virgins shriek in vain;
Thy infants perish on the plain.

What boots it then, in every clime,
Through the wide-spreading waste of time,
Thy martial glory, crown'd with praise,
Still shone with undiminished blaze?
Thy towering spirit now is broke,
Thy neck is bended to the yoke:
What foreign arms could never quell
By civil rage and rancour fell.

The rural pipe and merry lay
No more shall cheer the happy day;
No social scenes of gay delight
Beguile the dreary winter night;
No strains but those of sorrow flow,
And nought be heard but sounds of woe,
While the pale phantoms of the slain
Glide nightly o'er the silent plain.

O baneful cause, O fatal morn,
Accursed to ages yet unborn!
The sons against the father stood,
The parent shed his children's blood.
Yet, when the rage of battle ceased
The victor's soul was not appeased;
The naked and folorn must feel
Devouring flames and murdering steel!

The pious mother, doom'd to death,
Forsaken, wanders o'er the heath;
The bleak air whistles round her head,
Her helpless orphans cry for bread;
Bereft of shelter, food and friend,
She views the shades of night descend;
And, stretch'd beneath the inclement skies,
Weeps o'er her tender babes, and dies.

While the warm blood bedews my veins,
And unimpair'd remembrance reigns,
Resentment of my country's fate
Within my filial breast shall beat;
And, spite of her insulting foe,
My sympathising verse shall flow.
Mourn, hapless Caledonia, mourn
Thy banish'd peace, thy laurels torn!

TOBIAS SMOLLETT (1747)

Loss of the Royal George

Toll for the brave –
The brave! that are no more:
   All sunk beneath the wave,
Fast by their native shore.

   Eight hundred of the brave,
Whose courage well was tried,
   Had made the vessel heel
And laid her on her side;

   A land-breeze shook the shrouds,
And she was overset;
   Down went the *Royal George*
With all her crew complete.

Toll for the brave –
Brave Kempenfelt is gone,
   His last sea-fight is fought,
His work of glory done.

   It was not in the battle,
No tempest gave the shock,
   She sprang no fatal leak,
She ran upon no rock;

   His sword was in the sheath,
His fingers held the pen,
   When Kempenfelt went down
With twice four hundred men.

Weigh the vessel up,
Once dreaded by our foes,
And mingle with your cup
The tears that England owes;
Her timbers yet are sound,
And she may float again,
Full charged with England's thunder,
And plough the distant main;
But Kempenfelt is gone,
His victories are o'er;
And he and his eight hundred
Must plough the wave no more.

WILLIAM COWPER (*c*.1786)

The Battle of Blenheim

1

It was a summer evening,
Old Kaspar's work was done,
And he before his cottage door
Was sitting in the sun,
And by him sported on the green
His little grandchild Wilhelmine.

2

She saw her brother Peterkin
Roll something large and round,
Which he beside the rivulet
In playing there had found;
He came to ask what he had found,
That was so large, and smooth, and round.

3

Old Kaspar took it from the boy,
Who stood expectant by;
And then the old man shook his head
And with a natural sigh,
' 'Tis some poor fellow's skull,' said he,
'Who fell in the great victory.

4

'I find them in the garden,
    For there's many here about;
And often when I go to plough,
    The ploughshare turns them out!
For many thousand men,' said he,
'Were slain in that great victory.'

5

'Now tell us what 't was all about,'
    Young Peterkin, he cries;
And little Wilhelmine looks up
    With wonder-waiting eyes;
'Now tell us all about the war,
And what they fought each other for.'

6

'It was the English,' Kaspar cried,
    'Who put the French to rout;
But what they fought each other for,
    I could not well make out;
But everybody said,' quoth he,
'That 't was a famous victory.

7

'My father lived at Blenheim then,
    Yon little stream hard by;
They burnt his dwelling to the ground,
    And he was forced to fly;
So with his wife and child he fled,
Nor had he where to rest his head.

8

'With fire and sword the country round
    Was wasted far and wide,
And many a childing mother then,
    And new-born baby died;
But things like that, you know, must be
At every famous victory.

9

'They say it was a shocking sight
    After the field was won;
For many thousand bodies here
    Lay rotting in the sun;
But things like that, you know, must be
After a famous victory.

10

'Great praise the Duke of Marlbro' won,
    And our good Prince Eugene.'
'Why 't was a very wicked thing!'
    Said little Wilhelmine.
'Nay . . . nay . . . my little girl,' quoth he,
'It was a famous victory.

11

'And everybody praised the Duke
    Who this great fight did win.'
'But what good came of it at last?'
    Quoth little Peterkin.
'Why that I cannot tell,' said he,
'But 't was a famous victory.'

ROBERT SOUTHEY (1798)

Fire, Famine and Slaughter

A WAR ECLOGUE

The scene is a desolated Tract in La Vendee. FAMINE *is discovered lying on the ground; to her enter* FIRE *and* SLAUGHTER.

FAMINE	Sisters! sisters! who sent you here?
SLAUGHTER	(to FIRE) I will whisper it in her ear.
FIRE	No! no! no!
	Spirits hear what spirits tell;
	'Twill make a holiday in Hell.
	No! no! no!
	Myself; I named him once below,
	And all the souls that damned be
	Leaped up at once in anarchy,
	Clapped their hands and danced for glee.
	They no longer heeded me;
	But laughed to hear Hell's burning rafters
	Unwittingly re-echo laughters!
	No! no! no!
	Spirits hear what spirits tell;
	'Twill make a holiday in Hell!
FAMINE	Whisper it, sister! so and so
	In a dark hint, soft and slow.
SLAUGHTER	Letters four do form his name –
	And who sent you?
BOTH	The same! the same!
SLAUGHTER	He came by stealth and unlocked my den,
	And I have drunk the blood since then
	Of thrice three hundred thousand men.
BOTH	Who bade you do't?
SLAUGHTER	The same! the same!
	Letters four do form his name.
	He let me loose, and cried Halloo!
	To him alone the praise is due.
FAMINE	Thanks, sister, thanks! the men have bled,
	Their wives and children faint for bread,
	I stood in a swampy field of battle;

With bones and skulls I made a rattle,
To frighten the wolf and the carrion-crow
And the homeless dog, but they would not go.
So off I flew: for how could I bear
To see them gorge their dainty fare?
I heard a groan and a peevish squall,
And through the chink of a cottage wall –
Can you guess what I saw there?

BOTH Whisper it, sister, in our ear.

FAMINE A baby beat its dying mother:
    I had starved the one and was starving the other!

BOTH Who bade you do't?

FAMINE   The same! the same!
Letters four do form his name.
He let me loose, and cried, Halloo!
To him alone the praise is due.

FIRE Sisters! I from Ireland came!
Hedge and cornfields all on flame,
I triumphed o'er the setting sun!
And all the while the work was done,
On as I strode with my huge strides,
I flung back my head and held my sides,
It was so rare a piece of fun
To see the sweltered cattle run
With uncouth gallop through the night,
Scared by the red and noisy light!
By the light of his own blazing cot
Was many a naked Rebel shot;
The house-stream met the flame and hissed,
While crash! fell in the roof, I wist,
On some of those old bed-ridden nurses,
That deal in discontent and curses.

BOTH Who bade you do 't?

FIRE   The same! the same!
Letters four do form his name.
He let me loose and cried Halloo!
To him alone the praise is due.

ALL He let us loose, and cried Halloo!
How shall we yield him honour due?

FAMINE Wisdom comes with lack of food.

I'll gnaw, I'll gnaw the multitude,
Till the cup of rage o'erbrim:
They shall seize him and his brood –

SLAUGHTER They shall tear him limb from limb!

FIRE O thankless beldames and untrue!
And is this all that you can do
For him who did so much for you?
Ninety months he, by my troth!
Hath richly catered for you both;
And in an hour would you repay
An eight years' work? – Away! away!
I alone am faithful, I
Cling to him everlastingly.

SAMUEL TAYLOR COLERIDGE
(published 1798)

Coleridge later apologised for this vividly dramatised attack on Pitt the Younger, the great war-time prime minister, but it clearly reflects his youthful feelings about Britain's activities in France and Ireland at the end of the century. 'Halloo' was the cry used by huntsmen urging the hunt on towards the prey, and it is, of course, in Hell that Fire will 'cling to him everlastingly'.

11
THE LIGHTER SIDE
Part Two

An Elegy on Mrs Mary Blaize

Good people all, with one accord
    Lament for Madam BLAIZE,
Who never wanted a good word –
    From those who spoke her praise.

The needy seldom passed her door,
    And always found her kind;
She freely lent to all the poor,
    Who left a pledge behind.

She strove the neighbourhood to please,
    With manners wondrous winning,
And never followed wicked ways,
    Unless when she was sinning.

At church, in silks and satins new,
    With hoop of monstrous size,
She never slumbered in her pew,
    But when she shut her eyes.

Her love was sought, I do aver,
    By twenty beaux and more;
The king himself has followed her,
    When she has walked before.

But now her wealth and finery fled,
    Her hangers-on cut short all;
The doctors found, when she was dead,
    Her last disorder mortal.

Let us lament, in sorrow sore,
    For Kent-Street well may say,
That had she lived a twelvemonth more,
    She had not died today.

OLIVER GOLDSMITH (1759)

The Mouse's Petition to
Doctor Priestley Found in the Trap
where He Had Been Confined All Night

Oh! hear a pensive captive's prayer,
For liberty that sighs;
And never let thine heart be shut
Against the prisoner's cries.

For here forlorn and sad I sit,
Within the wiry grate;
And tremble at th' approaching morn,
Which brings impending fate.

If e'er thy breast with freedom glowed,
And spurned a tyrant's chain,
Let not thy strong oppressive force
A free-born mouse detain.

Oh! do not stain with guiltless blood
Thy hospitable hearth;
Nor triumph that thy wiles betrayed
A prize so little worth.

The scattered gleanings of a feast
My scanty meals supply;
But if thine unrelenting heart
That slender boon deny,

The cheerful light, the vital air,
Are blessings widely given;
Let nature's commoners enjoy
The common gifts of heaven.

The well-taught philosophic mind
To all compassion gives;
Casts round the world an equal eye,
And feels for all that lives.

If mind, as ancient sages taught,
A never-dying flame,
Still shifts through matter's varying forms,
In every form the same,

Beware, lest in the worm you crush
A brother's soul you find;
And tremble lest thy luckless hand
Dislodge a kindred mind.

Or, if this transient gleam of day
Be *all* of life we share,
Let pity plead within thy breast
That little *all* to spare.

So may thy hospitable board
With health and peace be crowned;
And every charm of heartfelt ease
Beneath thy roof be found.

So, when unseen destruction lurks,
Which mice like men may share,
May some kind angel clear thy path,
And break the hidden snare.

ANNA LAETITIA BARBAULD (1773)

Hermit Hoar

Hermit hoar, in solemn cell,
   Wearing out life's evening gray;
Smite thy bosom, sage, and tell,
   Where is bliss? and which the way?

Thus I spoke; and speaking sigh'd;
   Scarce repress'd the starting tear;
When the smiling sage reply'd –
   Come, my lad, and drink some beer.

SAMUEL JOHNSON (1779)

One-and-Twenty

Long-expected One-and-twenty,
   Ling'ring year, at length is flown:
Pride and pleasure, pomp and plenty,
   Great [Sir John], are now your own.

Loosen'd from the minor's tether,
   Free to mortgage or to sell,
Wild as wind and light as feather,
   Bid the sons of thrift farewell.

Call the Betsies, Kates, and Jennies,
   All the names that banish care;
Lavish of your grandsire's guineas,
   Show the spirit of an heir.

All that prey on vice and folly
   Joy to see their quarry fly:
There the gamester, light and jolly,
   There the lender, grave and sly.

Wealth, my lad, was made to wander,
   Let it wander as it will;
Call the jockey, call the pander,
   Bid them come and take their fill.

When the bonny blade carouses,
   Pockets full, and spirits high –
What are acres? What are houses?
   Only dirt, or wet or dry.

Should the guardian friend or mother
   Tell the woes of wilful waste,
Scorn their counsel, scorn their pother –
   You can hang or drown at last!

SAMUEL JOHNSON (1780)

Sir John Lade was a nephew of a member of Johnson's circle, Henry Thrale. Johnson's prediction that he would ruin himself, now he had come of age and was in control of his estate, proved accurate.

Dr Johnson's Ghost

ON BOSWELL'S *JOURNAL OF A TOUR OF THE HEBRIDES*

'Twas at the solemn hour of night,
   When men and spirits meet,
That Johnson, huge majestic sprite,
   Repaired to Boswell's feet.

His face was like the full-orbed moon
   Wrapped in a threatening cloud,
That bodes the tempest bursting soon,
   And winds that bluster loud.

Terrific was his angry look,
   His pendent eyebrows frowned;
Thrice in his hand he waved a book,
   Then dashed it on the ground.

'Behold,' he cried, 'perfidious man,
   This object of my rage:
Bethink thee of the sordid plan
   That formed this venal page.

'Was it to make this base record
   That you my friendship sought;
Thus to retain each vagrant word,
   Each undigested thought?

'Dar'st thou pretend that, meaning praise,
   Thou seek'st to raise my name,
When all thy babbling pen betrays
   But gives me churlish fame?

'Do readers in these annals trace
   The man that's wise and good?
No! – rather one of savage race,
   Illiberal, fierce and rude.

'A traveller, whose discontent
   No kindness can appease;
Who finds for spleen perpetual vent
   In all he hears and sees.

'One whose ingratitude displays
   The most ungracious guest;
Who hospitality repays
   With bitter, biting jest.

'Ah! would, as o'er the hills we sped,
   And climbed the sterile rocks,
Some vengeful stone had struck thee dead,
   Or steeple, spared by Knox!

'Thy adulation now I see,
   And all its schemes unfold:
Thy avarice, Boswell, cherished me
   To turn me into gold.

'So keepers guard the beasts they show,
   And for their wants provide;
Attend their steps where'er they go,
   And travel by their side.

'O! were it not that, deep and low,
   Beyond thy reach I'm laid,
Rapacious Boswell had ere now
   Johnson a mummy made.'

He ceased, and stalked from Boswell's sight
   With fierce indignant mien,
Scornful as Ajax' sullen sprite
   By sage Ulysses seen.

Dead paleness Boswell's cheek o'erspread,
   His limbs with horror shook;
With trembling haste he left his bed,
   And burnt his fatal book.

And thrice he called on Johnson's name.
    Forgiveness to implore!
Then thrice repeated – 'injured fame!'
    And word – wrote never more.

             ELIZABETH MOODY (1786)

The Diverting History of John Gilpin

SHOWING HOW HE WENT FARTHER THAN HE INTENDED, AND CAME SAFE HOME AGAIN

John Gilpin was a citizen
    Of credit and renown,
A train-band captain eke was he
    Of famous London town.

John Gilpin's spouse said to her dear –
    Though wedded we have been
These twice ten tedious years, yet we
    No holiday have seen.

To-morrow is our wedding-day,
    And we will then repair
Unto the Bell at Edmonton
    All in a chaise and pair.

My sister, and my sister's child,
    Myself, and children three,
Will fill the chaise; so you must ride
    On horseback after we.

He soon replied – I do admire
    Of womankind but one,
And you are she, my dearest dear,
    Therefore it shall be done.

I am a linen-draper bold,
    As all the world doth know,
And my good friend the calender
    Will lend his horse to go.

Quoth Mrs Gilpin – That's well said;
    And, for that wine is dear,
We will be furnish'd with our own,
    Which is both bright and clear.

John Gilpin kiss'd his loving wife;
    O'erjoy'd was he to find
That, though on pleasure she was bent,
    She had a frugal mind.

The morning came, the chaise was brought,
    But yet was not allow'd
To drive up to the door, lest all
    Should say that she was proud.

So three doors off the chaise was stay'd,
    Where they did all get in;
Six precious souls, and all agog
    To dash through thick and thin!

Smack went the whip, round went the wheels.
    Were never folk so glad,
The stones did rattle underneath,
    As if Cheapside were mad.

John Gilpin at his horse's side
    Seiz'd fast the flowing mane,
And up he got, in haste to ride,
    But soon came down again;

For saddle-tree scarce reach'd had he,
    His journey to begin,
When, turning round his head, he saw
    Three customers come in.

So down he came; for loss of time,
   Although it griev'd him sore,
Yet loss of pence, full well he knew,
   Would trouble him much more.

'Twas long before the customers
   Were suited to their mind,
When Betty screaming came down stairs –
   'The wine is left behind!'

Good lack! quoth he – yet bring it me,
   My leathern belt likewise,
In which I bear my trusty sword
   When I do exercise.

Now mistress Gilpin (careful soul!)
   Had two stone bottles found,
To hold the liquour that she lov'd
   And keep it safe and sound.

Each bottle had a curling ear,
   Through which the belt he drew,
And hung a bottle on each side,
   To make is balance true.

Then, over all, that he might be
   Equipp'd from top to toe,
His long red cloak, well brush'd and neat,
   He manfully did throw.

Now see him mounted once again
   Upon his nimble steed,
Full slowly pacing o'er the stones,
   With caution and good heed!

But, finding soon a smoother road
   Beneath his well-shod feet,
The snorting beast began to trot,
   Which gall'd him in his seat.

So, Fair and softly, John he cried,
  But John he cried in vain;
That trot became a gallop soon,
  In spite of curb and rein.

So stooping down, as needs he must
  Who cannot sit upright,
He grasp'd the mane with both his hands,
  And eke with all his might.

His horse, who never in that sort
  Had handled been before,
What thing upon his back had got
  Did wonder more and more.

Away went Gilpin, neck or nought;
  Away went hat and wig! –
He little dreamt, when he set out,
  Of running such a rig!

The wind did blow, the cloak did fly,
  Like streamer long and gay,
Till, loop and button failing both,
  At last it flew away.

Then might all people well discern
  The bottles he had slung;
A bottle swinging at each side,
  As hath been said or sung.

The dogs did bark, the children scream'd,
  Up flew the windows all;
And ev'ry soul cried out – Well done!
  As loud as he could bawl.

Away went Gilpin – who but he?
  His fame soon spread around –
He carries weight! he rides a race!
  'Tis for a thousand pound!

And still, as fast as he drew near,
   'Twas wonderful to view
How in a trice the turnpike-men
   Their gates wide open threw.

And now, as he went bowing down
   His reeking head full low,
The bottles twain behind his back
   Where shatter'd at a blow.

Down ran the wine into the road,
   Most piteous to be seen,
Which made his horse's flanks to smoke
   As they had basted been.

But still he seem'd to carry weight,
   With leathern girdle brac'd;
For all might see the bottle-necks
   Still dangling at his waist.

Thus all through merry Islington
   These gambols he did play,
And till he came unto the Wash
   Of Edmonton so gay.

And there he threw the wash about
   On both sides of the way,
Just like unto a trundling mop,
   Or a wild goose at play.

At Edmonton his loving wife
   From the balcony spied
Her tender husband, wond'ring much
   To see how he did ride.

Stop, stop, John Gilpin! – Here's the house –
   They all at once did cry;
The dinner waits, and we are tir'd:
   Said Gilpin – So am I!

But yet his horse was not a whit
    Inclin'd to tarry there;
For why? – his owner had a house
    Full ten miles off, at Ware.

So like an arrow swift he flew,
    Shot by an archer strong;
So did he fly – which brings me to
    The middle of my song.

Away went Gilpin, out of breath,
    And sore against his will,
Till at his friend the calender's
    His horse at last stood still.

The calender, amaz'd to see
    His neighbour in such trim,
Laid down his pipe, flew to the gate,
    And thus accosted him:

What news? What news? your tidings tell;
    Tell me you must and shall –
Say why bare-headed you are come,
    Or why you come at all?

Now Gilpin had a pleasant wit,
    And lov'd a timely joke;
And thus unto the calender
    In merry guide he spoke:

I came because your horse would come;
    And, if I well forebode,
My hat and wig will soon be here –
    They are upon the road.

The calender, right glad to find
    His friend in merry pin,
Return'd him not a single word,
    But to the house went in;

Whence straight he came with hat and wig;
   A wig that flow'd behind,
A hat not much the worse for wear,
   Each comely in its kind.

He held them up, and, in his turn,
   Thus show'd his ready wit –
My head is twice as big as your's,
   They therefore needs must fit.

But let me scrape the dirt away
   That hangs upon your face;
And stop and eat, for well you may
   Be in a hungry case.

Said John – It is my wedding-day,
   And all the world would stare,
If wife should dine at Edmonton
   And I should dine at Ware!

So, turning to this horse, he said –
   I am in haste to dine;
'Twas for your pleasure you came here,
   You shall go back for mine.

Ah, luckless speech, and bootless boast!
   For which he paid full dear;
For, while he spake, a braying ass
   Did sing most loud and clear;

Whereat his horse did snort, as he
   Had heard a lion roar,
And gallop'd off with all his might,
   As he had done before.

Away went Gilpin, and away
   Went Gilpin's hat and wig!
He lost them sooner than at first –
   For why? – they were too big!

Now, mistress Gilpin, when she saw
    Her husband posting down
Into the country far away,
    She pull'd out half a crown;

And thus unto the youth she said
    That drove them to the Bell –
This shall be yours when you bring back
    My husband safe and well.

The youth did ride, and soon did meet
    John coming back amain;
Whom in a trice he tried to stop,
    By catching at his rein;

But, not performing what he meant,
    And gladly would have done,
The frightened steed he frighted more,
    And made him faster run.

Away went Gilpin, and away
    Went post-boy at his heels! –
The post-boy's horse right glad to miss
    The lumb'ring of the wheels.

Six gentlemen upon the road,
    Thus seeing Gilpin fly,
With post-boy scamp'ring in the rear,
    They rais'd the hue and cry:

Stop thief! stop thief! – a highwayman!
    Not one of them was mute;
And all and each that pass'd that way
    Did join in the pursuit.

And now the turnpike gates again
    Flew open in short space;
The toll-men thinking, as before,
    That Gilpin rode a race.

And so he did - and won it too! –
   For he got first to town;
Nor stopp'd till where he had got up
   He did again get down.

Now let us sing – Long live the king,
   And Gilpin long live he;
And, when he next doth ride abroad,
   May I be there to see!

WILLIAM COWPER (1782)

Holy Willie's Prayer

O thou, wha in the Heavens dost dwell,
Wha, as it pleases best thysel',
Sends ane to heaven and ten to hell,
      A' for thy glory,
And no for ony guid or ill
      They've done afore thee!

I bless and praise thy matchless might,
Whan thousands thou hast left in night,
That I am here afore thy sight,
      For gifts an' grace
A burnin' an' a shinin' light,
      To a' this place.

What was I, or my generation,
That I should get sic exaltation?
I, wha deserve most just damnation,
      For broken laws,
Sax thousand years 'fore my creation,
      Thro' Adam's cause.

When frae my mither's womb I fell,
Thou might hae plungèd me in hell,
To gnash my gums, to weep and wail,
      In burnin' lakes,
Where damnèd devils roar and yell,
      Chain'd to their stakes;

Yet I am here a chosen sample,
To show thy grace is great and ample;
I'm here a pillar in thy temple,
            Strong as a rock,
A guide, a buckler, an example
            To a' thy flock.

O Lord, thou kens what zeal I bear,
When drinkers drink, and swearers swear,
And singin' there and dancin' here,
            Wi' great an' sma':
For I am keepit by thy fear
            Free frae them a'.

But yet, O Lord! confess I must
At times I'm fash'd wi' fleshy lust;
An' sometimes too, in warldly trust,
            Vile self gets in;
But thou remembers we are dust,
            Defil'd in sin.

O Lord! yestreen, thou kens, wi' Meg –
Thy pardon I sincerely beg;
O! may't ne'er be a livin' plague
            To my dishonour,
An' I'll ne'er lift a lawless leg
            Again upon her.

Besides I farther maun allow,
Wi' Lizzie's lass, three times I trow –
But, Lord, that Friday I was fou,
            When I cam near her,
Or else thou kens thy servant true
            Wad never steer her.

May be thou lets this fleshly thorn
Beset thy servant e'en and morn
Lest he owre high and proud should turn,
            That he's sae gifted;
If sae, thy hand maun e'en be borne,
            Until thou lift it.

Lord, bless thy chosen in this place,
For here thou hast a chosen race;
But God confound their stubborn face,
And blast their name,
Wha bring thy elders to disgrace
An' public shame.

Lord, mind Gawn Hamilton's deserts,
He drinks, an' swears, an' plays at cartes,
Yet has sae mony takin' arts
Wi' grit an' sma',
Frae God's ain priest the people's hearts
He steals awa'.

An' when we chasten'd him therefor,
Thou kens how he bred sic a splore[1]
As set the warld in a roar
O' laughin' at us;
Curse thou his basket and his store,
Kail and potatoes.

Lord, hear my earnest cry an' pray'r,
Against that presbyt'ry o' Ayr;
Thy strong right hand, Lord, make it bare
Upo' their heads;
Lord, weigh it down, and dinna spare,
For their misdeeds.

O Lord my God, that glib-tongu'd Aiken,
My very heart and soul are quakin',
To think how we stood sweatin', shakin',
An' piss'd wi' dread,
While he, wi' hingin' lips and snakin',
Held up his head.

Lord, in the day of vengeance try him;
Lord, visit them wha did employ him,
And pass not in thy mercy by them,
Nor hear their pray'r:
But, for thy people's sake, destroy them,
And dinna spare.

[1] merrymaking

But, Lord, remember me and mine
Wi' mercies temp'ral and divine,
That I for gear and grace may shine
   Excell'd by nane,
And a' the glory shall be thine,
   Amen, Amen!

     ROBERT BURNS (1785)

This entertaining satire on a Calvinist hypocrite who sees himself as
one of the elect, predestined for Heaven, was occasioned by his
denunciation of Gavin Hamilton, a friend of Burns's, for ungodly
behaviour. Aiken was the lawyer who defended Hamilton and had
the case laughed out of court.

To a Louse

ON SEEING ONE ON A LADY'S BONNET AT CHURCH

Ha! wh'are ye gaun, ye crowlin' ferlie![1]
Your impudence protects you sairly:
I canna say but ye strunt[2] rarely,
   Owre gauze and lace;
Tho' faith! I fear ye dine but sparely
   On sic a place.

Ye ugly, creepin', blastit wonner,[3]
Detested, shunn'd by saunt an' sinner!
How dare ye set your fit upon her,
   Sae fine a lady?
Gae somewhere else, and seek your dinner
   On some poor body.

Swith, in some beggar's haffet[4] squattle;
There ye may creep, and sprawl, and sprattle[5]
Wi' ither kindred jumping cattle,
   In shoals and nations;

[1] wonder   [2] strut   [3] wonder   [4] temple   [5] struggle

Where horn nor bane ne'er dare unsettle
        Your thick plantations.

Now haud ye there, ye're out o' sight,
Below the fatt'rels,[6] snug an' tight;
Na, faith ye yet! ye'll no be right
        Till ye've got on it,
The very tapmost tow'ring height
        O' Miss's bonnet.

My sooth! right bauld ye set your nose out,
As plump and gray as onie grozet;[7]
O for some rank mercurial rozet,[8]
        Or fell red smeddum!
I'd gie you sic a hearty doze o't,
        Wad dress your droddum!

I wad na been surpris'd to spy
You on an auld wife's flannen toy;[9]
Or aiblins[10] some bit duddie[11] boy,
        On's wyliecoat;
But Miss's fine Lunardi![12] fie,
        How daur ye do't?

O Jenny, dinna toss your head,
An' set your beauties a' abroad!
Ye little ken what cursèd speed
        The blastie's makin'!
Thae winks and finger-ends, I dread,
        Are notice takin'!

O wad some Pow'r the giftie gie us
To see oursels as others see us!
It wad frae mony a blunder free us,
        And foolish notion:
What airs in dress an' gait wad lea'e us,
        And ev'n devotion!

ROBERT BURNS (1786)

---

[6] ribbon-ends   [7] gooseberry   [8] resin   [9] flannel headgear   [10] perhaps
[11] ragged   [12] fashionable bonnet

12
THE ARTS &
THEIR CRITICS

A Song for St Cecilia's Day

1

From harmony, from heavenly harmony
    This universal frame began:
    When Nature underneath a heap
        Of jarring atoms lay,
    And could not heave her head,
The tuneful voice was heard from high:
      'Arise, ye more than dead.'
Then cold, and hot, and moist, and dry,
In order to their stations leap,
      And Music's power obey.
From harmony, from heavenly harmony
    This universal frame began:
    From harmony to harmony
Through all the compass of the notes it ran,
The diapason closing full in man.

2

What passion cannot Music raise and quell!
    When Jubal struck the corded shell,
    His listening brethren stood around,
    And, wondering, on their faces fell
    To worship that celestial sound.
Less than a god they thought there could not dwell
    Within the hollow of that shell
    That spoke so sweetly and so well.
What passion cannot Music raise and quell!

3

    The trumpet's loud clangor
      Excites us to arms,
    With shrill notes of anger,
      And mortal alarms.
    The double double double beat
      Of the thundering drum
Cries: 'Hark! the foes come;
Charge, charge, 'tis too late to retreat.'

4

The soft complaining flute
In dying notes discovers
The woes of hopeless lovers,
Whose dirge is whispered by the warbling lute.

5

Sharp violins proclaim
Their jealous pangs, and desperation,
Fury, frantic indignation,
Depth of pains, and height of passion,
For the fair, disdainful dame.

6

But O! what art can teach,
What human voice can reach,
The sacred organ's praise?
Notes inspiring holy love,
Notes that wing their heavenly ways
To mend the choirs above.

7

Orpheus could lead the savage race;
And trees unrooted left their place,
Sequacious of the lyre;
But bright Cecilia raised the wonder higher:
When to her organ vocal breath was given,
An angel heard, and straight appeared,
Mistaking earth for heaven.

GRAND CHORUS

As from the power of sacred lays
The spheres began to move,
And sung the great Creator's praise
To all the blest above;
So, when the last and dreadful hour
This crumbling pageant shall devour,
The trumpet shall be heard on high,
The dead shall live, the living die,
And Music shall untune the sky.

JOHN DRYDEN (1687)

MacFlecknoe

OR A SATIRE UPON THE TRUE
BLUE PROTESTANT POET, T. S.

In this brilliant example of the witty use of the couplet for purposes of
ridicule Dryden describes in mock heroic terms the coronation of his
political opponent the dramatist Thomas Shadwell as king of the bad
poets. Flecknoe, who crowns him, was an undistinguished writer
attacked earlier in the century by Andrew Marvell, and therefore
MacFlecknoe means 'spiritual son of Flecknoe'. At one point Dryden
makes the latter into a John the Baptist, ushering in a new Kingdom of
dullness, at another he is equated to Ascanius the son of Aeneas whose
descendants reputedly founded the Roman Empire. Shadwell's enormous
size and fondness for ale were well known.

> All human things are subject to decay,
> And when fate summons, monarchs must obey.
> This Flecknoe found, who, like Augustus, young
> Was called to empire, and had governed long;
> In prose and verse, was owned, without dispute,
> Through all the realms of Nonsense, absolute.
> This aged prince, now flourishing in peace,
> And blest with issue of a large increase,
> Worn out with business, did at length debate
> To settle the succession of the state;
> And, pondering which of all his sons was fit
> To reign, and wage immortal war with wit,
> Cried: ' 'Tis resolved; for nature pleads that he
> Should only rule, who most resembles me.
> Sh— alone my perfect image bears,
> Mature in dullness from his tender years:
> Sh— alone, of all my sons, is he
> Who stands confirmed in full stupidity.
> The rest to some faint meaning make pretense,
> But Sh— never deviates into sense.
> Some beams of wit on other souls may fall,

Strike through, and make a lucid interval;
But Sh——'s genuine night admits no ray,
His rising fogs prevail upon the day.
Besides, his goodly fabric fills the eye,
And seems designed for thoughtless majesty:
Thoughtless as monarch oaks that shade the plain,
And, spread in solemn state, supinely reign.
Heywood and Shirley were but types of thee,
Thou last great prophet of tautology.
Even I, a dunce of more renown than they,
Was sent before but to prepare thy way;
And, coarsely clad in Norwich drugget, came
To teach the nations in thy greater name.

   Now Empress Fame had published the renown
Of Sh——'s coronation through the town.
Roused by report of Fame, the nations meet,
From near Bunhill, and distant Watling Street.
No Persian carpets spread the imperial way,
But scattered limbs of mangled poets lay;
From dusty shops neglected authors come,
Martyrs of pies, and relics of the bum.
Much Heywood, Shirley, Ogilby there lay,
But loads of Sh—— almost choked the way.
Bilked stationers for yeomen stood prepared,
And Herringman was captain of the guard.
The hoary prince in majesty appeared,
High on a throne of his own labors reared.
At his right hand our young Ascanius sate,
Rome's other hope, and pillar of the state.
His brows thick fogs, instead of glories, grace,
And lambent dullness played around his face.
As Hannibal did to the altars come,
Sworn by his sire a mortal foe to Rome,
So Sh—— swore, nor should his vow be vain,
That he till death true dullness would maintain;
And, in his father's right, and realm's defense,
Ne'er to have peace with wit, nor truce with sense.
The king himself the sacred unction made,
As king by office, and as priest by trade.

In his sinister hand, instead of ball,
He placed a mighty mug of potent ale;
Love's Kingdom to his right he did convey,
At once his scepter, and his rule of sway;
Whose righteous lore the prince had practiced young,
And from whose loins recorded *Psyche* sprung.
His temples, last, with poppies were o'erspread,
That nodding seemed to consecrate his head.
Just at that point of time, if fame not lie,
On his left hand twelve reverend owls did fly.
So Romulus, 'tis sung, by Tiber's brook,
Presage of sway from twice six vultures took.
The admiring throng loud acclamations make,
And omens of his future empire take.
The sire then shook the honors of his head,
And from his brows damps of oblivion shed
Full on the filial dullness: long he stood,   ⎫
Repelling from his breast the raging god;   ⎬
At length burst out in this prophetic mood: ⎭
    'Heavens bless my son, from Ireland let him reign
To far Barbadoes on the western main;
Of his dominion may no end be known,
And greater than his father's be his throne;
Beyond *Love's Kingdom* let him stretch his pen!'
He paused, and all the people cried, 'Amen.'
Then thus continued he: 'My son, advance
Still in new impudence, new ignorance.
Success let others teach, learn thou from me
Pangs without birth, and fruitless industry.
Nor let false friends seduce thy mind to fame,
By arrogating Jonson's hostile name.
Let father Flecknoe fire thy mind with praise,
And uncle Ogilby thy envy raise.
Thou art my blood, where Jonson has no part:
What share have we in nature, or in art?
Where did his wit on learning fix a brand,
And rail at arts he did not understand?
Where made he love in Prince Nicander's vein,
Or swept the dust in *Psyche*'s humble strain?
Where sold he bargains, "whip-stitch, kiss my arse,"

Promised a play and dwindled to a farce?
When did his Muse from Fletcher scenes purloin
As thou whole Eth'rege dost transfuse to thine?
But so transfused, as oil on water's flow,
His always floats above, thine sinks below.
This is thy province, this thy wondrous way,
New humors to invent for each new play:
This is that boasted bias of thy mind,
By which one way, to dullness, 'tis inclined;
Which makes thy writings lean on one side still,
And, in all changes, that way bends thy will.
Nor let thy mountain-belly make pretense
Of likeness; thine's a tympany of sense.
A tun of man in thy large bulk is writ,
But sure thou'rt but a kilderkin of wit.
Like mine, thy gentle numbers feebly creep;
Thy tragic Muse gives smiles, thy comic sleep.
With whate'er gall thou sett'st thyself to write,
Thy inoffensive satires never bite.
In thy felonious heart though venom lies,
It does but touch thy Irish pen, and dies.
Thy genius calls thee not to purchase fame
In keen iambics, but mild anagram.
Leave writing plays, and choose for thy command
Some peaceful province in acrostic land.
There thou may'st wings display and altars raise,
And torture one poor word ten thousand ways.
Or, if thou wouldst thy different talent suit,
Set thy own songs, and sing them to thy lute.'

   He said: but his last words were scarcely heard
For Bruce and Longville had a trap prepared,
And down they sent the yet declaiming bard.
Sinking he left his drugget robe behind,
Borne upwards by a subterranean wind.
The mantle fell to the young prophet's part,
With double portion of his father's art.

JOHN DRYDEN (*c.*1679)
see further note overleaf

FURTHER NOTE: Heywood, Shirley and Ogilby were writers despised by Dryden, more or less justifiably. Ben Jonson, whose literary heir Shadwell apparently felt himself to be, John Fletcher and 'gentle' George Etherege, Dryden's distinguished contemporary, were playwrights he admired. Shadwell stole ideas from all of them. There are references to Shadwell's plays *Love's Kingdom* and *Virtuoso*, and the piece ends with two of his characters from the latter play operating a theatrical trapdoor, an incident also borrowed from it.

The Playhouse

Where gentle Thames through stately channels glides,
And England's proud metropolis divides;
A lofty fabric does the sight invade,
And stretches o'er the waves a pompous shade;
Whence sudden shouts the neighbourhood surprise,
And thundering claps and dreadful hissings rise.
    Here thrifty R— hires monarchs by the day,
And keeps his mercenary kings in pay;
With deep-mouthed actors fills the vacant scenes,
And rakes the stews for goddesses and queens:
Here the lewd punk, with crowns and sceptres graced,
Teaches her eyes a more majestic cast;
And hungry monarchs with a numerous train
Of suppliant slaves, like Sancho, starve and reign.
    But enter in, my Muse; the stage survey,
And all its pomp and pageantry display;
Trap-doors and pit-falls, form th'unfaithful ground,
And magic walls encompass it around:
On either side maimed temples fill our eyes,
And intermixed with brothel-houses rise;
Disjointed palaces in order stand,
And groves obedient to the mover's hand
O'ershade the stage, and flourish at command.
A stamp makes broken towns and trees entire:
So when Amphion struck the vocal lyre,
He saw the spacious circuit all around,

With crowding woods and rising cities crowned.
   But next the tiring-room survey, and see
False titles, and promiscuous quality,
Confus'dly swarm, from heroes and from queens,
To those that swing in clouds and fill machines.
Their various characters they choose with art,
The frowning bully fits the tyrant's part:
Swoll'n cheeks and swaggering belly make an host,
Pale meagre looks and hollow voice a ghost;
From careful brows and heavy downcast eyes,
Dull cits and thick-skulled aldermen arise:
The comic tone, inspired by Congreve, draws
At every word, loud laughter and applause:
The whining dame continues as before,
Her character unchanged, and acts a whore.
   Above the rest, the prince with haughty stalks
Magnificent in purple buskins walks:
The royal robes his awful shoulders grace,
Profuse of spangles and of copper-lace:
Officious rascals to his mighty thigh,
Guiltless of blood, th'unpointed weapon tie:
Then the gay glittering diadem put on,
Ponderous with brass, and starred with Bristol-stone.
His royal consort next consults her glass,
And out of twenty boxes culls a face;
The whitening first her ghastly looks besmears,
All pale and wan th'unfinished form appears;
Till on her cheeks the blushing purple glows,
And a false virgin-modesty bestows.
Her ruddy lips the deep vermilion dyes;
Length to her brows the pencil's art supplies,
And with black bending arches shades her eyes.
Well pleased at length the picture she beholds,
And spots it o'er with artificial moulds;
Her countenance complete, the beaux she warms
With looks not hers: and, spite of nature, charms.
   Thus artfully their persons they disguise,
Till the last flourish bids the curtain rise.
The prince then enters on the stage in state;
Behind, a guard of candle-snuffers wait:

There swoll'n with empire, terrible and fierce,
He shakes the dome, and tears his lungs with verse:
His subjects tremble; the submissive pit,
Wrapped up in silence and attention, sit;
Till, freed at length, he lays aside the weight
Of public business and affairs of state:
Forgets his pomp, dead to ambitious fires,
And to some peaceful brandy-shop retires;
Where in full gills his anxious thoughts he drowns,
And quaffs away the care that waits on crowns.
   The princess next her painted charms displays,
Where every look the pencil's art betrays;
The callow squire at distance feeds his eyes,
And silently for paint and washes dies:
But if the youth behind the scenes retreat,
He sees the blended colours melt with heat,
And all the trickling beauty run in sweat.
The borrowed visage he admires no more,
And nauseates every charm he loved before:
So the famed spear, for double force renowned,
Applied the remedy that gave the wound.
In tedious lists 'twere endless to engage,
And draw at length the rabble of the stage,
Where one for twenty years has given alarms,
And called contending monarchs to their arms;
Another fills a more important post,
And rises every other night a ghost;
Through the cleft stage his mealy face he rears,
Then stalks along, groans thrice, and disappears;
Others, with swords and shields, the soldier's pride,
More than a thousand times have changed their side,
And in a thousand fatal battles died.
   Thus several persons several parts perform;
Soft lovers whine, and blustering heroes storm.
The stern exasperated tyrants rage,
Till the kind bowl of poison clears the stage.
Then honours vanish, and distinctions cease;
Then, with reluctance, haughty queens undress.
Heroes no more their fading laurels boast,
And mighty kings in private men are lost.

He, whom such titles swelled, such power made proud,
To whom whole realms and vanquished nations bowed,
Throws off the gaudy plume, the purple train,
And in his own vile tatters stinks again.

JOSEPH ADDISON

The Progress of Poetry

The farmer's goose, who in the stubble,
Has fed without restraint, or trouble;
Grown fat with corn and sitting still,
Can scarce get o'er the barn-door sill:
And hardly waddles forth, to cool
Her belly in the neighbouring pool:
Nor loudly cackles at the door;
For cackling shows the goose is poor.

But when she must be turned to graze,
And round the barren common strays,
Hard exercise, and harder fare,
Soon make my dame grow lank and spare:
Her body light, she tries her wings,
And scorns the ground, and upward springs,
While all the parish, as she flies,
Hear sounds harmonious from the skies.

Such is the poet, fresh in pay,
(The third night's profits of his play;)
His morning-draughts till noon can swill,
Among his brethren of the quill:
With good roast beef his belly full,
Grown lazy, foggy, fat, and dull:
Deep sunk in plenty, and delight,
What poet e'er could take his flight?
Or stuffed with phlegm up to the throat,
What poet e'er could sing a note?
Nor Pegasus could bear the load,

Along the high celestial road;
The steed, oppressed, would break his girth,
To raise the lumber from the earth.

But, view him in another scene,
When all his drink is Hippocrene;
His money spent, his patrons fail,
His credit out for cheese and ale;
His two-year's coat so smooth and bare,
Through every thread it lets in air;
With hungry meals his body pined,
His guts and belly full of wind;
And, like a jockey in a race,
His flesh brought down to flying case:
Now his exalted spirit loathes
Incumbrances of food and clothes;
And up he rises like a vapour,
Supported high on wings of paper;
He singing flies, and flying sings,
While from below all Grub Street rings.

JONATHAN SWIFT

Epistle to Mr Jervas

WITH DRYDEN'S TRANSLATION OF FRESNOY'S *ART OF PAINTING*

This verse be thine, my friend, nor thou refuse
This, from no venal or ungrateful Muse.
Whether thy hand strike out some free design,
Where life awakes, and dawns at ev'ry line;
Or blend in beauteous tints the colour'd mass,
And from the canvas call the mimic face:
Read these instructive leaves, in which conspire
Fresnoy's close art, and *Dryden*'s native fire:
And reading wish, like theirs, our fate and fame,
So mix'd our studies, and so join'd our name,

Like them to shine thro' long succeeding age,
So just thy skill, so regular my rage.
　　Smit with the love of Sister-arts we came,
And met congenial, mingling flame with flame;
Like friendly colours found them both unite,
And each from each contract new strength and light.
How oft' in pleasing tasks we wear the day,
While summer suns roll unperceiv'd away?
How oft' our slowly-growing works impart,
While images reflect from art to art?
How oft' review; each finding like a friend
Something to blame, and something to commend?
What flatt'ring scenes our wand'ring fancy wrought,
Rome's pompous glories rising to our thought!
Together o'er the *Alps* methinks we fly,
Fir'd with ideas of fair *Italy*.
With thee, on *Raphael*'s Monument I mourn,
Or wait inspiring dreams at *Maro*'s Urn:
With thee repose, where *Tully* once was laid,
Or seek some ruin's formidable shade;
While fancy brings the vanish'd piles to view,
And builds imaginary *Rome* a-new.
Here thy well-study'd Marbles fix our eye;
A fading Fresco here demands a sigh:
Each heav'nly piece unweary'd we compare,
Match *Raphael*'s grace, with thy lov'd *Guido*'s air,
Caracci's strength, *Correggio*'s softer line,
Paulo's free stroke, and *Titian*'s warmth divine.
　　How finish'd with illustrious toil appears
This small, well-polish'd gem, the work of years!
Yet still how faint by precept is exprest
The living image in the Painter's breast?
Thence endless streams of fair ideas flow,
Strike in the sketch, or in the picture glow;
Thence beauty, waking all her forms, supplies
An Angel's sweetness, or *Bridgewater*'s eyes.
　　Muse! at that name thy sacred sorrows shed,
Those tears eternal, that embalm the dead:
Call round her tomb each object of desire,
Each purer frame inform'd with purer fire:

Bid her be all that chears or softens life,
The tender sister, daughter, friend and wife;
Bid her be all that makes mankind adore;
Then view this marble, and be vain no more!

Yet still her charms in breathing paint engage;
Her modest cheek shall warm a future age.
Beauty, frail flow'r that ev'ry season fears,
Blooms in thy colours for a thousand years.
Thus *Churchill*'s race shall other hearts surprize,
And other Beauties envy *Worsley*'s eyes,
Each pleasing *Blount* shall endless smiles bestow,
And soft *Belinda*'s blush for ever glow.

Oh lasting as those colours may they shine,
Free as thy stroke, yet faultless as thy line!
New graces yearly, like thy works, display;
Soft without weakness, without glaring gay;
Led by some rule, that guides, but not constrains;
And finish'd more thro' happiness than pains!
The kindred arts shall in their praise conspire,
One dip the pencil, and one string the lyre.
Yet should the Graces all thy figures place,
And breathe an air divine on ev'ry face;
Yet should the Muses bid my numbers roll,
Strong as their charms, and gentle as their soul;
With *Zeuxis' Helen* thy *Bridgewater* vie,
And these be sung 'till *Granville's Myra* die;
Alas! how little from the grave we claim?
Thou but preserv'st a Face and I a Name.

ALEXANDER POPE (*c.*1715)

Charles Jervas was a pupil of the distinguished painter Sir Godfrey
Kneller, and was regarded very highly in Pope's day, though
modern critics do not share this opinion.

from *An Essay on Criticism*

Of all the Causes which conspire to blind
Man's erring Judgment, and misguide the Mind,
What the weak Head with strongest Byass rules,
Is *Pride*, the *never-failing Vice of Fools*.
Whatever Nature has in *Worth* deny'd,
She gives in large Recruits of *needful Pride*;
For as in *Bodies*, thus in *Souls*, we find
What wants in *Blood* and *Spirits*, swell'd with *Wind*;
Pride, where Wit fails, steps in to our Defence,
And fills up all the *mighty Void* of *Sense*!
If once right Reason drives *that Cloud* away,
Truth breaks upon us with *resistless Day*;
Trust not your self; but your Defects to know,
Make use of ev'ry *Friend* – and ev'ry *Foe*.

A *little Learning* is a dang'rous Thing;
Drink deep, or taste not the *Pierian* Spring:
There *shallow Draughts* intoxicate the Brain,
And drinking *largely* sobers us again.
Fir'd at first Sight with what the *Muse* imparts,
In *fearless Youth* we tempt the Heights of Arts,
While from the bounded *Level* of our Mind,
Short Views we take, nor see the *Lengths behind*,
But *more advanc'd*, behold with strange Surprize
New, distant Scenes of *endless* Science rise!
So pleas'd at first, the towring *Alps* we try,
Mount o'er the Vales, and seem to tread the Sky;
Th' Eternal Snows appear already past,
And the first *Clouds* and *Mountains* seem the last:
But *those attain'd*, we tremble to survey
The growing Labours of the lengthen'd Way,
Th' *increasing* Prospect *tires* our wandring Eyes,
Hills peep o'er Hills, and *Alps* on *Alps* arise!

A perfect Judge will *read* each Work of Wit
With the same Spirit that its Author *writ*,
Survey the *Whole*, nor seek slight Faults to find,
Where *Nature moves*, and *Rapture warms* the Mind;

Nor lose, for that malignant dull Delight,
The *gen'rous Pleasure* to be charm'd with Wit.
But in such Lays as neither *ebb*, nor *flow*,
Correctly cold, and *regularly low*,
That shunning Faults, one quiet *Tenour* keep;
We cannot *blame* indeed – but we may *sleep*.
In Wit, as Nature, what affects our Hearts
Is not th' Exactness of peculiar Parts;
'Tis not a *Lip*, or *Eye*, we Beauty call,
But the joint Force and full *Result* of *all*.
Thus when we view some well-proportion'd Dome,
(The *World*'s just Wonder, and ev'n *thine* O *Rome*!)
No single Parts unequally surprize;
All comes *united* to th' admiring Eyes;
No monstrous Height, or Breadth, or Length appear;
The *Whole* at once is *Bold*, and *Regular*.

  Whoever thinks a faultless Piece to see,
Thinks what ne'er was, nor is, nor e'er shall be.
In ev'ry Work regard the *Writer's End*,
Since none can compass more than they *Intend*;
And if the *Means* be just, the *Conduct* true,
Applause, in spite of trivial Faults, is due.
As Men of Breeding, sometimes Men of Wit,
T' avoid *great Errors*, must the *less* commit,
Neglect the Rules each *Verbal Critick* lays,
For *not* to know some Trifles, is a Praise.
Most Criticks, fond of some subservient Art,
Still make the *Whole* depend upon a *Part*,
They talk of *Principles*, but Notions prize,
And All to one lov'd Folly Sacrifice.

                *   *   *

  Some to *Conceit* alone their Taste confine,
And glitt'ring Thoughts struck out at ev'ry Line;
Pleas'd with a Work where nothing's just or fit;
One *glaring Chaos* and *wild Heap* of *Wit*:
Poets like Painters, thus, unskill'd to trace
The *naked Nature* and the *living Grace*,
With *Gold* and *Jewels* cover ev'ry Part,
And hide with *Ornaments* their *Want of Art*.

True Wit is *Nature* to Advantage drest,
What oft was *Thought*, but ne'er so well *Exprest*,
Something, whose Truth convinc'd at Sight we find,
That gives us back the Image of our Mind:
As Shades more sweetly recommend the Light,
So modest Plainness sets off sprightly Wit:
For *Works* may have more *Wit* than does 'em good,
As *Bodies* perish through Excess of *Blood*.
    Others for *Language* all their Care express,
And value *Books*, as Women *Men*, for *Dress*:
Their Praise is still – *The Style is excellent*:
The *Sense*, they humbly take upon Content.
Words are like *Leaves*; and where they most abound,
Much *Fruit* of *Sense* beneath is rarely found.
False Eloquence, like the *Prismatic Glass*,
Its gawdy Colours spreads on *ev'ry place*;
The Face of Nature we no more Survey,
All glares *alike*, without *Distinction* gay:
But true *Expression*, like th' unchanging *Sun*, ⎫
Clears, and *improves* whate'er it shines upon, ⎬
It *gilds* all Objects, but it *alters* none. ⎭
Expression is the *Dress* of *Thought*, and still
Appears more *decent* as more *suitable*;
A vile Conceit in pompous Words exprest,
Is like a Clown in regal Purple drest;
For diff'rent *Styles* with diff'rent *Subjects* sort,
As several Garbs with Country, Town, and Court.

ALEXANDER POPE (1711)

A conceit was an extravagant or ingenious comparison or
use of imagery.

from the *Epistle to Burlington*

BAD TASTE IN ARCHITECTURE
AND LANDSCAPE GARDENING

At Timon's Villa let us pass a day,
Where all cry out, 'What sums are thrown away!'
So proud, so grand, of that stupendous air,
Soft and Agreeable come never there.
Greatness, with Timon, dwells in such a draught
As brings all Brobdignag before your thought.
To compass this, his building is a Town,
His pond an Ocean, his parterre a Down:
Who but must laugh, the Master when he sees,
A puny insect, shiv'ring at a breeze!
Lo, what huge heaps of littleness around!
The whole, a labour'd Quarry above ground.
Two Cupids squirt before: a Lake behind
Improves the keenness of the Northern wind.
His Gardens next your admiration call,
On ev'ry side you look, behold the Wall!
No pleasing Intricacies intervene,
No artful wildness to perplex the scene;
Grove nods at grove, each Alley has a brother,
And half the platform just reflects the other.
The suff'ring eye inverted Nature sees,
Trees cut to Statues, Statues thick as trees,
With here a Fountain, never to be play'd,
And there a Summer-house, that knows no shade;
Here Amphitrite sails thro' myrtle bow'rs;
There Gladiators fight, or die, in flow'rs;
Un-water'd see the drooping sea-horse mourn,
And swallows roost in Nilus' dusty Urn.
My Lord advances with majestic mien,
Smit with the mighty pleasure, to be seen:
But soft – by regular approach – not yet –
First thro' the length of yon hot Terrace sweat,
And when up ten steep slopes you've dragg'd your
        thighs,

Just at his Study-door he'll bless your eyes.
  His Study! with what Authors is it stor'd?
In Books, not Authors, curious is my Lord;
To all their dated Backs he turns you round,
These Aldus printed, those Du Suëil has bound.
Lo some are Vellom, and the rest as good
For all his Lordship knows, but they are Wood.
For Locke or Milton 'tis in vain to look,
These shelves admit not any modern book.
  And now the Chapel's silver bell you hear,
That summons you to all the Pride of Pray'r:
Light quirks of Musick, broken and uneven,
Make the soul dance upon a Jig to Heaven.
On painted Cielings you devoutly stare,
Where sprawl the Saints of Verrio or Laguerre,
On gilded clouds in fair expansion lie,
And bring all Paradise before your eye.
To rest, the Cushion and soft Dean invite,
Who never mentions Hell to ears polite.
  But hark! the chiming Clocks to dinner call;
A hundred footsteps scrape the marble Hall:
The rich Buffet well-colour'd Serpents grace,
And gaping Tritons spew to wash your face.
Is this a dinner? this a Genial room?
No, 'tis a Temple, and a Hecatomb.
A solemn Sacrifice, perform'd in state,
You drink by measure, and to minutes eat.
So quick retires each flying course, you'd swear
Sancho's dread Doctor and his Wand were there.
Between each Act the trembling salvers ring,
From soup to sweet-wine, and God bless the King.
In plenty starving, tantaliz'd in state,
And complaisantly help'd to all I hate,
Treated, caress'd, and tir'd, I take my leave,
Sick of his civil Pride from Morn to Eve;
I curse such lavish cost, and little skill,
And swear no Day was ever past so ill.
  Yet hence the Poor are cloath'd, the Hungry fed;
Health to himself, and to his Infants bread
The Lab'rer bears: What his hard Heart denies,

   His charitable Vanity supplies.
     Another age shall see the golden Ear
Imbrown the Slope, and nod on the Parterre,
Deep Harvests bury all his pride has plann'd,
And laughing Ceres[1] re-assume the land.

                  ALEXANDER POPE (by 1735)

from the *Epistle to Dr Arbuthnot*

POPE TRIES TO ESCAPE FROM BAD POETS
SEEKING ENDORSEMENT OF THEIR WORK

The scene is his villa at Twickenham; the Dog Star was supposed to
drive people mad, Bedlam was the Bethlehem Hospital for the insane,
Parnassus was the Greek mountain associated with poetry and the arts.
The Greek and Latin names describe typical supplicants – one of whose
names, Cornus, suggest that his literary activities had driven his wife to
infidelity; Drury Lane garrets were the haunts of unsuccessful writers,
and Lintot was a printer/publisher.

POPE   Shut, shut the door, good John! (fatigued, I said),
        Tie up the knocker, say I'm sick, I'm dead.
        The Dog Star rages! nay 'tis past a doubt
        All Bedlam, or Parnassus, is let out:
        Fire in each eye, and papers in each hand,
        They rave, recite, and madden round the land.
           What walls can guard me, or what shades can hide?
        They pierce my thickets, through my grot they glide,
        By land, by water, they renew the charge,
        They stop the chariot, and they board the barge.
        No place is sacred, not the church is free;
        Even Sunday shines no Sabbath day to me:
        Then from the Mint walks forth the man of rhyme,
        Happy to catch me just at dinner time.
           Is there a parson, much bemused in beer,
        A maudlin poetess, a rhyming peer,

[1] here as goddess of nature

A clerk foredoomed his father's soul to cross,
Who pens a stanza when he should engross?
Is there who, locked from ink and paper, scrawls
With desperate charcoal round his darkened walls?
All fly to Twit'nam, and in humble strain
Apply to me to keep them mad or vain.
Arthur, whose giddy son neglects the laws,
Imputes to me and my damned works the cause:
Poor Cornus sees his frantic wife elope,
And curses wit, and poetry, and Pope.

   Friend to my life (which did not you prolong,
The world had wanted many an idle song)
What drop or nostrum can this plague remove?
Or which must end me, a fool's wrath or love?
A dire dilemma! either way I'm sped,
If foes, they write, if friends, they read me dead.
Seized and tied down to judge, how wretched I!
Who can't be silent, and who will not lie:
To laugh, were want of goodness and of grace,
And to be grave, exceeds all power of face.
I sit with sad civility, I read
With honest anguish, and an aching head:
And drop at last, but in unwilling ears,
This saving counsel, 'Keep your piece nine years.'

   'Nine years!' cries he, who high in Drury Lane,
Lulled by soft zephyrs through the broken pane,
Rhymes ere he wakes, and prints before term ends,
Obliged by hunger and request of friends:
'The piece, you think, is incorrect? why, take it,
I'm all submission, what you'd have it, make it.'

   Three things another's modest wishes bound,
My friendship! and a prologue, and ten pound.

   Pitholeon sends to me: 'You know his Grace,
I want a patron; ask him for a place.'
Pitholeon libeled me – 'but here's a letter
Informs you, sir, 'twas when he knew no better.
Dare you refuse him? Curll invites to dine,
He'll write a *Journal*, or he'll turn divine.'
Bless me! a packet – ' 'Tis a stranger sues,
A virgin tragedy, an orphan Muse.'

If I dislike it, 'Furies, death, and rage!'
If I approve, 'Commend it to the stage.'
There (thank my stars) my whole commission ends,
The players and I are, luckily, no friends.
Fired that the house reject him, ' 'Sdeath, I'll print it,
And shame the fools – Your interest, sir, with Lintot!'
Lintot, dull rogue, will think your price too much.
'Not, sir, if you revise it, and retouch.'
All my demurs but double his attacks;
At last he whispers, 'Do; and we go snacks.' [1]
Glad of a quarrel, straight I clap the door,
'Sir, let me see your works and you no more.'

ALEXANDER POPE (1735)

from *An Epistle to William Hogarth*

A VIEW OF HOGARTH

The distinguished popular painter and print-maker had caricatured
Churchill's friend Wilkes. He had recently painted a picture,
Sigismunda Weeping over the Heart of Tancred, to display his powers
as a 'classical' painter, and it had been a disaster.

Whilst a dear Country, and an injur'd Friend,
Urge my strong anger to the bitt'rest end,
Whilst honest trophies to revenge are rais'd,
Let not One real Virtue pass unprais'd.
Justice with equal course bids Satire flow,
And loves the Virtue of her greatest foe.

O! that I here could that rare Virtue mean
Which scorns the rule of Envy, Pride and Spleen,
Which springs not from the labour'd Works of Art,
But hath its rise from Nature in the heart,

---

[1] split the profits

Which in itself with happiness is crown'd,
And spreads with joy the blessing all around!
But Truth forbids, and in these simple lays,
Contented with a diff'rent kind of Praise,
Must HOGARTH stand; that Praise which GENIUS gives,
In Which to latest time the *Artist* lives,
But not the *Man*; which, rightly understood,
May make Us great, but cannot make us good.
That Praise be HOGARTH's; freely let him wear
That Wreath which GENIUS wove, and planted there.
Foe as I am, should Envy tear it down,
Myself would labour to replace the Crown.

In walks of Humor, in that cast of Style,
Which, probing to the quick, yet makes us smile;
In Comedy, thy nat'ral road to fame,
Nor let me call it by a meaner name,
Where a beginning, middle, and an end
Are aptly joined; where parts on parts depend,
Each made for each, as bodies for their soul,
So as to form one true and perfect whole,
Where a plain story to the eye is told,
Which we conceive the moment we behold,
HOGARTH unrivall'd stands, and shall engage
Unrivall'd praise to the most distant age.

How could'st Thou then to Shame perversely run,
And tread that path which Nature bad Thee shun,
Why did ambition overleap her rules,
And thy vast parts become the sport of Fools?
By diff'rent methods diff'rent Men excell,
But where is He, who can do all things well?
Humour thy Province, for some monstrous crime
Pride struck Thee with the frenzy of *Sublime*.
But, when the work was finish'd, could thy mind
So partial be, and to herself so blind,
What with contempt All view'd, to view with awe,
Nor see those faults which ev'ry Blockhead saw?
Blush, Thou vain Man, and if desire of Fame,

Founded on real Art, thy thoughts inflame,
To quick destruction SIGISMUNDA give,
And let her mem'ry die, that thine may live.

But should fond Candour, for her Mercy sake,
With pity view, and pardon this mistake;
Or should Oblivion, to thy wish most kind,
Wipe off that stain, nor leave one trace behind;
Of ARTS *despis'd*, of ARTISTS by thy frown
Aw'd from just hopes, of *rising Worth kept down,*
Of all thy meanness thro' this mortal race,
Can'st Thou the living memory erase,
Or shall not Vengeance follow to the grave,
And give back just that measure which You gave?
With so much merit, and so much success,
With so much pow'r to curse, so much to bless,
Would He have been Man's friend, instead of foe,
HOGARTH had been a little God below.
Why then, like savage Giants, fam'd of old,
Of whom in Scripture Story we are told,
Dost Thou in cruelty that strength employ,
Which Nature meant to save, not to destroy,
Why dost Thou, all in horrid pomp array'd,
Sit grinning o'er the ruins Thou hast made?
Most rank Ill-nature must applaud thy art;
But even Candour must condemn thy heart.

CHARLES CHURCHILL (1763)

Lines on Thomas Warton's Poems

Wheresoe'er I turn my View,
All is strange, yet nothing new;
Endless Labour all along,
Endless Labour to be wrong;
Phrase that Time has flung away,
Uncouth Words in Disarray:
Trickt in Antique Ruff and Bonnet,
Ode and Elegy and Sonnet.

SAMUEL JOHNSON (d.1784)

13
A GALLERY OF
CHARACTERS

from *Hudibras*

PORTRAIT OF A PURITAN

In this extract Samuel Butler is ridiculing what he saw as the hypocrisy and religious fanaticism of the middle-class bourgeoisie who had supported the Parliamentary side in the Civil War. He uses the burlesque technique of pretending that his hero is a knight errant (i.e. wandering) from the age of chivalry, riding out in search of adventures inspired by his lady, Dame Religion. The charges he makes against them echo ones made against the Puritans in the plays of Ben Jonson and others as much as sixty years before, not only because of their humourlessness and anti-royalism, but also because of their general ignorance, concealed through long-winded abuse of language and their disapproval of drama and imaginative literature in general. Their short hair, leading to their nicknames of 'roundhead' and 'long-ears', together with their sober dress also made them figures of fun. Butler is thought to have been thinking of a particular City knight and magistrate (hence the references to being dubbed – the blow on the shoulder – and to 'binding over'). There are a few further notes at the end of the extracts.

> When civil dudgeon first grew high,
> And men fell out, they knew not why;
> When hard words, jealousies and fears
> Set folks together by the ears,
> And made them fight, like mad or drunk,
> For Dame Religion, as for punk,[1]
> Whose honesty they all durst swear for,
> Though not a man of them knew wherefore,
> When gospel trumpeter surrounded
> With long eared rout, to battle sounded,
> And pulpit, drum ecclesiastic
> Was beat with fist instead of stick;
> Then did Sir Knight abandon dwelling
> And out he rode a colonelling.
>   A wight[2] he was whose very sight would
> Entitle him Mirror of Knighthood,

[1] whore   [2] man

That never bowed his stubborn knee
To anything but chivalry,
Nor put up blow but that which laid
Right Worshipful on shoulder-blade;
Chief of domestic knights and errant,
Either for chartel or for warrant,
Great on the bench, great on the saddle,
That could as well bind o'er as swaddle;[3]
Mighty he was at both of these,
And styled of war as well as peace.
(So some rats, of ambiguous nature,
Are either for the land or water.)
But here our authors make a doubt
Whether he were more wise or stout.
Some hold the one and some the other;
But howsoe'er they make a pother,
The difference was so small his brain
Outweighed his rage but half a grain;
Which made some take him for a fool.
For it has been held by many that,
As Montaigne playing with his cat,
Complains that she thought him an ass,
Much more she would Sir Hudibras;
(For that's the name our valiant knight
To all his challenges would write).
But they're mistaken very much;
'Tis plain enough he was no such.
We grant, although he had much wit,
He was very shy of using it,
As being loath to wear it out,
And therefore bore it not about,
Unless on holidays or so,
As men their best apparel do.
Besides, 'tis known he could speak Greek
As naturally as pigs squeak;
That Latin was no more difficile,
Than to a blackbird 'tis to whistle.
Being rich in both, he never scanted

---

[3] tie up or beat up

His bounty unto such as wanted;
But much of either would afford
To many that had not one word.
For Hebrew roots, although they're found
To flourish most in barren ground,
He had such plenty as sufficed
To make some think him circumcised.
And truly so he was perhaps,
Not as a proselyte, but for claps.

* * *

For rhetoric, he could not ope
His mouth but out there flew a trope,[4]
And when he happened to break off
In the middle of his speech, or cough,
He had hard[5] words ready to show why,
And tell what rules he did it by.
Else, when with greatest art he spoke,
You'd think he spoke like other folk;
For all a rhetorician's rules
Teach nothing but to name his tools.
But when he pleased to show it, his speech
In loftiness of sound was rich,
A Babylonish dialect
Which learned pedants much affect.
It was a parti-coloured dress
Of patched and piebald languages;
'Twas English cut on Greek and Latin,
Like fustian[6] heretofore on satin.
It had an odd promiscuous tone,
As if he had talked three parts in one;
Which made some think, when he did gabble,
They had heard three labourers of Babel,
Or Cerberus himself pronounce
A leash of languages at once.
This he as volubly did vent
As if his stock would ne'er be spent;
And truly, to support that charge,

---

[4] figure of speech   [5] long and unfamiliar   [6] cheap coarse cloth

He had supplies as vast and large;
For he could coin or counterfeit
New words with little or no wit,
Words so debased and hard no stone
Was hard enough to touch them on;
And when with hasty noise he spoke 'em,
The ignorant for current took 'em –
That had the orator who once
Did fill his mouth with pebble stones
When he harangued but known his phrase
He would have used no other ways.

*   *   *

   In school divinity as able
As he that hight[7] Irrefragable;
A second Thomas, or at once
To name them all, another Duns,
Profound in all the nominal
And real ways beyond them all,
For he a rope of sand could twist
As tough as learned Sorbonist;
And weave fine cobwebs, fit for skull
That's empty when the moon is full:
Such as take lodgings in a head
That's to be let unfurnished.
He could raise scruples dark and nice
And after solve 'em in a trice;
As if divinity had catched
The itch on purpose to be scratched;
Or like a mountebank did wound
And stab herself with doubts profound,
Only to show with how small pain
The sores of faith are cured again;
Although, by woeful proof, we find
They always leave a scar behind.
He knew the seat of Paradise,
Could tell in what degree it lies,
And, as he was disposed, could prove it
Below the moon, or else above it;

---

[7] was called

What Adam dreamt of when his bride
Came from her closet to his side;
Whether the Devil tempted her
By a High Dutch interpreter,
If either of them had a navel;
Who first made music malleable;
Whether the Serpent at the Fall
Had cloven feet, or none at all.
All this, without a gloss or comment,
He could unriddle in a moment,
In proper terms, such as men smatter,
When they throw out and miss the matter.
     For his religion, it was fit
To match his learning and his wit,
'Twas Presbyterian True Blue,
For he was of that stubborn crew
Of errant saints whom all men grant
To be the True Church Militant;
Such as do build their faith upon
The holy text of Pike and Gun;
Decide all controversies by
Infallible Artillery;
And prove their doctrine orthodox,
By Apostolic Blows and Knocks;
Call fire and sword and desolation
A Godly Thorough Reformation,
Which always must be carried on,
And still be doing, never done;
As if Religion were intended
For nothing else but to be mended –
A sect whose chief Devotion lies
In odd, perverse Antipathies,
In falling out with that or this,
And finding somewhat still amiss,
More peevish, cross and splenetic,
Than dog distract or monkey sick;
That with more care keep Holy-day
The wrong, than others the right, way;
Compound for sins they are inclined to,
By damning those they have no mind to;

Still so perverse and opposite,
As if they worshipped God for spite.
The self-same thing they will abhor
One way and long another for.
Free Will they one way disavow,
Another, nothing else allow.
All piety consists therein
In them, in other men all sin.

SAMUEL BUTLER (1663)

Cerberus was the three-headed dog who guarded the entrance to the Classical underworld; the three heads are imagined as barking in different languages. The reference at the beginning of the third extract is to three famous Doctors of the Church. A 'rope of sands' is an argument without a sound basis. The orator who filled his mouth with pebbles was the great Greek political speaker Demosthenes. The name Hudibras is borrowed from Spenser's knightly romance epic *The Faerie Queene* (Book 2). The original Sir Hudibras 'not so good of deedes, as great of name' is noted for rashness and humourlessness, and associated with the maiden Elissa who disapproves of pleasure.

from *Absalom and Achitophel*

CHARACTERS OF CHARLES II'S ENEMIES

1

THE DUKE OF BUCKINGHAM

In the first rank of these did Zimri stand;
A man so various, that he seemed to be
Not one, but all mankind's epitome:
Stiff in opinions, always in the wrong;
Was everything by starts, and nothing long;
But, in the course of one revolving moon,
Was chymist, fiddler, statesman, and buffoon:
Then all for women, painting, rhyming, drinking,
Besides ten thousand freaks that died in thinking.
Blest madman, who could every hour employ,

With something new to wish, or to enjoy!
Railing[1] and praising were his usual themes;
And both (to show his judgment) in extremes:
So over-violent, or over-civil,
That every man, with him, was God or Devil.
In squandering wealth was his peculiar art:
Nothing went unrewarded but desert.
Beggared by fools, whom still he found too late,
He had his jest, and they had his estate.

2

SLINGSBY BETHELL, A SHERIFF OF LONDON

Shimei, whose youth did early promise bring
Of zeal to God and hatred to his king,
Did wisely from expensive sins refrain,
And never broke the Sabbath, but for gain;
Nor ever was he known an oath to vent,
Or curse, unless against the government.
Thus heaping wealth, by the most ready way
Among the Jews, which was to cheat and pray,
The city, to reward his pious hate
Against his master, chose him magistrate.
His hand a vare[2] of justice did uphold;
His neck was loaded with a chain of gold.
During his office, treason was no crime;
The sons of Belial[3] had a glorious time;
For Shimei, though not prodigal of pelf,
Yet loved his wicked neighbor as himself.
When two or three were gathered to declaim ⎫
Against the monarch of Jerusalem,   ⎬
Shimei was always in the midst of them;   ⎭
And if they cursed the king when he was by,
Would rather curse than break good company.
If any durst his factious friends accuse,
He packed a jury of dissenting Jews;
Whose fellow-feeling in the godly cause
Would free the suffering saint from human laws.

---

[1] attacking verbally   [2] staff   [3] a Miltonic devil

For laws are only made to punish those
Who serve the king, and to protect his foes.
If any leisure time he had from power
(Because 'tis sin to misemploy an hour),
His business was, by writing, to persuade
That kings were useless, and a clog to trade;
And, that his noble style he might refine,
No Rechabite[4] more shunned the fumes of wine.
Chaste were his cellars, and his shrieval board[5]
The grossness of a city feast abhorred:
His cooks, with long disuse, their trade forgot;
Cool was his kitchen, though his brains were hot,
Such frugal virtue malice may accuse,
But sure 'twas necessary to the Jews:
For towns once burnt such magistrates require
As dare not tempt God's providence by fire.
With spiritual food he fed his servants well,
But free from flesh that made the Jews rebel;
And Moses' laws he held in more account,
For forty days of fasting in the mount.
To speak the rest, who better are forgot,
Would tire a well-breathed witness of the Plot.

3

TITUS OATES

Yet, Corah, thou shalt from oblivion pass:
Erect thyself, thou monumental brass,
High as the serpent of thy metal made,
While nations stand secure beneath thy shade.
What though his birth were base, yet comets rise
From earthy vapors, ere they shine in skies.
Prodigious actions may as well be done
By weaver's issue, as by prince's son.
This arch-attestor for the public good
By that one deed ennobles all his blood.
Who ever asked the witnesses' high race
Whose oath with martyrdom did Stephen grace?

---

[4] Jewish ascetic   [5] dinner table

Ours was a Levite, and as times went then,
His tribe were God Almighty's gentlemen.
Sunk were his eyes, his voice was harsh and loud,
Sure signs he neither choleric was nor proud:
His long chin proved his wit; his saintlike grace
A church vermilion, and a Moses' face.
His memory, miraculously great,
Could plots, exceeding man's belief, repeat;
Which therefore cannot be accounted lies,
For human wit could never such devise.
Some future truths are mingled in his book;
But where the witness failed, the prophet spoke:
Some things like visionary flights appear;
The spirit caught him up, the Lord knows where,
And gave him his rabbinical degree,
Unknown to foreign university.
His judgment yet his memory did excel;
Which pieced his wondrous evidence so well,
And suited to the temper of the times,
Then groaning under Jebusitic crimes.
Let Israel's foes suspect his heavenly call,
And rashly judge his writ apocryphal;
Our laws for such affronts have forfeits made:
He takes his life, who takes away his trade.
Were I myself in witness Corah's place,
The wretch Who did me such a dire disgrace
Should whet my memory, though once forgot,
To make him an appendix of my plot.
His zeal to heaven made him his prince despise,
And load his person with indignities;
But zeal peculiar privilege affords,
Indulging latitude to deeds and words;
And Corah might for Agag's murder call,
In terms as coarse as Samuel used to Saul.
What others in his evidence did join
(The best that could be had for love or coin),
In Corah's own predicament will fall;
For *witness* is a common name to all.

JOHN DRYDEN (1681)

Resolution, in Four Sonnets,

OF A POETICAL QUESTION PUT TO ME BY A
FRIEND, CONCERNING FOUR RURAL SISTERS

1

Alice is tall and upright as a Pine,
White as blaunch'd Almonds, or the falling Snow,
Sweet as are Damask Roses when they blow,
And doubtless fruitful as the swelling Vine.

Ripe to be cut, and ready to be press'd,
Her full cheek'd beauties very well appear,
And a year's fruit she loses e'ery year,
Wanting a man t'improve her to the best.

Full fain she would be husbanded, and yet,
Alass! she cannot a fit Lab'rer get
To cultivate her to her own content:

Fain would she be (God wot) about her task,
And yet (forsooth) she is too proud to ask,
And (which is worse) too modest to consent.

2

Marg'ret of humbler stature by the head
Is (as it oft falls out with yellow hair)
Than her fair Sister, yet so much more fair,
As her pure white is better mixt with red.

This, hotter than the other ten to one,
Longs to be put unto her Mother's trade,
And loud proclaims she lives too long a Maid,
Wishing for one t'untie her Virgin Zone.

She finds Virginity a kind of ware,
That's very very troublesome to bear,
And being gone, she thinks will ne'er be mist:

And yet withall, the Girl has so much grace,
To call for help I know she wants the face,
Though ask'd, I know not how she would resist.

3

Mary is black, and taller than the last,
Yet equal in perfection and desire,
To the one's melting snow, and t'other's fire,
As with whose black their fairness is defac'd.

She pants as much for love as th'other two,
But she so vertuous is, or else so wise,
That she will win or will not love a prize,
And but upon good terms will never doe:

Therefore who her will conquer ought to be
At least as full of love and wit as she,
Or he shall ne'er gain favour at her hands:

Nay, though he have a pretty store of brains,
Shall only have his labour for his pains,
Unless he offer more than she demands.

4

Martha is not so tall, nor yet so fair
As any of the other lovely three,
Her chiefest Grace is poor simplicity,
Yet were the rest away, she were a Star.

She's fair enough, only she wants the art
To set her Beauties off as they can doe,
And that's the cause she ne'er heard any woo,
Nor ever yet made conquest of a heart:

And yet her bloud's as boiling as the best,
Which, pretty soul, does so disturb her rest,
And makes her languish so, she's fit to die.

Poor thing, I doubt she still must lie alone,
For being like to be attack'd by none,
Sh'as no more wit to ask than to deny.

CHARLES COTTON (*d.*1687)

The Sluggard

'Tis the voice of the sluggard; I heard him complain,
'You have waked me too soon, I must slumber again.'
As the door on its hinges, so he on his bed,
Turns his sides and his shoulders and his heavy head.

'A little more sleep, and a little more slumber;'
Thus he wastes half his days and his hours without number;
And when he gets up, he sits folding his hands,
Or walks about sauntering, or trifling he stands.

I passed by his garden, and saw the wild brier,
The thorn and the thistle grow broader and higher;
The clothes that hang on him are turning to rags;
And his money still wastes, till he starves or he begs.

I made him a visit, still hoping to find
He had took better care for improving his mind:
He told me his dreams, talked of eating and drinking;
But he scarce reads his bible, and never loves thinking.

Said I then to my heart, 'Here's a lesson for me;
That man's but a picture of what I might be:
But thanks to my friends for their care in my breeding,
Who taught me betimes to love working and reading.'

ISAAC WATTS (c.1715)

The Character of Sir Robert Walpole

With favour and fortune fastidiously blessed,
He's loud in his laugh and he's coarse in his jest;
Of favour and fortune unmerited vain,
A sharper in trifles, a dupe in the main.
Achieving of nothing, still promising wonders,
By dint of experience improving in blunders;

Oppressing true merit, exalting the base,
And selling his country to purchase his peace.
A jobber of stocks by retailing false news;
A prater at court in the style of the stews;
Of virtue and worth by profession a giber,
Of juries and senates the bully and briber:
Though I name not the wretch you know who I mean —
'Tis the cur-dog of Britain and spaniel of Spain.

JONATHAN SWIFT (c.1727)

Stella's Birthday, 1721

All travellers at first incline
Where'er they see the fairest sign,
And, if they find the chambers neat,
And like the liquour and the meat,
Will call again and recommend
The Angel Inn to every friend.
And, though the painting grows decayed
The house will never lose its trade;
Nay, though the trecherous rascal Thomas
Hangs a new Angel two doors from us
As fine as daubers hands can make it
In hopes that strangers may mistake it,
They think it both a shame and sin
To quit the true old angel Inn.
    Now, this is Stella's case in fact,
An angels's face, a little cracked
(Could poets or could painters fix
How angels look at thirty-six);
This drew us in at first to find
In such a form an angel's mind,
And every virtue now supplies
The fainting rays of Stella's eyes.
See, at her levee, crowding swains
Whom Stella freely entertains
With breeding, humour, wit and sense,

And puts them to so small expense,
Their minds so plentifully fills,
And makes such reasonable bills,
So little gets for what she gives,
We really wonder how she lives,
And, had her stock been less, no doubt
She must have long ago run out.
    Then who can think we'll quit the place
When Doll hangs out a newer face,
Or stop and light at Cloe's head
With scraps and leavings to be fed?
    Then Chloe, still go on to prate
Of thirty-six and thirty-eight;
Pursue thy trade of scandal picking,
Thy hints that Stella is no chicken,
Your innuendos, when you tell us
That Stella loves to talk with fellows;
But let me warn you to believe
A truth for which your soul should grieve;
That, should you live to see the day
When Stella's locks must all be grey;
When age must print a furrowed trace
On every feature of her face;
Though you and all your senseless tribe,
Could art, or time, or nature bribe,
To make you look like beauty's queen,
And hold forever at fifteen,
No bloom of youth can ever blind
The cracks and wrinkles of you mind,
And men of sense will pass your door,
And crowd to Stella's at fourscore.

JONATHAN SWIFT (1720–1)

This is one of Swift's several birthday letters to his 'most valuable friend' Esther Johnson whom he persuaded to move to Dublin, where he lived, in 1701 and who eventually died there in 1728. There has always been much speculation about the nature of their relationship. A more directly affectionate letter, written six years later, is in Section 9.

from *Verses on the Death of Dean Swift*

SELF-PORTRAIT OF SWIFT

'The Dean, if we believe report,
Was never ill received at court:
As for his works in verse and prose,
I own myself no judge of those:
Nor, can I tell what critics thought 'em;
But, this I know, all people bought 'em;
As with a moral view designed
To cure the vices of mankind:
His vein, ironically grave,
Exposed the fool, and lashed the knave:
To steal a hint was never known,
But what he writ was all his own.

'He never thought an honour done him,
Because a duke was proud to own him:
Would rather slip aside, and choose
To talk with wits in dirty shoes:
Despised the fools with stars and garters,
So often seen caressing Chartres:
He never courted men in station,
Nor persons had in admiration;
Of no man's greatness was afraid,
Because he sought for no man's aid.
Though trusted long in great affairs,
He gave himself no haughty airs:
Without regarding private ends,
Spent all his credit for his friends:
And only chose the wise and good;
No flatterers; no allies in blood;
But succoured virtue in distress,
And seldom failed of good success;
As numbers in their hearts must own,
Who, but for him, had been unknown.

'With princes kept a due decorum,
But never stood in awe before 'em:

And to her Majesty, God bless her,
Would speak as free as to her dresser,
She thought it his peculiar whim,
Nor took it ill as come from him.
He followed David's lesson just,
"In princes never put thy trust."
And, would you make him truly sour;
Provoke him with a slave in power:
The Irish senate, if you named,
With what impatience he declaimed!
Fair LIBERTY was all his cry;
For her he stood prepared to die;
For her he boldly stood alone;
For her he oft exposed his own.
Two kingdoms, just as factions led,
Had set a price upon his head;
But, not a traitor could be found,
To sell him for six hundred pound.

'Had he but spared his tongue and pen,
He might have rose like other men:
But, power was never in his thought;
And, wealth he valued not a groat:
Ingratitude he often found,
And pitied those who meant the wound:
But, kept the tenor of his mind,
To merit well of humankind:
Nor made a sacrifice of those
Who still were true, to please his foes.
He laboured many a fruitless hour
To reconcile his friends in power;
Saw mischief by a faction brewing,
While they pursued each other's ruin.
But, finding vain was all his care,
He left the court in mere despair.

* * *

'In exile with a steady heart,
He spent his life's declining part;
Where folly, pride, and faction sway,
Remote from St John, Pope, and Gay.

'His friendship there to few confined,
Were always of the middling kind:
No fools of rank, a mongrel breed,
Who fain would pass for lords indeed:
Where titles give no right or power,
And peerage is a withered flower,
He would have held it a disgrace,
If such a wretch had known his face.
On rural squires, that kingdom's bane,
He vented oft his wrath in vain:
Biennial squires, to market brought;
Who sell their souls and votes for naught;
The nation stripped, go joyful back,
To rob the church, their tenants rack,
Go snacks with thieves and rapparees,
And keep the peace, to pick up fees:
In every job to have a share,
A gaol or barrack to repair;
And turn the tax for public roads
Commodious to their own abodes.

'Perhaps I may allow the Dean
Had too much satire in his vein;
And seemed determined not to starve it,
Because no age could more deserve it.
Yet, malice never was his aim;
He lashed the vice but spared the name.
No individual could resent,
Where thousands equally were meant.
His satire points at no defect,
But what all mortals may correct;
For he abhorred that senseless tribe,
Who call it humour when they jibe:
He spared a hump or crooked nose,
Whose owners set not up for beaux.
True genuine dullness moved his pity,
Unless it offered to be witty.
Those, who their ignorance confessed,
He ne'er offended with a jest;
But laughed to hear an idiot quote,
A verse from Horace, learnt by rote.

'He knew an hundred pleasant stories,
With all the turns of Whigs and Tories:
Was cheerful to his dying day,
And friends would let him have his way.

'He gave the little wealth he had,
To build a house for fools and mad:
And showed by one satiric touch,
No nation wanted it so much:
That kingdom he hath left his debtor,
I wish it soon may have a better.'

JONATHAN SWIFT (1731)

from the *Epistle to A Lady*

ON THE CHARACTERS OF FIVE WOMEN

See Sin in State, majestically drunk,
Proud as a Peeress, prouder as a Punk;
Chaste to her Husband, frank to all beside,
A teeming Mistress, but a barren Bride.
What then? let Blood and Body bear the fault,
Her Head's untouch'd, that noble Seat of Thought:
Such this day's doctrine – in another fit
She sins with Poets thro' pure Love of Wit.
What has not fir'd her bosom or her brain?
Caesar and Tall-boy, Charles and Charlema'ne.
As Helluo, late Dictator of the Feast,
The Nose of Hautgout, and the Tip of Taste,
Critick'd your wine, and analyz'd your meat,
Yet on plain Pudding deign'd at-home to eat;
So Philomedé, lect'ring all mankind
On the soft Passion, and the Taste refin'd,
Th' Address, the Delicacy – stoops at once,
And makes her hearty meal upon a Dunce.
Flavia's a Wit, has too much sense to Pray,
To Toast our wants and wishes, is her way;

Nor asks of God, but of her Stars to give
The mighty blessing, 'while we live, to live.'
Then all for Death, that Opiate of the soul!
Lucretia's dagger, Rosamonda's bowl.
Say, what can cause such impotence of mind?
A Spark too fickle, or a Spouse too kind.
Wise Wretch! with Pleasures too refin'd to please,
With too much Spirit to be e'er at ease,
With too much Quickness ever to be taught,
With too much Thinking to have common Thought:
Who purchase Pain with all that Joy can give,
And die of nothing but a Rage to live.
    Turn then from Wits; and look on Simo's Mate,
No Ass so meek, no Ass so obstinate:
Or her, that owns her Faults, but never mends,
Because she's honest, and the best of Friends:
Or her, whose life the Church and Scandal share,
For ever in a Passion, or a Pray'r:
Or her, who laughs at Hell, but (like her Grace)
Cries, 'Ah! how charming if there's no such place!'
Or who in sweet vicissitude appears
Of Mirth and Opium, Ratafie and Tears,
The daily Anodyne, and nightly Draught,
To kill those foes to Fair ones, Time and Thought.
Woman and Fool are two hard things to hit,
For true No-meaning puzzles more than Wit.
    But what are these to great Atossa's mind?
Scarce once herself, by turns all Womankind!
Who, with herself, or others, from her birth
Finds all her life one warfare upon earth:
Shines, in exposing Knaves, and painting Fools,
Yet is, whate'er she hates and ridicules.
No Thought advances, but her Eddy Brain
Whisks it about, and down it goes again.
Full sixty years the World has been her Trade,
The wisest Fool much Time has ever made.
From loveless youth to unrespected age,
No Passion gratify'd except her Rage.
So much the Fury still out-ran the Wit,
The Pleasure miss'd her, and the Scandal hit.

Who breaks with her, provokes Revenge from Hell,
But he's a bolder man who dares be well:
Her ev'ry turn with Violence pursu'd,
Nor more a storm her Hate than Gratitude.
To that each Passion turns, or soon or late;
Love, if it makes her yield, must make her hate:
Superiors? death! and Equals? what a curse!
But an Inferior not dependant? worse.
Offend her, and she knows not to forgive;
Oblige her, and she'll hate you while you live:
But die, and she'll adore you – Then the Bust
And Temple rise – then fall again to dust.
Last night, her Lord was all that's good and great,
A Knave this morning, and his Will a Cheat.
Strange! by the Means defeated of the Ends,
By Spirit robb'd of Pow'r, by Warmth of Friends,
By Wealth of Follow'rs! without one distress
Sick of herself thro' very selfishness!
Atossa, curs'd with ev'ry granted pray'r,
Childless with all her Children, wants an Heir.
To Heirs unknown descends th' unguarded store
Or wanders, Heav'n-directed, to the Poor.

    Pictures like these, dear Madam, to design,
Asks no firm hand, and no unerring line;
Some wand'ring touch, or some reflected light,
Some flying stroke alone can hit 'em right:
For how should equal Colours do the knack?
Chameleons who can paint in white and black?

    'Yet Cloe sure was form'd without a spot – '
Nature in her then err'd not, but forgot.
'With ev'ry pleasing, ev'ry prudent part,
Say, what can Cloe want?' – she wants a Heart.
She speaks, behaves, and acts just as she ought;
But never, never, reach'd one gen'rous Thought.
Virtue she finds too painful an endeavour,
Content to dwell in Decencies for ever.
So very reasonable, so unmov'd,
As never yet to love, or to be lov'd.
She, while her Lover pants upon her breast,
Can mark the figures on an Indian chest;

And when she sees her Friend in deep despair,
Observes how much a Chintz exceeds Mohair.
Forbid it Heav'n, a Favour or a Debt
She e'er should cancel – but she may forget.
Safe is your Secret still in Cloe's ear;
But none of Cloe's shall you ever hear.
Of all her Dears she never slander'd one,
But cares not if a thousand are undone.
Would Cloe know if you're alive or dead?
She bids her Footman put it in her head.
Cloe is prudent – would you too be wise?
Then never break your heart when Cloe dies.

ALEXANDER POPE (1731–5)

from the *Epistle to Dr Arbuthnot*

ADDISON AND HERVEY

Peace to all such! but were there one whose fires
True Genius kindles, and fair Fame inspires;
Blessed with each talent and each art to please,
And born to write, converse, and live with ease:
Should such a man, too fond to rule alone,
Bear, like the Turk, no brother near the throne;
View him with scornful, yet with jealous eyes,
And hate for arts that caused himself to rise;
Damn with faint praise, assent with civil leer,
And without sneering, teach the rest to sneer;
Willing to wound, and yet afraid to strike,
Just hint a fault, and hesitate dislike;
Alike reserved to blame or to commend,
A timorous foe, and a suspicious friend;
Dreading even fools; by flatterers besieged,
And so obliging that he ne'er obliged;
Like Cato, give his little senate laws,
And sit attentive to his own applause;
While wits and Templars every sentence raise,

And wonder with a foolish face of praise –
Who but must laugh, if such a man there be?
Who would not weep, if Atticus were he?

*   *   *

PORE   Yet let me flap this bug with gilded wings,
This painted child of dirt, that stinks and stings;
Whose buzz the witty and the fair annoys,
Yet wit ne'er tastes, and beauty ne'er enjoys;
So well-bred spaniels civilly delight
In mumbling of the game they dare not bite.
Eternal smiles his emptiness betray,
As shallow streams run dimpling all the way.
Whether in florid impotence he speaks,
And, as the prompter breathes, the puppet squeaks;
Or at the ear of Eve, familiar toad,
Half froth, half venom, spits himself abroad,
In puns, or politics, or tales, or lies,
Or spite, or smut, or rhymes, or blasphemies.
His wit all seesaw between *that* and *this*,
Now high, now low, now master up, now miss, ⎱
And he himself one vile antithesis.   ⎰
Amphibious thing! that acting either part,
The trifling head or the corrupted heart,
Fop at the toilet, flatterer at the board,
Now trips a lady, and now struts a lord.
Eve's tempter thus the rabbins have expressed,
A cherub's face, a reptile all the rest;
Beauty that shocks you, parts that none will trust,
Wit that can creep, and pride that licks the dust.

ALEXANDER POPE (published 1735)

Pope had been a member of Addison's circle but had later taken
offence when Addison's friends had criticised his translation of
Homer. Lord Hervey and Pope, both small sickly men who spent
much of their time in feminine company, were very jealous of each
other. As this extract shows Pope was not called the 'Wasp of
Twickenham' for nothing!

from *The Ghost*

AN UNFLATTERING VIEW OF DR JOHNSON

Churchill was a close friend of John Wilkes, the radical politician, whom the conservative Johnson regarded as a scoundrel. The picture of Johnson, affected by Churchill's strongly partisan feelings, is very unlike the generous-minded (though strongly opinionated) and spiritually tortured figure we know from Boswell and elsewhere. The second extract's reference to his cheating his subscribers (i.e. the people who, in the absence of a publishing system such as exists today, were his financial backers) relates to his great edition of Shakespeare, which was eventually triumphantly produced, but took twelve years to appear. The personal remarks refer to his ungainly appearance, partly due to childhood illness, and huge size. The English language owes an immense debt to Johnson's great pioneering *Dictionary*, and it is amazing that the GPO chose not to commemorate the bicentenary of his death in 1984 with a stamp, preferring instead to celebrate cattle breeders. Few other countries would have made such a choice, let alone one whose language has become so international!

POMPOSO (insolent and loud,
Vain idol of a *scribbling* crowd,
Whose very name inspires an awe,
Whose ev'ry word is Sense and Law,
For what his Greatness hath decreed,
Like Laws of PERSIA and of MEDE,
Sacred thro' all the realm of *Wit*,
Must never of Repeal admit;
Who, cursing flatt'ry, is the tool
Of ev'ry fawning flatt'ring fool;
Who Wit with jealous eye surveys,
And sickens at another's praise;
Who, proudly seiz'd of *Learning*'s throne,
Now damns all Learning but his own;
Who scorns those common wares to trade in,
Reas'ning, *Convincing*, and *Persuading*,
But makes each Sentence current pass
With *Puppy*, *Coxcomb*, *Scoundrel*, Ass;

For 'tis with *him* a certain rule,
The Folly 's prov'd, when he calls Fool;
Who, to increase his native strength,
Draws words, six syllables in length,
With which, assisted with a frown
By way of Club, he knocks us down;
Who 'bove the Vulgar dares to rise,
And sense of *Decency* defies,
For this same *Decency* is made
Only for Bunglers in the trade;
And, like the *Cobweb Laws*, is still
Broke thro' by *Great ones* when they will) –
POMPOSO, with *strong sense* supplied,
Supported, and confirm'd by *Pride*,
His Comrades' terrors to beguile,
Grinn'd horribly a ghastly smile:
Features so horrid, were it light,
Would put the Devil himself to flight.

*   *   *

Horrid, *unwieldy*, *without Form*,
Savage, as OCEAN in a Storm,
Of size prodigious, in the rear,
That Post of Honour, should appear
POMPOSO; *Fame* around should tell
How he a slave to int'rest fell,
How, for *Integrity* renown'd,
Which Booksellers have often found,
He for *Subscribers* baits his hook,
And takes their cash – but where 's the Book?
No matter where – *Wise* Fear, we know,
Forbids the robbing of a Foe,
But what, to serve our private ends,
Forbids the cheating of our Friends?
No Man alive, who would not swear
All's *safe*, and therefore *honest* there.
For spite of all the learned say,
If we to Truth attention pay,
The word *Dishonesty* is meant
For nothing else but *Punishment*.

Fame too should tell, nor heed the threat
Of Rogues, who Brother Rogues abet,
Nor tremble at the terrors hung
Aloft, *to make her hold her tongue*,
How to all Principles untrue,
Nor fix'd to *old* Friends, nor to *New*,
He damns the *Pension* which he takes,
And loves the STUART he forsakes.
NATURE (who justly regular
Is very seldom known to err,
But now and then in *sportive mood*,
As some *rude* wits have understood,
Or *through much work requir'd in haste*,
Is with a random stroke disgrac'd)
POMPOSO form'd on *doubtful* plan,
Not quite a *Beast*, nor quite a *Man*,
Like – *God knows what* – for never yet
Could the most subtle human Wit,
Find out a Monster, which might be
The Shadow of a *Simile*.

CHARLES CHURCHILL (1762–3)

from *The Traveller*

NATIONAL CHARACTERS OF THE ITALIANS AND SWISS

Far to the right where Apennine ascends,
Bright as the summer, Italy extends;
Its uplands sloping deck the mountain's side,
Woods over woods in gay theatric pride;
While oft some temple's mould'ring tops between
With venerable grandeur mark the scene.

Could Nature's bounty satisfy the breast,
The sons of Italy were surely blest.
Whatever fruits in different climes were found,
That proudly rise, or humbly court the ground;

Whatever blooms in torrid tracts appear,
Whose bright succession decks the varied year;
Whatever sweets salute the northern sky
With vernal lives that blossom but to die;
These here disporting own the kindred soil,
Nor ask luxuriance from the planter's toil;
While sea-born gales their gelid wings expand
To winnow fragrance round the smiling land.

But small the bliss that sense alone bestows,
And sensual bliss is all the nation knows.
In florid beauty groves and fields appear,
Man seems the only growth that dwindles here.
Contrasted faults through all his manners reign;
Though poor, luxurious; though submissive, vain;
Though grave, yet trifling; zealous, yet untrue;
And e'en in penance planning sins anew.
All evils here contaminate the mind,
That opulence departed leaves behind;
For wealth was theirs, not far removed the date,
When commerce proudly flourished through the state;
At her command the palace learned to rise,
Again the long-fall'n column sought the skies;
The canvas glowed beyond e'en Nature warm,
The pregnant quarry teemed with human form;
Till, more unsteady than the southern gale,
Commerce on other shores displayed her sail:
While nought remained of all that riches gave,
But towns unmanned, and lords without a slave;
And late the nation found, with fruitless skill,
Its former strength was but plethoric ill.

Yet still the loss of wealth is here supplied
By arts, the splendid wrecks of former pride;
From these the feeble heart and long-fall'n mind
An easy compensation seem to find.
Here may be seen, in bloodless pomp arrayed,
The paste-board triumph and the cavalcade;
Processions formed for piety and love,
A mistress or a saint in every grove.

By sports like these are all their cares beguiled,
The sports of children satisfy the child;
Each nobler aim, repressed by long control,
Now sinks at last, or feebly mans the soul;
While low delights, succeeding fast behind,
In happier meanness occupy the mind:
As in those domes, where Caesars once bore sway,
Defaced by time and tottering in decay,
There in the ruin, heedless of the dead,
The shelter-seeking peasant builds his shed,
And, wond'ring man could want the larger pile,
Exults, and owns his cottage with a smile.

My soul, turn from them; turn we to survey
Where rougher climes a nobler race display,
Where the bleak Swiss their stormy mansions tread,
And force a churlish soil for scanty bread;
No product here the barren hills afford,
But man and steel, the soldier and his sword;
No vernal blooms their torpid rocks array,
But winter ling'ring chills the lap of May;
No Zephyr fondly sues the mountain's breast,
But meteors glare, and stormy glooms invest.

Yet still, e'en here, content can spread a charm,
Redress the clime, and all its rage disarm.
Though poor the peasant's hut, his feasts though small,
He sees his little lot the lot of all;
Sees no contiguous palace rear its head
To shame the meanness of his humble shed;
No costly lord the sumptuous banquet deal
To make him loathe his vegetable meal;
But calm, and bred in ignorance and toil,
Each wish contracting, fits him to the soil.
Cheerful at morn he wakes from short repose,
Breasts the keen air, and carols as he goes;
With patient angle trolls the finny deep,
Or drives his vent'rous plough-share to the steep;
Or seeks the den where snow-tracks mark the way,
And drags the struggling savage into day.

At night returning, every labour sped,
He sits him down the monarch of a shed;
Smiles by his cheerful fire, and round surveys
His children's looks, that brighten at the blaze;
While his loved partner, boastful of her hoard,
Displays her cleanly platter on the board:
And haply too some pilgrim, thither led,
With many a tale repays the nightly bed.

Thus every good his native wilds impart,
Imprints the patriot passion on his heart,
And e'en those ills, that round his mansion rise,
Enhance the bliss his scanty fund supplies.
Dear is that shed to which his soul conforms,
And dear that hill which lifts him to the storms;
And as a child, when scaring sounds molest,
Clings close and closer to the mother's breast,
So the loud torrent, and the whirlwind's roar,
But bind him to his native mountains more.

OLIVER GOLDSMITH (published 1764)

from *The Deserted Village*

THE VILLAGE PARSON AND SCHOOLMASTER

Near yonder copse, where once the garden smiled,
And still where many a garden flower grows wild;
There, where a few torn shrubs the place disclose,
The village preacher's modest mansion rose.
A man he was to all the country dear,
And passing rich with forty pounds a year;
Remote from towns he ran his godly race,
Nor e'er had changed, nor wished to change his place;
Unpractised he to fawn, or seek for power,
By doctrines fashioned to the varying hour;
Far other aims his heart had learned to prize,
More skilled to raise the wretched than to rise.

His house was known to all the vagrant train,
He chid their wand'rings, but relieved their pain;
The long-remembered beggar was his guest,
Whose beard descending swept his aged breast;
The ruined spendthrift, now no longer proud,
Claimed kindred there, and had his claims allowed;
The broken soldier, kindly bade to stay,
Sat by his fire, and talked the night away;
Wept o'er his wounds, or tales of sorrow done,
Shouldered his crutch, and showed how fields were won.
Pleased with his guests, the good man learned to glow,
And quite forgot their vices in their woe;
Careless their merits, or their faults to scan,
His pity gave ere charity began.

Thus to relieve the wretched was his pride,
And e'en his failings leaned to virtue's side;
But in his duty prompt at every call,
He watched and wept, he prayed and felt, for all.
And, as a bird each fond endearment tries
To tempt its new-fledged offspring to the skies,
He tried each art, reproved each dull delay,
Allured to brighter worlds, and led the way.

Beside the bed where parting life was laid,
And sorrow, guilt, and pain, by turns dismayed,
The reverend champion stood. At his control,
Despair and anguish fled the struggling soul;
Comfort came down the trembling wretch to raise,
And his last falt'ring accents whispered praise.

At church, with meek and unaffected grace,
His looks adorned the venerable place;
Truth from his lips prevailed with double sway,
And fools, who came to scoff, remained to pray.
The service passed, around the pious man,
With steady zeal, each honest rustic ran;
E'en children followed with endearing wile,
And plucked his gown, to share the good man's smile.
His ready smile a parent's warmth expressed,

Their welfare pleased him, and their cares distressed;
To them his heart, his love, his griefs were given,
But all his serious thoughts had rest in Heaven.
As some tall cliff, that lifts its awful form,
Swells from the vale, and midway leaves the storm,
Though round its breast the rolling clouds are spread,
Eternal sunshine settles on its head.

Beside yon straggling fence that skirts the way,
With blossomed furze unprofitably gay,
There, in his noisy mansion, skilled to rule,
The village master taught his little school;
A man severe he was, and stern to view;
I knew him well, and every truant knew;
Well had the boding tremblers learned to trace
The day's disasters in his morning face;
Full well they laughed, with counterfeited glee,
At all his jokes, for many a joke had he;
Full well the busy whisper, circling round,
Conveyed the dismal tidings when he frowned;
Yet he was kind; or if severe in aught,
The love he bore to learning was in fault;
The village all declared how much he knew;
'Twas certain he could write, and cypher too;
Lands he could measure, terms and tides presage.
And e'en the story ran that he could gauge.
In arguing too, the parson owned his skill,
For e'en though vanquished, he could argue still;
While words of learned length and thund'ring sound
Amazed the gazing rustics ranged around,
And still they gazed, and still the wonder grew,
That one small head could carry all he knew.

OLIVER GOLDSMITH (published 1770)

The Solitude of Alexander Selkirk

I am monarch of all I survey,
   My right there is none to dispute;
From the centre all round to the sea
   I am lord of the fowl and the brute.
O solitude! where are the charms
   That sages have seen in thy face?
Better dwell in the midst of alarms
   Than reign in this horrible place.

I am out of humanity's reach,
   I must finish my journey alone,
Never hear the sweet music of speech;
   I start at the sound of my own.
The beasts that roam over the plain
   My form with indifference see;
They are so unacquainted with man,
   Their tameness is shocking to me.

Society, friendship, and love
   Divinely bestowed upon man,
O had I the wings of a dove
   How soon would I taste you again!
My sorrows I then might assuage
   In the ways of religion and truth,
Might learn from the wisdom of age,
   And be cheered by the sallies of youth.

Ye winds that have made me your sport,
   Convey to this desolate shore
Some cordial endearing report
   Of a land I shall visit no more:
My friends, do they now and then send
   A wish or a thought after me?
O tell me I yet have a friend,
   Though a friend I am never to see.

How fleet is a glance of the mind!
   Compared with the speed of its flight,
The tempest itself lags behind,
   And the swift-wingèd arrows of light.
When I think of my own native land
   In a moment I seem to be there;
But, alas! recollection at hand
   Soon hurries me back to despair.

But the seafowl is gone to her nest,
   The beast is laid down in his lair;
Even here is a season of rest,
   And I to my cabin repair.
There is mercy in every place,
   And mercy, encouraging thought!
Gives even affliction a grace
   And reconciles man to his lot.

WILLIAM COWPER (1782)

14
MEDIEVALISM, LEGEND, DREAM, NIGHTMARE & THE SUPERNATURAL

from *Paradise Lost*

MILTON'S SATAN

He scarce had ceased when the superior fiend
Was moving towards the shore, his ponderous shield
Ethereal temper, massy, large and round,
Behind him cast; the broad circumference
Hung on his shoulders like the moon, whose orb
Through optic glass the Tuscan artist views
At evening from the top of Fesole
Or in Valdarno, to descry new lands,
Rivers, or mountains in her spotty globe.
His spear, to equal which the tallest pine,
Hewn on Norwegian hills, to be the mast
Of some great ammiral, were but a wand,
He walked with, to support uneasy steps
Over the burning marl, not like those steps
On heaven's azure; and the torrid clime
Smote on him sore besides, vaulted with fire:
Natheless he so endured, till on the beach
Of that inflamed sea he stood and call'd
His legions, angel forms, who lay entranced
Thick as autumnal leaves that strew the brooks
In Vallombrosa, where the Etrurian shades,
High overarch'd imbower; or scatter'd sedge
Afloat, when with fierce winds Orion arm'd
Hath vex'd th Red Sea coast, whose waves o'erthrew
Busiris and his Memphian chivalry,
While with perfidious hatred they pursued
The sojourners of Goshen, who beheld
From the safe shore their floating carcases
And broken chariot wheels: so thick-bestrewn,
Abject and lost lay these, covering the flood,
Under amazement of their hideous change.

Vallombrosa, 'the shady valley', is in Tuscany, but the name clearly recalls the Valley of the Shadow of Death. The end of the passage recalls the army of Pharaoh destroyed pursuing the Israelites across the Red Sea.

SATAN REVIEWS HIS TROOPS

                                      And now his heart
Distends with pride, and hardening in his strength
Glories: for never, since created man,
Met such embodied force, as named with those
Could merit more than that small infantry
Warr'd on by cranes; though all the giant brood
Of Phlegra with the heroic race were join'd
That fought at Thebes and Ilium, on each side
Mixed with auxiliar gods; and what resounds
In fable or romance of Uther's son
Begirt with British and Armoric knights;
And all who since, baptized or infidel,
Jousted in Aspramont, or Montalban,
Damasco, or Morocco, or Trebizond,
Or whom Biserta sent from Afric shore,
When Charlemain with all his peerage fell
By Fontarrabia. Thus far these beyond
Compare of mortal prowess, yet observed
Their dread commander: he, above the rest
In shape and gesture proudly eminent,
Stood like a tower; his form had not yet lost
All its original brightness; nor appeared
Less than archangel ruin'd, and the excess
Of glory obscured: as when the sun, new risen,
Looks through the horizontal misty air,
Shorn of his beams; or from behind the moon,
In dim eclipse, disastrous twilight sheds
On half the nations, and with fear of change
Perplexes monarchs. Darken'd So, yet shone
Above them all the archangel; but his face
Deep scars of thunder had intrench'd; and care
Sat on his faded cheek, but under brows
Of dauntless courage and considerate pride
Waiting revenge; cruel his eye, but cast
Signs of remorse and passion, to behold
The fellows of his crime, the followers rather
(Far other once beheld in bliss) condemn'd

For ever now to have their lot in pain;
Millions of spirits for his fault amerced
Of heaven, and from eternal splendours flung
For his revolt; yet faithful how they stood,
Their glory wither'd; as when heaven's fire
Hath scath'd the forest oaks, or mountain pines,
With singed top, their stately growth, though bare,
Stands on the blasted heath.

To emphasise the huge scale of the conflict between good and evil
he is describing, Milton compares Satan's troops here with all the
warrior armies that figure in the great epics and legends of the past,
the Giants that attacked Olympus, the knights of Arthurian legends,
and the heroes of Italian and French romance epics.

SATAN ENCOUNTERS SIN AND DEATH

Before the gates there sat
On either side a formidable shape;
The one seem'd woman to the waist and fair;
But ended foul in many a scaly fold
Voluminous and vast; a serpent arm'd
With mortal sting; about her middle round
A cry of hell-hounds never-ceasing bark'd,
With wide Cerberian mouths, full loud, and rung
A hideous peal; yet when they list would creep,
If aught disturb'd their noise, into her womb,
And kennel there; yet still there bark'd and howl'd
Within, unseen. Far less abhorr'd than these
Vex'd Scylla,[1] bathing in the sea that parts
Calabria from the hoarse Trinacrian shore;
Nor uglier follow the night-hag, when, call'd
In secret, riding through the air she comes,
Lured with the smell of infant blood, to dance
With Lapland witches, while the labouring moon

---

[1] a Classical sea monster

Eclipses at their charms. The other shape,
If shape it might be call'd, that shape had none
Distinguishable in member, joint or limb;
Or substance might be call'd that shadow seem'd,
For each seem'd either; black it stood as night,
Fierce as ten Furies, terrible as hell,
And shook a dreadful dart; what seem'd his head
The likeness of a kingly crown had on.

JOHN MILTON (1667)

William and Margaret

'Twas at the silent solemn hour,
    When night and morning meet;
In glided Margaret's grimly ghost,
    And stood at William's feet.

Her face was like an April morn,
    Clad in a wintry cloud;
And clay-cold was her lily hand
    That held her sable shroud.

So shall the fairest face appear,
    When youth and years are flown:
Such is the robe that kings must wear,
    When death has reft their crown.

Her bloom was like the springing flower,
    That sips the silver dew;
The rose was budded in her cheek,
    Just opening to the view.

But love had, like the canker-worm,
    Consumed her early prime;
The rose grew pale, and left her cheek;
    She died before her time.

'Awake!' she cried, 'thy true love calls,
   Come from her midnight grave:
Now let thy pity hear the maid,
   Thy love refused to save.

'This is the dark and dreary hour
   When injured ghosts complain;
When yawning graves give up their dead
   To haunt the faithless swain.

'Bethink thee, William, of the fault,
   Thy pledge and broken oath:
And give me back my maiden vow,
   And give me back my troth.

'Why did you promise love to me,
   And not that promise keep?
Why did you swear mine eyes were bright,
   Yet leave those eyes to weep?

'How could you say my face was fair,
   And yet that face forsake?
How could you win my virgin heart,
   Yet leave that heart to break?

'Why did you say, my lip was sweet,
   And made the scarlet pale?
And why did I, young, witless maid!
   Believe the flattering tale?

'That face, alas! no more is fair;
   Those lips no longer red:
Dark are my eyes, now closed in death,
   And every charm is fled.

'The hungry worm my sister is;
   This winding-shèet I wear:
And cold and weary lasts our night,
   Till that last morn appear.

'But hark! – the cock has warned me hence;
   A long and late adieu!
Come, see, false man, how low she lies,
   Who died for love of you.'

The lark sung loud; the morning smiled,
   With beams of rosy red:
Pale William quaked in every limb,
   And raving left his bed.

He hied him to the fatal place
   Where Margaret's body lay;
And stretched him on the grass-green turf,
   That wrapped her breathless clay.

And thrice he called on Margaret's name,
   And thrice he wept full sore;
Then laid his cheek to her cold grave,
   And word spake never more.

                         DAVID MALLET (1723)

from *Ode on the Popular Superstitions of the Highlands of Scotland*

THE KELPIE

6

What though far off, from some dark dell espied
   His glimm'ring mazes cheer th' excursive sight,
Yet turn, ye wand'rers, turn your steps aside,
   Nor trust the guidance of that faithless light;
For watchful, lurking 'mid th' unrustling reed,
   At those mirk hours the wily monster lies,
And listens oft to hear the passing steed,
   And frequent round him rolls his sullen eyes,
If chance his savage wrath may some weak wretch surprise.

7

Ah, luckless swain, o'er all unblest indeed!
   Whom late bewildered in the dank, dark fen,
Far from his flocks and smoking hamlet then!
   To that sad spot . . . :[1]
On him enraged, the fiend, in angry mood,
   Shall never look with pity's kind concern,
But instant, furious, raise the whelming flood
   O'er its drowned bank, forbidding all return.
Or, if he meditate his wished escape
   To some dim hill that seems uprising near,
To his faint eye the grim and grisly shape,
   In all its terrors clad, shall wild appear.
Meantime, the wat'ry surge shall around him rise,
   Poured sudden forth from every swelling source.
What now remains but tears and hopeless sighs?
   His fear-shook limbs have lost their youthly force,
And down the waves he floats, a pale and breathless corse.

---

[1] part of line missing

8

For him, in vain, his anxious wife shall wait,
   Or wander forth to meet him on his way;
For him, in vain, at to-fall of the day,
   His babes shall linger at th' unclosing gate!
Ah, ne'er shall he return! Alone, if night
   Her travelled limbs in broken slumbers steep,
With dropping willows dressed, his mournful sprite
   Shall visit sad, perchance, her silent sleep:
Then he, perhaps, with moist and wat'ry hand,
   Shall fondly seem to press her shudd'ring cheek
And with his blue swoln face before her stand,
   And, shiv'ring cold, these piteous accents speak:
'Pursue, dear wife, thy daily toils pursue
   At dawn or dusk, industrious as before;
Nor e'er of me one hapless thought renew,
   While I lie welt'ring on the oziered shore,
Drowned by the kelpie's wrath, nor e'er shall aid thee more

           WILLIAM COLLINS (1750)

The faithless light is the Will o' the Wisp that leads people to destruction on the marshes. The kelpie is a horse-shaped water monster that drowns its victims.

Minstrel's Song

This is from the play *Aella*, one of the pretendedly medieval works created by this young Bristol poet. He later committed suicide in London despairing of gaining the recognition he craved.

> O! synge untoe mie roundelaie,
> O! droppe the brynie teare wythe mee,
> Daunce ne moe atte hallie daie,[1]
> Lycke a reynynge ryver bee;
> > Mie love ys dedde,
> > Gon to hys death-bedde,
> > Al under the wyllowe tree.

> Blacke hys cryne[2] as the wyntere nyghte,
> Whyte hys rode[3] as the sommer snowe,
> Rodde hys face as the mornynge lyghte,
> Cale[4] he lyes ynne the grave belowe;
> > Mie love ys dedde,
> > Gon to hys deathe-bedde,
> > Al under the wyllowe tree.

> Swote[5] hys tyngue as the throstles note,
> Quycke ynn daunce as thoughte canne bee,
> Defte hys taboure, codgelle stote,
> O! hee lyes bie the wyllowe tree:
> > Mie love ys dedde,
> > Gonne to hys deathe-bedde,
> > Alle underre the wyllowe tree.

> Harke! the ravenne flappes hys wynge,
> In the briered delle belowe;
> Harke! the dethe-owle loude dothe synge,
> To the nyghte-mares as heie goe;
> > Mie love ys dedde,
> > Gonne to hys deathe-bedde,
> > Al under the wyllowe tree.

[1] holiday [2] hair [3] complexion [4] cold [5] sweet

See! the whyte moone sheenes onne hie;
Whyterre ys mie true loves shroude;
Whyterre yanne the mornynge skie,
Whyterre yanne the evenynge cloude;
  Mie love ys dedde,
  Gon to hys deathe-bedde,
  Al under the wyllowe tree.

Heere, uponne mie true loves grave,
Schalle the baren fleurs be layde,
Nee one hallie Seyncte to save
Al the celness[6] of a mayde.
  Mie love ys dedde,
  Gonne to hys death-bedde,
  Alle under the wyllowe tree.

Wythe mie hondes I'lle dente[7] the brieres
Rounde his hallie corse to gre,[8]
Ouphante[9] fairie, lyghte youre fyres,
Heere mie boddie stylle schalle bee,
  Mie love ys dedde,
  Gon to hys death-bedde,
  Al under the wyllowe tree.

Comme, wythe acorne-coppe & thorne,
Drayne mie hartys blodde awaie;
Lyfe & all yttes goode I scorne,
Daunce bie nete, or feaste by daie.
  Mie love ys dedde,
  Gon to hys death-bedde,
  Al under the wyllowe tree.

      THOMAS CHATTERTON (by 1768)

---

[6] coldness   [7] fasten, plant   [8] grow   [9] elfin

Tam O' Shanter

When chapman billies[1] leave the street,
And drouthy[2] neibors neibors meet,
As market-days are wearing late,
An' folk begin to tak the gate;[3]
While we sit bousing at the nappy,[4]
An' getting fou and unco happy,
We think na on the lang Scots miles,
The mosses, waters, slaps,[5] and stiles,
That lie between us and our hame,
Where sits our sulky sullen dame,
Gathering her brows like gathering storm,
Nursing her wrath to keep it warm.

    This truth fand honest Tam O' Shanter,
As he frae Ayr ae night did canter –
(Auld Ayr, wham ne'er a town surpasses
For honest men and bonnie lasses).

    O Tam! hadst thou but been sae wise
As ta'en thy ain wife Kate's advice!
She tauld thee weel thou was a skellum,
A bletherin', blusterin', drunken blellum;[6]
That frae November till October,
Ae market-day thou was na sober;
That ilka melder wi' the miller
Thou sat as lang as thou had siller;[7]
That every naig was ca'd a shoe on,[8]
The smith and thee gat roarin' fou on;
Thou at the Lord's house, even on Sunday,
Thou drank wi' Kirkton Jean till Monday.
She prophesied that, late or soon,
Thou would be found deep drowned in Doon;
Or catched wi' warlocks in the mirk
By Alloway's auld haunted kirk.

---

[1] market stallholders   [2] thirsty   [3] take to the road   [4] ale   [5] hedges
[6] lazybones   [7] cash (silver)   [8] every horse you ordered shod

Ah, gentle dames! it gars me greet[9]
To think how mony counsels sweet,
How mony lengthened sage advices,
The husband frae the wife despises!
   But to our tale: Ae market night,
Tam had got planted unco right,
Fast by an ingle, bleezing finely,
Wi' reaming swats,[10] that drank divinely;
And at his elbow, Souter[11] Johnny,
His ancient, trusty, drouthy crony;
Tam lo'ed him like a very brither;
They had been fou for weeks thegither.
The night drave on wi' sangs and clatter,
And aye the ale was growing better:
The landlady and Tam grew gracious,
Wi' favours secret, sweet, and precious;
The souter tauld his queerest stories;
The landlord's laugh was ready chorus:
The storm without might rair and rustle,
Tam did na mind the storm a whistle.
   Care, mad to see a man sae happy,
E'en drowned himsel amang the nappy.
As bees flee hame wi' lades o' treasure,
The minutes winged their way wi' pleasure;
Kings may be blest, but Tam was glorious,
O'er a' the ills o' life victorious!
   But pleasures are like poppies spread –
You seize the flow'r, its bloom is shed;
Or like the snow falls in the river –
A moment white, then melts for ever;
Or like the borealis race,[12]
That flit ere you can point their place;
Or like the rainbow's lovely form
Evanishing amid the storm.
Nae man can tether time nor tide;
The hour approaches Tam maun[13] ride;
That hour, o' night's black arch the key-stane,
That dreary hour, he mounts his beast in;

[9] makes me cry   [10] heady young ale   [11] cobbler   [12] aurora   [13] must

And sic a night he taks the road in,
As ne'er poor sinner was abroad in.
   The wind blew as 'twad blawn its last;
The rattling show'rs rose on the blast;
The speedy gleams the darkness swallowed;
Loud, deep, and lang, the thunder bellowed:
That night, a child might understand,
The Deil had business on his hand.
   Weel mounted on his gray mare, Meg,
A better never lifted leg,
Tam skelpit[14] on thro' dub[15] and mire,
Despising wind, and rain, and fire;
Whiles holding fast his gude blue bonnet;
Whiles crooning o'er some auld Scots sonnet;
Whiles glow'ring round wi' prudent cares,
Lest bogles[16] catch him unawares.
Kirk-Alloway was drawing nigh,
Whare ghaists and houlets nightly cry.
   By this time he was cross the ford,
Where in the snaw the chapman smoored;[17]
And past the birks[18] and meikle[19] stane,
Where drunken Charlie brak's neck-bane;
And thro' the whins,[20] and by the cairn,
Where hunters fand the murdered bairn;
And near the thorn, aboon the well,
Where Mungo's mither hanged hersel.
Before him Doon pours all his floods;
The doubling storm roars thro' the woods;
The lightnings flash from pole to pole;
Near and more near the thunders roll:
When, glimmering thro' the groaning trees,
Kirk-Alloway seemed in a bleeze;
Thro' ilka bore[21] the beams were glancing;
And loud resounded mirth and dancing.
   Inspiring bold John Barleycorn!
What dangers thou canst make us scorn!
Wi' tippenny,[22] we fear nae evil;

[14] hastened   [15] puddle   [16] spirits   [17] smothered   [18] birches   [19] huge
[20] gorse   [21] every gap   [22] cheap ale

Wi' usquebae,[23] we'll face the devil!
The swats sae reamed in Tammie's noddle,
Fair play,[24] he cared na deils a boddle![25]
But Maggie stood right sair astonished,
Till, by the heel and hand admonished,
She ventured forward on the light;
And, vow! Tam saw an unco sight!
Warlocks and witches in a dance!
Nae cotillon brent new frae France,
But hornpipes, jigs, strathspeys, and reels,
Put life and mettle in their heels.
A winnock-bunker in the east,
There sat auld Nick, in shape o' beast –
A touzie tyke,[26] black, grim, and large!
To gie them music was his charge:
He screwed the pipes and gart them skirl,
Till roof and rafters a' did dirl.[27]
Coffins stood round like open presses,
That shawed the dead in their last dresses;
And by some devilish cantraip sleight
Each in its cauld hand held a light,
By which heroic Tam was able
To note upon the haly table
A murderer's banes in gibbet-airns;
Twa span-lang,[28] wee, unchristened bairns;
A thief new-cutted frae the rape –
Wi' his last gasp his gab[29] did gape;
Five tomahawks, wi' blude red rusted;
Five scymitars, wi' murder crusted;
A garter, which a babe had strangled;
A knife, a father's throat had mangled,
Whom his ain son o' life bereft –
The gray hairs yet stack to the heft;
Wi' mair of horrible and awfu',
Which even to name wad be unlawfu'.
    As Tammie glowred, amazed, and curious,
The mirth and fun grew fast and furious:

[23] whisky [24] to be fair [25] the smallest coin [26] shaggy dog [27] rattle
[28] long as a hand-span [29] mouth

The piper loud and louder blew;
The dancers quick and quicker flew;
They reeled, they set, they crossed, they cleekit,[30]
Till ilka carlin[31] swat and reekit,
And coost her duddies[32] to the wark,
And linkit[33] at it in her sark![34]

 Now Tam, O Tam! had thae been queans,[35]
A' plump and strapping in their teens;
Their sarks, instead o' creeshie flannen,[36]
Been snaw-white seventeen hunder linen!
Thir breeks o' mine,[37] my only pair,
That ance were plush, o' gude blue hair,
I wad hae gi'en them off my hurdies,[38]
For ae blink o' the bonnie burdies![39]

 But withered beldams, auld and droll,
Rigwoodie[40] hags wad spean a foal,[41]
Louping and flinging[42] on a crummock,[43]
I wonder didna turn thy stomach.

 But Tam kent what was what fu' brawlie[44]
There was ae winsome wench and walie[45]
That night enlisted in the core,[46]
Lang after kent on Carrick shore!
(For mony a beast to dead she shot,
And perished mony a bonnie boat,
And shook[47] baith meikle corn and bear,[48]
And kept the country-side in fear.)
Her cutty sark,[49] o' Paisley harn,
That while a lassie she had worn,
In longitude tho' sorely scanty,
It was her best, and she was vauntie.[50]
Ah! little kent thy reverend grannie
That sark she coft[51] for her wee Nannie
Wi' twa pund Scots ('twas a' her riches)

---

[30] linked arms   [31] hag   [32] threw her clothes off (to dance more freely)
[33] tripped   [34] undergarments   [35] young girls   [36] greasy flannel
[37] those breeches of mine   [38] buttocks   [39] lasses   [40] rugged
[41] scare a mare into giving birth prematurely   [42] leaping and dancing
[43] staff with crooked tip   [44] well   [45] buxom   [46] corps   [47] scattered
[48] barley   [49] short tunic   [50] proud   [51] bought

Wad ever graced a dance of witches!
    But here my muse her wing maun cour;[52]
Sic flights are far beyond her pow'r –
To sing how Nannie lap and flang,
(A souple jade she was, and strang);
And how Tam stood, like ane bewitched,
And thought his very een enriched;
Even Satan glowred and fidged fu' fain,
And hotched[53] and blew wi' might and main:
Till first ae caper, syne[54] anither,
Tam tint his reason a' thegither,
And roars out 'Weel done, Cutty-sark!'
And in an instant all was dark!
And scarcely had he Maggie rallied,
When out the hellish legion sallied.
    As bees bizz out wi' angry fyke[55]
When plundering herds[56] assail their byke,[57]
As open[58] pussie's[59] mortal foes
When pop! she starts before their nose,
As eager runs the market-crowd,
When 'Catch the thief!' resounds aloud.
So Maggie runs; the witches follow,
Wi' mony an eldritch[60] skriech and hollow.
    Ah, Tam! ah, Tam! thou'll get thy fairin'![61]
In hell they'll roast thee like a herrin'!
In vain thy Kate awaits thy comin'!
Kate soon will be a woefu' woman!
Now do thy speedy utmost, Meg,
And win the key-stane o' the brig:
There at them thou thy tail may toss,
A running stream they darena cross.
But ere the key-stane she could make,
The fient a tail she had to shake!
For Nannie, far before the rest,
Hard upon noble Maggie prest,
And flew at Tam wi' furious ettle;[62]

---

[52] restrain [53] wriggled [54] then [55] fret [56] herdsman [57] hive
[58] bay (of hounds) [59] the hare [60] unearthly [61] what you deserve
[62] purpose

But little wist she Maggie's mettle!
Ae spring brought off her master hale,
But left behind her ain gray tail:
The carlin claught[63] her by the rump,
And left poor Maggie scarce a stump.

    Now, wha this tale o' truth shall read,
Each man and mother's son, take heed;
Whene'er to drink you are inclined,
Or cutty-sarks rin in your mind,
Think! ye may buy the joys o'er dear;
Remember Tam O' Shanter's mare.

[63] clutched   **ROBERT BURNS (1791)**

Kubla Khan

In Xanadu did Kubla Khan
A stately pleasure dome decree:
Where Alph, the sacred river, ran
Through caverns measureless to man
      Down to a sunless sea.
So twice five miles of fertile ground
With walls and towers were girdled round:
And there were gardens bright with sinuous rills,
Where blossomed many an incense bearing tree;
And here were forests ancient as the hills,
Enfolding sunny spots of greenery.

But oh! that deep romantic chasm which slanted
Down the green hill athwart a cedarn cover!
A savage place! as holy and enchanted
As e'er beneath a waning moon was haunted
By woman waiting for her demon lover!
  And from this chasm, with ceaseless turmoil
    breathing,
A mighty fountain momently was forced:
Amid whose swift half-intermitted burst
Huge fragments vaulted like rebounding hail,
Or chaffy grain beneath the thresher's flail:

And 'mid these dancing rocks at once and ever
It flung up momently the sacred river.
Four miles meandering with a mazy motion
Through wood and dale the sacred river ran,
Then reached the caverns measureless to man,
And sank in tumult to a lifeless ocean:
And mid this tumult Kubla heard from far
Ancestral voices prophesying war!
 The shadow of the dome of pleasure
 Floated midway on the waves;
 Where was heard the mingled measure
 From the fountain and the caves.
It was a miracle of rare device,
A sunny pleasure-dome with caves of ice!
 A damsel with a dulcimer
 In a vision once I saw:
 It was an Abyssinian maid,
 And on her dulcimer she played,
 Singing of Mount Abora.
 Could I revive within me
 Her symphony and song,
To such a deep delight 'twould win me,
That with music loud and long,
I would build that dome in air,
That sunny dome! those caves of ice!
And all who heard should see them there,
And all should cry, Beware! Beware!
His flashing eyes, his floating hair!
Weave a circle round him thrice,
And close your eyes with holy dread,
For he on honey dew hath fed,
And drunk the milk of Paradise.

SAMUEL TAYLOR COLERIDGE (1797–8)

This great visionary fragment was based, according to Coleridge, on memories of a dream inspired by reading about Kubla Khan's palace (almost certainly made more vivid by opium). It was allegedly unfinished because of the unwelcome arrival of 'a person on business from Porlock'. Busy scholars have traced in Coleridge's wide reading the sources of most of its imaginative detail.

The Ancient Mariner

1

It is an ancient Mariner
And he stoppeth one of three.
. . . 'By thy long gray beard and glittering eye,
Now wherefore stopp'st thou me?

The Bridegroom's doors are opened wide,
And I am next of kin;
The guests are met, the feast is set;
May'st hear the merry din.'

He holds him with his skinny hand,
'There was a ship,' quoth he.
'Hold off! unhand me, greybeard loon!'
Eftsoons his hand dropped he.

He holds him with his glittering eye -
The Wedding-Guest stood still,
And listens like a three years' child:
The Mariner hath his will.

The Wedding-Guest sat on a stone:
He cannot choose but hear;
And thus spake on that ancient man,
The bright-eyed Mariner.

'The ship was cheered, the harbor cleared,
Merrily did we drop
Below the kirk, below the hill,
Below the lighthouse top.

The Sun came up upon the left,
Out of the sea came he!
And he shone bright, and on the right
Went down into the sea.

Higher and higher every day,
Till over the mast at noon – '
The Wedding-Guest here beat his breast,
For he heard the loud bassoon.

The bride hath paced into the hall,
Red as a rose is she;
Nodding their heads before her goes
The merry minstrelsy.

The Wedding-Guest he beat his breast,
Yet he cannot choose but hear;
And thus spake on that ancient man,
The bright-eyed Mariner.

'And now the Storm-Blast came, and he
Was tyrannous and strong;
He struck with his o'ertaking wings,
And chased us south along.

With sloping masts and dipping prow,
As who pursued with yell and blow
Still treads the shadow of his foe,
And forward bends his head,
The ship drove fast, loud roared the blast,
And southward aye we fled.

And now there came both mist and snow,
And it grew wondrous cold:
And ice, mast-high, came floating by,
As green as emerald.

And through the drifts the snowy clifts
Did send a dismal sheen:
Nor shapes of men nor beasts we ken –
The ice was all between.

The ice was here, the ice was there,
The ice was all around:
It cracked and growled, and roared and howled,
Like noises in a swound!

At length did cross an Albatross,
Thorough the fog it came;
As if it had been a Christian soul,
We hailed it in God's name.

It ate the food it ne'er had eat,
And round and round it flew.
The ice did split with a thunder-fit;
The helmsman steered us through!

And a good south wind sprung up behind;
The Albatross did follow,
And every day, for food or play,
Came to the mariner's hollo!

In mist or cloud, on mast or shroud,
It perched for vespers nine;
Whiles all the night, through fog-smoke white,
Glimmered the white Moon-shine.'

'God save thee, ancient Mariner!
From the fiends, that plague thee thus! –
Why look'st thou so?' – 'With my crossbow
I shot the ALBATROSS.

2

The Sun now rose upon the right:
Out of the sea came he,
Still hid in mist, and on the left
Went down into the sea.

And the good south wind still blew behind,
But no sweet bird did follow,
Nor any day for food or play
Came to the mariners' hollo!

And I had done a hellish thing,
And it would work 'em woe:
For all averred, I had killed the bird
That made the breeze to blow.
Ah wretch! said they, the bird to slay,
That made the breeze to blow!

Nor dim nor red, like God's own head,
That glorious Sun uprist:
Then all averred, I had killed the bird
That brought the fog and mist.
'Twas right, said they, such birds to slay,
That bring the fog and mist.

The fair breeze blew, the white foam flew,
The furrow followed free;
We were the first that ever burst
Into that silent sea.

Down dropped the breeze, the sails dropped down,
'Twas sad as sad could be;
And we did speak only to break
The silence of the sea!

All in a hot and copper sky,
The bloody Sun, at noon,
Right up above the mast did stand,
No bigger than the Moon.

Day after day, day after day,
We stuck, nor breath nor motion;
As idle as a painted ship
Upon a painted ocean.

Water, water, everywhere,
And all the boards did shrink;
Water, water, everywhere,
Nor any drop to drink.

The very deep did rot: O Christ!
That ever this should be!
Yea, slimy things did crawl with legs
Upon the slimy sea.

About, about, in reel and rout
The death-fires danced at night;
The water, like a witch's oils,
Burnt green, and blue and white.

And some in dreams assured were
Of the Spirit that plagued us so;
Nine fathom deep he had followed us
From the land of mist and snow.

And every tongue, through utter drought,
Was withered at the root;
We could not speak, no more than if
We had been choked with soot.

Ah! well-a-day! what evil looks
Had I from old and young!
Instead of the cross, the Albatross
About my neck was hung.

3

There passed a weary time. Each throat
Was parched, and glazed each eye.
A weary time! a weary time!
How glazed each weary eye,
When looking westward, I beheld
A something in the sky.

At first it seemed a little speck,
And then it seemed a mist;
It moved and moved, and took at last
A certain shape, I wist.

A speck, a mist, a shape, I wist!
And still it neared and neared:
As if it dodged a water-sprite,
It plunged and tacked and veered.

With throats unslaked, with black lips baked,
We could nor laugh nor wail;
Through utter drought all dumb we stood!
I bit my arm, I sucked the blood,
And cried, A sail! a sail!

With throats unslaked, with black lips baked,
Agape they heard me call:
Gramercy! they for joy did grin,

And all at once their breath drew in,
As they were drinking all.

See! see! (I cried) she tacks no more!
Hither to work us weal;
Without a breeze, without a tide,
She steadies with upright keel!

The western wave was all aflame.
The day was well nigh done!
Almost upon the western wave
Rested the broad bright sun;
When that strange shape drove suddenly
Betwixt us and the Sun.

And straight the Sun was flecked with bars,
(Heaven's Mother send us grace!)
As if through a dungeon grate he peered
With broad and burning face.

Alas! (thought I, and my heart beat loud)
How fast she nears and nears!
Are those *her* sails that glance in the Sun,
Like restless gossameres?

Are those *her* ribs through which the Sun
Did peer, as through a grate?
And is that Woman all her crew?
Is that a DEATH? and are there two?
Is DEATH that woman's mate?

Her lips were red, her looks were free,
Her locks were yellow as gold:
Her skin was as white as leprosy,
The Night-mare Life-in-DEATH was she,
Who thicks man's blood with cold.

The naked hulk alongside came,
And the twain were casting dice;
"The game is done! I've won! I've won!"
Quoth she, and whistled thrice.

The Sun's rim dips; the stars rush out:
At one stride comes the dark;
With far-heard whisper, o'er the sea,
Off shot the spectre-bark.

We listened and looked sideways up!
Fear at my heart, as at a cup,
My lifeblood seemed to sip!
The stars were dim, and thick the night,
The steersman's face by his lamp gleamed white;
From the sails the dew did drip –
Till clomb above the eastern bar
The horned Moon, with one bright star
Within the nether tip.

One after one, by the star-dogged Moon,
Too quick for groan or sigh,
Each turned his face with a ghastly pang,
And cursed me with his eye.

Four times fifty living men,
(And I heard nor sigh nor groan)
With heavy thump, a lifeless lump,
They dropped down one by one.

The souls did from their bodies fly –
They fled to bliss or woe!
And every soul, it passed me by,
Like the whizz of my crossbow!'

4

'I fear thee, ancient Mariner!
I fear thy skinny hand!
And thou art long, and lank, and brown,
As in the ribbed sea-sand.

I fear thee and thy glittering eye,
And thy skinny hand, so brown.' –
'Fear not, fear not, thou Wedding-Guest!
This body dropped not down.

Alone, alone, all, all alone,
Alone on a wide wide sea!
And never a saint took pity on
My soul in agony.

The many men, so beautiful!
And they all dead did lie:
And a thousand thousand slimy things
Lived on; and so did I.

I looked upon the rotting sea,
And drew my eyes away;
I looked upon the rotting deck,
And there the dead men lay.

I looked to heaven, and tried to pray;
But or ever a prayer had gushed
A wicked whisper came, and made
My heart as dry as dust.

I closed my lids, and kept them close,
And the balls like pulses beat;
For the sky and the sea, and the sea and the sky
Lay like a load on my weary eye,
And the dead were at my feet.

The cold sweat melted from their limbs,
Nor rot nor reek did they:
The look with which they looked on me
Had never passed away.

An orphan's curse would drag to hell
A spirit from on high;
But oh! more horrible than that
Is the curse in a dead man's eye!
Seven days, seven nights, I saw that curse,
And yet I could not die.

The moving Moon went up the sky,
And nowhere did abide:
Softly she was going up,
And a star or two beside —

Her beams bemocked the sultry main,
Like April hoar-frost spread;
But where the ship's huge shadow lay,
The charmed water burnt alway
A still and awful red.

Beyond the shadow of the ship,
I watched the water snakes:
They moved in tracks of shining white,
And when they reared, the elfish light
Fell off in hoary flakes.

Within the shadow of the ship
I watched their rich attire:
Blue, glossy green, and velvet black,
They coiled and swam; and every track
Was a flash of golden fire.

O happy living things! no tongue
Their beauty might declare:
A spring of love gushed from my heart,
And I blessed them unaware:
Sure my kind saint look pity on me,
And I blessed them unaware.

The self-same moment I could pray;
And from my neck so free
The Albatross fell off, and sank
Like lead into the sea.

5

Oh sleep! it is a gentle thing,
Beloved from pole to pole!
To Mary Queen the praise be given!
She sent the gentle sleep from Heaven,
That slid into my soul.

The silly buckets on the deck,
That had so long remained,
I dreamt that they were filled with dew;
And when I awoke, it rained.

My lips were wet, my throat was cold,
My garments all were dank;
Sure I had drunken in my dreams,
And still my body drank.

I moved, and could not feel my limbs:
I was so light – almost
I thought that I had died in sleep,
And was a blessed ghost.

And soon I heard a roaring wind
It did not come anear;
But with its sound it shook the sails,
That were so thin and sere.

The upper air burst into life!
And a hundred fire-flags sheen,
To and fro they were hurried about!
And to and fro, and in and out?
The wan stars danced between.

And the coming wind did roar more loud,
And the sails did sigh like sedge;
And the rain poured down from one black cloud;
The Moon was at its edge.

The thick black cloud was cleft, and still
The Moon was at its side:
Like waters shot from some high crag,
The lightning fell with never a jag,
A river steep and wide.

The loud wind never reached the ship,
Yet now the ship moved on!
Beneath the lightning and the Moon
The dead men gave a groan.

They groaned, they stirred, they all uprose,
Nor spake, nor moved their eyes;
It had been strange, even in a dream,
To have seen those dead men rise.

The helmsman steered, the ship moved on;
Yet never a breeze up-blew;
The mariners all 'gan work the ropes,
Where they were wont to do;
They raised their limbs like lifeless tools -
We were a ghastly crew.

The body of my brother's son
Stood by me, knee to knee:
The body and I pulled at one rope,
But he said nought to me.'

'I fear thee, ancient Mariner!'
'Be calm, thou Wedding-Guest!
'Twas not those souls that fled in pain,
Which to their corses came again,
But a troop of spirits blest:

For when it dawned – they dropped their arms,
And clustered round the mast;
Sweet sounds rose slowly through their mouths,
And from their bodies passed.

Around, around, flew each sweet sound,
Then darted to the Sun;
Slowly the sounds came back again,
Now mixed, now one by one.

Sometimes a-dropping from the sky
I heard the sky-lark sing;
Sometimes all little birds that are,
How they seemed to fill the sea and air
With their sweet jargoning!

And now 'twas like all instruments,
Now like a lonely flute;
And now it is an angel's song,
That makes the heavens be mute.

It ceased; yet still the sails made on
A pleasant noise till noon,
A noise like of a hidden brook
In the leafy month of June,

That to the sleeping woods all night
Singeth a quiet tune.

Till noon we quietly sailed on,
Yet never a breeze did breathe:
Slowly and smoothly went the ship,
Moved onward from beneath.

Under the keel nine fathom deep,
From the Land of mist and snow,
The spirit slid: and it was he
That made the ship to go.
The sails at noon left off their tune,
And the ship stood still also.

The Sun, right up above the mast,
Had fixed her to the ocean:
But in a minute she 'gan stir,
With a short uneasy motion –
Backwards and forwards half her length
With a short uneasy motion.

Then like a pawing horse let go,
She made a sudden bound:
It flung the blood into my head,
And I fell down in a swound.

How long in that same fit I lay,
I have not to declare;
But ere my living life returned,
I heard and in my soul discerned
Two voices in the air.

"Is it he?" quoth one, "Is this the man?
By him who died on cross,
With his cruel bow he laid full low
The harmless Albatross.

The spirit who bideth by himself
In the land of mist and snow,
He loved the bird that loved the man
Who shot him with his bow."

The other was a softer voice,
As soft as honeydew:
Quoth he, "The man hath penance done,
And penance more will do."

6

First Voice
"But tell me, tell me! speak again,
Thy soft response renewing –
What makes that ship drive on so fast?
What is the ocean doing?"

Second Voice
"Still as a slave before his lord,
The ocean hath no blast;
His great bright eye most silently
Up to the Moon is cast –

If he may know which way to go;
For she guides him smooth or grim.
See, brother, see! how graciously
She looketh down on him."

First Voice
"But why drives on that ship so fast,
Without or wave or wind?"

Second Voice
"The air is cut away before,
And closes from behind.

Fly, brother, fly! more high, more high!
Or we shall be belated:
For slow and slow that ship will go,
When the Mariner's trance is abated."

I woke, and we were sailing on
As in a gentle weather:
'Twas night, calm night, the moon was high;
The dead men stood together.

All stood together on the deck,
For a charnel-dungeon fitter:
All fixed on me their stony eyes,
That in the Moon did glitter.

The pang, the curse, with which they died,
Had never passed away:
I could not draw my eyes from theirs,
Nor turn them up to pray.

And now this spell was snapped: once more
I viewed the ocean green,
And looked far forth, yet little saw
Of what had else been seen –

Like one, that on a lonesome road
Doth walk in fear and dread,
And having once turned round walks on,
And turns no more his head;
Because he knows, a frightful fiend
Doth close behind him tread.

But soon there breathed a wind on me,
Nor sound nor motion made:
Its path was not upon the sea,
In ripple or in shade.

It raised my hair, it fanned my cheek
Like a meadow-gale of spring –
It mingled strangely with my fears,
Yet it felt like a welcoming.

Swiftly, swiftly flew the ship,
Yet she sailed softly too:
Sweetly, sweetly blew the breeze –
On me alone it blew.

Oh! dream of joy! is this indeed
The lighthouse top I see?
Is this the hill? is this the kirk?
Is this mine own countree?

We drifted o'er the harbour bar,
And I with sobs did pray –
O let me be awake, my God!
Or let me sleep alway.

The harbour bay was clear as glass,
So smoothly it was strewn!
And on the bay the moonlight lay,
And the shadow of the Moon.

The rock shone bright, the kirk no less,
That stands above the rock:
The moonlight steeped in silentness
The steady weathercock.

And the bay was white with silent light,
Till rising from the same,
Full many shapes, that shadows were,
In crimson colours came.

A little distance from the prow
Those crimson shadows were:
I turned my eyes upon the deck –
Oh, Christ! what saw I there!

Each corse lay flat, lifeless and flat,
And, by the holy rood!
A man all light, a seraph man,
On every corse there stood.

This seraph band, each waved his hand:
It was a heavenly sight!
They stood as signals to the land,
Each one a lovely light;

This seraph band, each waved his hand,
No voice they did impart –
No voice; but oh! the silence sank
Like music on my heart.

But soon I heard the clash of oars,
I heard the Pilot's cheer;
My head was turned perforce away
And I saw a boat appear.

The Pilot and the Pilot's boy,
I heard them coming fast:
Dear Lord in Heaven! it was a joy
The dead men could not blast.

I saw a third – I heard his voice:
It is the Hermit good!
He singeth loud his goodly hymns
That he makes in the wood.
He'll shrieve my soul, he'll wash away
The Albatross's blood.

7

This Hermit good lives in that wood
Which slopes down to the sea.
How loudly his sweet voice he rears!
He loves to talk with marineres
That come from a far countree.

He kneels at morn, and noon, and eve –
He hath a cushion plump:
It is the moss that wholly hides
The rotted old oak-stump.

The skiff-boat neared: I heard them talk,
"Why, this is strange, I trow!
Where are those lights so many and fair,
That signal made but now?"

"Strange, by my faith!" the Hermit said –
"And they answered not our cheer!
The planks looked warped! and see those sails
How thin they are and sere!
I never saw aught like to them,
unless perchance it were

Brown skeletons of leaves that lag
My forest-brook along;
When the ivy-tod is heavy with snow,
And the owlet whoops to the wolf below
That eats the she-wolf's young."

"Dear Lord! it hath a fiendish look,"
(The Pilot made reply)
"I am a-feared" – "Push on, push on!"
Said the Hermit cheerily.

The boat came closer to the ship,
But I nor spake nor stirred;
The boat came close beneath the ship,
And straight a sound was heard.

Under the water it rumbled on,
Still louder and more dread:
It reached the ship, it split the bay;
The ship went down like lead.

Stunned by that loud and dreadful sound,
Which sky and ocean smote,
Like one that hath been seven days drowned
My body lay afloat;
But, swift as dreams, myself I found
Within the Pilot's boat.

Upon the whirl, where sunk the ship.
The boat spun round and round;
And all was still, save that the hill
Was telling of the sound.

I moved my lips – the Pilot shrieked
And fell down in a fit;
The holy Hermit raised his eyes,
And prayed where he did sit.

I took the oars: the Pilot's boy,
Who now doth crazy go,
Laughed loud and long, and all the while,
His eyes went to and fro.
"Ha! ha!"quoth he, "full plain I see,
The Devil knows how to row."

And now, all in my own countree,
I stood on the firm land!
The Hermit stepped forth from the boat,
And scarcely he could stand.

"O shrieve me, shrieve me, holy man!"
The Hermit crossed his brow.
"Say quick," quoth he, "I bid thee say –
What manner of man art thou?"

Forthwith this frame of mine was wrenched
With a woeful agony,
Which forced me to begin my tale;
And then it left me free.

Since then, at an uncertain hour,
That agony returns:
And till my ghastly tale is told,
This heart within me burns.

I pass, like night, from land to land;
I have strange power of speech;
That moment that his face I see,
I know the man that must hear me:
To him my tale I teach.

What loud uproar bursts from that door!
That wedding-guests are there:
But in the garden-bower the bride
And bride-maids singing are:
And hark the little vesper bell,
Which biddeth me to prayer!

O Wedding-Guest! this soul hath been
Alone on a wide wide sea:
So lonely 'twas, that God himself
Scarce seemed there to be.

O sweeter than the marriage feast,
'Tis sweeter far to me,
To walk together to the kirk
With a goodly company! –

To walk together to the kirk,
And all together pray,
While each to his great Father bends,
Old men, and babes, and loving friends
And youths and maidens gay!

Farewell, farewell! but this I tell
To thee, thou Wedding-Guest!
He prayeth well, who loveth well
Both man and bird and beast.

He prayeth best, who loveth best
All things both great and small;
For the dear God who loveth us,
He made and loveth all.'

The Mariner, whose eye is bright,
Whose beard with age is hoar,
Is gone: and now the Wedding-Guest
Turned from the bridegroom's door.

He went like one that hath been stunned,
And is of sense forlorn:
A sadder and a wiser man,
He rose the morrow morn.

SAMUEL TAYLOR COLERIDGE (1798)

The wandering albatross, often seen very far from land, clearly reminded sailors, with its outstretched wings, of the protective Cross of Christ. The poem can be seen as one about a sinner achieving grace after a long period of atonement through suffering, with his blessing of the water snakes in Part 4 his first step to redemption. With its layers of meaning and its relevance to the modern world's increasing concern with the environment and with spiritual if not necessarily formal religious values, this seemed a suitable poem with which to bring this anthology to a close.

INDEX OF POEM TITLES

INDEX OF FIRST LINES

The Wordsworth Poetry Library

Works of

Matthew Arnold

William Blake

The Brontë Sisters

Rupert Brooke

Robert Browning

Elizabeth Barrett Browning

Robert Burns

Lord Byron

Geoffrey Chaucer

G. K. Chesterton

John Clare

Samuel Taylor Coleridge

Emily Dickinson

John Donne

John Dryden

Thomas Hardy

George Herbert

Gerard Manley Hopkins

A. E. Housman

James Joyce

John Keats

Rudyard Kipling

D. H. Lawrence

Henry Wadsworth Longfellow

Macaulay

Andrew Marvell

John Milton

Wilfred Owen

'Banjo' Paterson

Edgar Allen Poe

Alexander Pope

John Wilmot, Earl of Rochester

Christina Rossetti

Sir Walter Scott

William Shakespeare

P. B. Shelley

Edmund Spenser

Algernon Swinburne

Alfred Lord Tennyson

Edward Thomas

Walt Whitman

Oscar Wilde

William Wordsworth

W. B. Yeats

Anthologies & Collections

Restoration and
Eighteenth-Century Verse

Nineteenth-Century Verse

The Wordsworth Book of
First World War Poetry

Love Poems

The Metaphysical Poets

The Wordsworth Book of Sonnets